WHEN WE WENT FIRST CLASS

When We Went

First Class

Ellen Williamson

Iowa State University Press / Ames

I·O·W·A
HERITAGE
COLLECTION

Burma Shave jingle used by permission from Philip Morris, Inc.

This printing produced from the original edition published by Doubleday & Co., Inc. Published by arrangement with Doubleday, a division of Bantam Doubleday Dell Publishing Group, Inc. Text reprinted from the original without correction.

♾ Printed on acid-free paper in the United States of America

First edition, 1977
First Iowa Heritage Collection edition, 1990

Library of Congress Cataloging-in-Publication Data

Williamson, Ellen
     When we went first class/Ellen Williamson.—1st Iowa heritage collection ed.
         p.   cm.—(Iowa heritage collection)
     Reprint. Originally published: Garden City, N.Y.: Doubleday, 1977.
     ISBN 0-8138-1083-3
     1. United States—Description and travel—1920–1949. 2. United States—Social life and customs—1918–1945. 3. Williamson, Ellen—Journeys—United States. I. Title. II. Series.
E169.W64   1990
917.304′91—dc20   90—4825

The last digit is the print number: 1 0 9 8 7 6 5 4

Grateful Acknowledgments to the following friends:
Betty Fisher, Lois Cole, Barbara Vanneck, Barbara Dixon, Gloria Bakey, William J. Harris, John Mifflin, Courtney Campbell, and, above all, Karen Van Westering.

Contents

Preface

ONE DAY THIS past summer found me leaving New York from La Guardia Airport on a large jet, a 727 or something similar, bound for Detroit, where I disembarked and walked briskly through the airport to another airline. After a half-hour wait I boarded a smaller turboprop and headed for northern Michigan. An hour later we reached the airport of Traverse City, where I was met by Joe McPhillips, who hurried me to his charter plane, waiting nearby. After Joe helped me up the little iron step and fastened my seat belt, he said, "Be sure your door is fastened tight. It sometimes has a way of popping open."

Putting my luggage in the single back seat, he jumped in and we took off, heading straight up the middle of Grand Traverse Bay. Twenty minutes later we came down on the bumpy grass landing field of the town of Charlevoix. Joe helped me down to the ground and into the little yellow Gremlin that was waiting for me.

A short time later I walked into our log-cabin living room, the family gathering place on Oyster Bay of Lake Charlevoix, and found a group of teen-agers sprawled around the large oval table. A niece of mine was there, and two godchildren and four or five others. Paper cups of yogurt or some such thing lay about, as well as half-empty bottles of soft drinks and chocolate cookie crumbs. Stevie Wonder's voice, or somebody who sounded like him, came plaintively from the phonograph. It was a typical sight, and we greeted each other cheerily.

"You're just in time to settle an argument for us, Aunt Ellen!" my niece Francie exclaimed. "What was the fastest way to get to Charlevoix before airplanes, and how long did it take?"

"The train, of course," I answered promptly.

"There! I told you so," somebody shouted gleefully. "I said the train all along."

Francie looked disappointed. "The train was faster than a fast automobile?" she inquired.

I paused for a minute and thought. "Yes, the old Pere Marquette railroad train the Resort Special would beat the auto every time," I said firmly, "especially since there were no superhighways—only narrow sandy roads, with lots of turns."

"What about a fast motorboat going up Lake Michigan from Chicago to Charlevoix? Wouldn't that beat the train?" someone else asked.

"Maybe, but I never heard of anyone doing it. It was too far and the water was too rough," I replied. "But the lake steamers left Chicago late in the afternoon, at about the same time as the train, and they didn't arrive until noon the next day. The train pulled in at seven-thirty in the morning."

"Before the train I suppose you went on horseback or maybe by horse and buggy?" asked a beau of Francie's.

"Heavens no," I said. "Trains were running when I was a little girl. A horse and buggy would have taken forever."

"You never rode in a stagecoach?" my godchild Susie asked.

"Did you ever ride in a horsecar?" someone else wanted to know.

I shook my head. "No, but I do remember seeing a very noisy early automobile somewhere in downtown Cedar Rapids when I was quite young. This car must have backfired or something because it scared all the horses on the street. They reared and stampeded and tried to run away, all of them whinnying, delivery wagons tipping over every which way, and people screaming. My pony cart seemed much safer than automobiles for a long time after that."

Francie, and I guess the others too, were looking at me sad-eyed.

"Aunt Ellen." She spoke pityingly. "How perfectly awful it must be to be so old. Oh, I feel so sorry for you." The rest shook their heads and murmured things like "Yeah, yeah."

Anger rose up in me like a black fog. I could almost feel sparks flying out of my ears.

"Listen, brats." I spoke loud and clearly. "Even though you seem to think that I was born in a covered wagon and helped write the Monroe Doctrine, I don't mind being old at all. It has its advantages, and I will be happy to name a few, but before I do I have some news for you." I paused impressively.

"Someday all of you will be exactly my age or you won't," I continued slowly. "You have no choice—you'll be old or six feet under."

The little group gasped simultaneously, and looked at one another horrified.

"It's not as bad as you think, so stop feeling sorry for me right this minute," I continued briskly. "The best thing about being *mature* (that's a stylish new word for old, by the way) is self-assurance. When I was your age I worried all the time: what to say to the new boy who took me to the dance, what to wear to the beach party so that I would look like all the other girls, and how to behave when the date got expectedly drunk and so on.

"Nowadays I talk and dress and behave exactly as I please, having enough confidence in myself so that I don't have to stop and wonder if I am doing or saying the right thing: it comes automatically. It's a great feeling."

I paused for breath. No one said a word, they just stared owl-eyed.

"As you may have figured out," I continued, "you change your status as you grow up, from time to time. You should do as good a job as you possibly can with each change or stepping-stone in your life—first a good, polite child, then a teen-ager whom everyone likes, then the best college undergraduate possible, and then on to a popular jobholder as well as becoming a good wife or husband, and later a tip-top parent. The effort is well worth it, for there you are, finally, with all kinds of pleasant and interesting experiences behind you, and a rosy future ahead because of the fact that you have worked hard at becoming a first-class finished product: a sort of Man or Woman for All Seasons."

I moved to the door, everyone watching silently. The anger departed and I added, "That's all I have to say, and I hope that you will enjoy life at my age—being a finished product, that is—as much as I do."

I went off to Mushroom Palace (the name of my own little log cabin) and wrote:

Idea for a Book:

1. A book about us, the Finished Products of the Space Age, the generation which started off in a world where the train and ship were the most important means of transportation.
2. By comparison we traveled slowly, but certainly more elegantly, taking this less hurried and refined way of travel for granted.
3. The Cunard Line's slogan was correct: Getting there is half the fun.

There are not many of us left who have this unique heritage, and that is why I've written this little book for those who will never know the experiences and pleasures of When We Went First Class.

WHEN WE WENT FIRST CLASS

~ 1

San Francisco: The Earthquake and Fire

I AM TOLD THAT I was born at exactly midnight on October 31, 1905, and was therefore rather like the people who are born on a Turkish ship that is sailing in French waters and who can take their choice of being a citizen of either country: I could have a birthday on October 31 or November 1. My family chose the former because it was Halloween and makes for excellent birthday parties. Otherwise, mine must have been an uneventful birth, as I never remember hearing much about it, and furthermore never even had a birth certificate, which makes acquiring a passport and Social Security benefits as difficult as taking a poodle or bloodhound to England.

My traveling days started then, it seems, for after the Christmas holidays, the Douglas family left for Santa Barbara, as usual, spending the rest of the winter amid the pepper trees and mountain lilac bushes and eucalyptus of Mission Canyon, and everyone but me riding horseback through the trails in the foothills or galloping on the beaches along the Pacific.

We left for home on April 15, taking the train to San Francisco, where we were to spend two nights. Rooms had been engaged on the twelfth and top floor of the St. Francis Hotel, newly built by the Crocker family, and also we had reservations from Oakland to Cedar Rapids on the Union Pacific's best train, the Overland Limited. There were nine of us altogether: my parents, my elder sister, aged ten at the time, her nurse, who was a British-nanny type named Nora, my nurse, who was a German and known as Fräulein, my mother's French maid, Rosie, me the little pink bundle, and Mr. and Mrs. Clark Duncan of Sioux City, who were great friends of my parents and had been visiting them in Santa Barbara.

Everything went smoothly after we arrived, and my father told me that on Tuesday evening (April 17) he and Mother and the Duncans went to the opera. It was the second night of the Metropolitan's season in San Francisco and the opera was *Carmen*, starring Enrico Caruso, Olive Fremstad, Antonio Scotti, and Louise Homer. He said that Caruso sang magnificently, really brought down the house, and described all the diamond stomachers and tiaras that the dressy ladies of San Francisco were wearing. I also remember his telling me what a gay and prosperous place San Francisco was in those days. He told me, chuckling at the thought, that he and Mr. Duncan had wanted after the opera to go to a place in San Francisco known as Ye Olde Whore Shoppe, just to see what it was really like, but that instead they had prudently gone with the ladies to dine at the Palace Hotel, celebrating the festive evening with champagne and a soufflé Grand Marnier.

He went on to tell about how large and ever-growing San Francisco was in those days. He was proud of it and its progress. There were almost a half million people living in the Bay Area at this time, whereas in Los Angeles the population was a mere 204,000. He thought that San Francisco was a terrible-looking city actually, filled with shanties and jerry-built houses, mixed in with hideous Victorian monstrosities.

Then, too, it was laid out all wrong, he maintained. There were, and still are, forty-odd hills in the city limits, but instead of building the streets to curve gracefully around the contours of the hills the whole thing was planned for a perfectly flat town with streets laid in a grid pattern. Consequently there are some frightfully steep streets which in some cases had to become stairways.

However, the hillsides give it a style all of its own, and so did the strange combination of ethnic and fortune-hunting groups who lived there: Chinese laborers, gold seekers, gamblers, Italian immigrants, Russian traders, sailors and seafarers from everywhere, hoodlums,* and Spanish families who had settled there as far back as the founding in 1776 of the Mission San Francisco de Asís (that would be Assisi).

My parents returned to the St. Francis that night after dinner at the Palace, and retired around midnight. At 5:13 in the morning of April 18 the earthquake struck. My father woke up to feel the brass bed in which he was lying slide all the way across the room and slam into the opposite wall. At the same time, through the window ahead he could see two tall buildings on the opposite side of Union Square, the park on which the St. Francis faces, and while he was looking at them they tipped toward each other, tops touching, and then with a shower of bricks falling from them, straightened themselves up again. Meanwhile books and magazines slid off whatever they were on, pictures that were hung from a molding up at the ceiling swung out from the walls and slammed back and forth.

He also told me that at first there was almost no noise, just the slamming of the pictures. It was a beautiful clear spring morning with no fog or wind. However, as the shaking continued a sort of low roar started, sounding like a subway train going by, then grew louder and louder until it seemed there was nothing else but terrific earsplitting noise. Actually it was girders being torn apart, wood being ground into splinters, and bricks falling, but most of all the bricks falling. Ninety-five percent of all the chimneys in San Francisco fell, either to the streets or through the roofs of houses.

It lasted forty-seven seconds, and it was caused by a rift in the ancient San Andreas fault, which runs from Point Arena on the California coast about one hundred miles north of San Francisco down to the south almost another hundred miles to the Pajaro Valley in Monterey County.

This strange moving force started at Point Arena and traveled

* The word "hoodlum" originated in San Francisco just before this time. It came from a street gang of thieves who would surround a rich man or a pair of them. "Huddle 'em!" a lookout would shout, and the gang would rob them and run.

straight south. As it proceeded the earth opened up along the fault and then closed again, but the land on the western side was now sixteen feet north of where it was before, just imagine. Buildings collapsed completely if they straddled the fault, bridges buckled, roads and railroad tracks moved sixteen feet away, houses close to the rift's path slid downhill or tipped over. When it crossed hilly country, the land fell away, leaving chasms, some as wide as twenty feet. When it crossed flat ground the earth closed again, leaving no sign of ever having opened up. Absolutely nothing could stop this titanic force. Redwood trees, and you know how huge they are, if they happened to be astride the fault, were ripped in two.

As the rift continued south the sixteen-foot displacement of earth grew less, fortunately, but the shock remained as violent as ever. It bypassed Alcatraz completely, the island in the Golden Gate, which was a military prison in those days, then went straight through San Francisco with full force, and on south, where the rift managed to break up the conduit to San Francisco's water supply. It then went on to wreck Palo Alto and Stanford University, and finally, after severe damage to the Pajaro Valley, ran out of steam, although the San Andreas fault goes on underground for hundreds of miles farther.

There were additional shocks at 5:18, 5:20, and 5:25, but they were small ones. At the St. Francis Hotel, according to my sister Margaret, she and my father got dressed and went downstairs.

She wore a starchy pink linen dress and insisted on carrying a stuffed Easter rabbit she prized highly. The elevators weren't working, so they walked down the twelve flights, and saw that as they descended the damage to each floor became worse and worse. Plaster had fallen a little from the ceilings on the eleventh and tenth floors; down below, the plaster was thick on the floors, doors were hanging crazily from wrenched hinges, broken glass was everywhere.

When they reached the lobby they found terrible destruction. All the wall panels there, made of veined green marble, had crashed to the floor, and there were obviously bodies lying under them. They made their way out through the revolving door and crossed Powell Street to get to Union Square, stepping carefully through and over the rubble. Margaret remembers sitting on the grass and looking up at the windows where the rest of us were, and Mother appeared at a window, dressed in a gray suit complete with black hat and veil. She held the baby (me, of course), waved to them, and pointed down, implying that she'd be down soon.

As far as Margaret can remember all nine of us met somewhere in the lobby around eight o'clock, leaving the thirty-eight pieces of luggage neatly packed upstairs. The chef and his assistants were bravely serving warmed-up coffee and yesterday's rolls in one of the dining rooms, and althought it was jammed with people they found a table for us and we squeezed around it. Mother was carrying her jewel case, a small dark leather box, because Rosie was very near to hysterics, and kept moaning that she had left her *postiche* (that would be a wiglet) upstairs and here she was at the end of the world and with a *coiffure* that the *Bon Dieu* would find a *déshonneur*.

Just then (at 8:14) there was another earthquake, the strongest since the first one, and everyone scrambled to get out. Margaret remembered some pillars in the dining room wobbling back and forth. As they were pushing their way to the revolving doors, a tall red-haired man came up to Mother and said, "Madame, I will save you." Then he reached for the jewel case, which he apparently thought was worth saving too, and at that Mr. Duncan and my father stepped between them and off went the man.

I am told that we got outside and again sat in Union Square. Nora had swept the rolls off the table into a napkin, so the others finished breakfast, and after that I got mine, my mother nursing me quietly under a palm tree. After I had finished a young man came up to her carrying a little baby. He explained that the baby's mother had been killed by a falling chimney, that he was her brother, and could she possibly give the poor little thing some milk. Of course mother obliged, and Margaret said that Nora and Fräulein, who was holding me, and Mother and Mrs. Duncan all cried quietly the whole time.

After that we all walked to some friend's house nearby, only to find the house in ruins and the owners sitting forlornly on the curb. That is when my father decided that we should all get out of town as quickly as possible. Perhaps he smelled smoke, or wondered what he would do with all of us if there were a fire.

He walked over to the edge of the street, Geary or Post, I imagine, and stood there carefully watching the wagons and automobiles going by. When a large Pierce-Arrow appeared he held up his hand. The car stopped and he asked if it was available for transporting all of us out to the Presidio, where my parents had friends. The lady in the back seat was a Mrs. Spreckels, and she said that she was carrying a carload of blankets to the hospital but that she would come back and would be delighted to take us then if we would wait.

Just as she was speaking Daddy saw out of the corner of his eye a large comfortable carriage approaching, so he thanked her, and stopped the horse and buggy.

"I'll give you five hundred dollars for your rig," he said.

"Sold!" said the man, and climbed down, accepted the cash, handed the reins to my father, and walked off. We all got in, and away we went, mostly at a snail's pace, threading our way around rubble. It was getting dark when we finally reached Dr. and Mrs. Walker's house. Mother remembered it well, described it as a big brown comfortable house, encircled by a wide porch, where they were welcomed so heartily that she broke down and cried in Mrs. Walker's arms.

The Duncans went on with the carriage to some friends of theirs, and Margaret remembers that as she waved goodbye to them she noticed that the sky in the direction of San Francisco was a glowing red. The city seemed to be on fire everywhere. She also remembers a Tiffany lamp over the dining-room table that swayed back and forth every few minutes, for there were still tremors occurring, but she felt safe although tired. She said the pink linen dress was a real mess.

My mother said that after Margaret was put to bed she and Nora and Fräulein were up all night long. Dr. Walker and his wife got no sleep either. The poor doctor went in and out constantly. First he was off to fix up a family whose house had collapsed and who had been buried in the ruins, then he'd go off in the opposite direction to see a patient whose leg had to be amputated. Then he would come wearily in, put down his black bag, and while he drank some coffee Mrs. Walker would replenish his bag, adding fresh bandages and dressings and morphine, and a man in the stable would unharness his horse and hitch up a fresh animal to his light four-wheeler and away he would go again.

However, after he had left the second time, two women came to the house, almost at exactly the same time, and each one in labor. Apparently the shock of the earthquake precipitated childbirth, and in less than half an hour each of the two had been delivered of a baby. One so premature that it was no more than a miscarriage, but the other was a healthy little boy who yelled his head off and seemed to weigh eight or nine pounds.

And who assisted at these births? My mother, Nora, and Fräulein. Both the nurses had a knowledge of midwifery, especially Fräulein, and Mother was the daughter of a doctor and had always been interested in medicine, and had in fact watched her father perform surgical operations ever since she was a young girl.

The three of them organized themselves into an almost professional team, and during the long night were responsible for the safe arrival of twenty-two babies. Rosie, who was over her hysterics, but was much too squeamish to have anything to do with the continuing obstetrics, was put into the kitchen, where she boiled water, and at the same time Mrs. Walker and her maid were busy all night long looking after the new arrivals.

It was this pair who took care of the babies. They washed them, then marked which one belonged to the proper mother, putting the mother's initials (in red ink) on her own baby's little bottom. Then they made each one a little warm nest out of a rolled-up blanket.

Mother had only one moment of near-panic. It was when one mother was brought in about four in the morning. She was in great pain, and was in advanced labor. Mother reassured the father, put him out on the porch with a group of other fathers and attendants, and got the lady ready for the actual birth. To her surprise she saw a little foot appear where the baby's head should have been. Luckily Dr. Walker appeared at this point and showed the team how to maneuver the baby around so that it would arrive head first.

By daylight several trained nurses who usually took care of Dr. Walker's patients arrived, and the Walker household got some rest and sleep. The fire was spreading, however, and although the Walker's house never burned, nevertheless there were fires in the neighborhood, for Margaret remembers going to watch a big white house nearby which had a garden and a beautiful round lily pond. The owners doused many blankets in the pond (remember that the whole San Francisco area was without water) and plastered them all over the roof, thereby saving the house.

The Douglas family left the following morning in the Walkers' large carriage (don't ask about the Duncans and what became of them and the borrowed five-hundred-dollar horse and buggy; no one can recall) and managed to get to the Market Street ferry. There were fires smoldering everywhere amid the ruins and blocked-off streets, and soldiers shooting at looters, but they made it.

As an aside, sixty-nine years later, April 18, 1975, the Navy released a long-secret report written by Lieutenant Frederick N. Freeman of a navy relief force sent to the stricken city. He wrote: "The crowds rushed saloon after saloon and looted the stock, becoming intoxicated during the day. In my opinion, great loss of life resulted from men and women becoming stultified by liquor and being too tired and exhausted to get out of the way of the fire."

The two-page report was declassified recently by the Navy, after it was discovered by San Francisco author Frederick A. Goerner while researching at the Western Regional Archives of the federal government in San Francisco.

At the ferry where we arrived, Margaret in the wilted pink linen dress was still clutching the Easter rabbit, otherwise there was no luggage whatsoever except a paper sack containing some sour little oranges that Rosie had managed to pick before leaving the Walkers' place.

The ferry was so crowded with literally hundreds and hundreds of homeless Chinese that our family could only find a spot on the roof of the ferry. Margaret told me that the ordeal of standing there with no railing, hemmed in by pig-tailed coolies all muttering and pushing, was almost more terrifying than the earthquake itself.

At last we arrived in Oakland, sometime before noon, and spent the rest of the day sitting in the overcrowded Oakland station waiting for the train to appear. Just about this time, I am told, I began to fret. I had been a good quiet baby until that afternoon, and when the train finally pulled in, all solidly electric-lighted, full of food and drink and porters and polished mahogany drawing rooms, sparkling silver and snow-white napery, I yelled like a coyote and continued to howl for most of the three-day trip.

In fact, it was so bad that my father wired ahead to Cedar Rapids for our doctor to be on hand as soon as we arrived. He was on the platform when the train pulled in, took one fast look at little red-faced me, and said that I was just plain hungry. Mother's milk had departed as a result of shock and fatigue.

Margaret said the trip home was one vast shopping spree. Everyone aboard jumped off every time the train stopped and bought shoelaces, handkerchiefs, stockings, and toothbrushes. Then came one glorious forty-five-minute stop in Ogden, Utah, where passengers took hacks (the forerunners of the taxi) to the stores and shops of downtown Ogden. That's when Margaret acquired a piece of blue gingham cloth, and Nora and Rosie made it into a dress that very afternoon. And she also recalls that my mother sent off a telegram to Marshall Field's asking them to send a whole new layette for her baby sister, and I'm sure that whatever came proved useful.

Since that earthquake of 1906 I have been in three others. None was anywhere near as serious, but they are the three that I was old enough to remember.

The first one was in Santa Barbara and it happened early one morning in 1915 while my younger sister Barbara and I were getting dressed. I was sitting on the floor pulling on my brown cotton ribbed stockings when the whole big wooden house in which we lived began swaying and creaking, back and forth and back and forth with a diagonal motion—first we pitched toward one corner of the room, then were rocked toward the opposite corner.

I remember seeing the mountains out of the window, and they looked all fuzzy and blurred. From downstairs we could hear the noise of crashing china (our room was just over the dining room), and even though it was scary I couldn't help laughing at our little rocking chair, which was rocking away furiously all by itself. Our nurse Danny lurched in from her room and yelled at us to hurry and stand with her in the doorway in case the ceiling fell in, but before we could get there the quaking stopped and I remember that we were disappointed because there was almost no damage anywhere, and we were hustled off to school at the usual time. It was an anticlimax because my father had often told me about the San Francisco one, and had solemnly said that he had thought at the time that it was surely the end of the world.

There was only one nice thing (I thought) about this minor quake: my orthodontist was knocked down his cellar steps, sprained his ankle, and canceled all appointments for three weeks.

The next earthquake occurred when I was walking arm in arm down a street in San Francisco with a teen-age cousin from Cedar Rapids, Anne Hamilton. We were walking downhill from the Fairmont Hotel on our way to Chinatown (just a little sight-seeing trip) and we were laughing and chattering away, and paying little attention to anything except ourselves, but we did notice that people were really behaving peculiarly.

"Crazy grown-ups," we remarked, "daffy Friscans!" as increasing numbers dashed out of their houses and apartments, all looking up and down, some of them actually running. We edged around some of them, jostled others, and never did know that an earthquake was taking place until we returned to the Fairmont for lunch. Our parents reported that it was a fairly severe quake and that they had been nervous about us; in fact, as I recall, we were scolded for not taking the earthquake seriously.

When I was watching a play one evening at Vassar College in

1925, the third earthquake took place. We were in the Students'
Building, almost the entire student body, and all of us looking at
the stage, when suddenly the big chandelier high above us began
swinging wildly, a low rumbling noise came from the ground
below us, and at the same time I could see the balcony above (I
was in the orchestra) begin to creak and undulate.

Instantly I knew what it was and instinctively jumped to my
feet and vaulted nimbly over the three friends sitting next to me,
landed in the aisle and tore out the nearest exit, clattered down
the steps to the big green lawn and pulled up short. Others were
there ahead of me, all out of breath too, and we were joined by
dozens more. It turned out that everyone there was from California and other mountain states, Japan, and the Hawaiian Islands.

A stage manager had come on stage after I had left and had reassured the puzzled audience that everything was fine and said to
stay where they were. None of us returned, but sat around in the
moonlight talking about our earthquake experiences.

The next day I ran into Dean Ella McCaleb, a retired charming
old friend. "I was so relieved to learn that it was an earthquake,"
she told me. "I thought I was having a stroke."

And that is enough about San Francisco and earthquakes, except for one strange thing that I have always wondered about. In
an almanac printed in those days in California called Zeitler's was
the following message:

> Some time during the early part of the year 1906, a severe under-
> ground earthquake will occur in the San Francisco area, doing
> great damage, probably in the month of February.

ℯ𝒻ℴ 2

Scotland in Iowa

CEDAR RAPIDS, IOWA, had a population in 1837 of one: a horse thief by the name of Osgood Shepherd. In 1838 the population rose to five when he built a log cabin by the Cedar River and brought his wife there and their two children and his aged father.

Osgood vanished several years later, but other settlers were arriving and it was thought that he was caught at his racket. In those days it was easy to walk off with someone's bay horse, dye it black during the night, and sell it the next morning to a traveler or settler on his way down the river. When a good rainstorm came along, the black horse turned brown again, and thus originated the phrase "a horse of a different color."

In the year I was born—1905—Cedar Rapids had a population of about twenty thousand people. The Douglas family must have seemed an odd group to the other residents, for they never discarded their Scotch ways and customs, but stuck firmly by them. Not only did we have collie and sheltie dogs with names like Jeanie and Roderick Dhu, but we children drove around in a wicker-basket-type cart behind a cross little black Shetland pony called Neddie. Out by the barn and stables was a little round dog-kennel house with runways where West Highland terriers were raised commercially.

Why had the Douglases come to Cedar Rapids in the first place? Because my grandfather George Douglas, a stonecutter and construction engineer who lived in Thurso, Scotland, was asked to come to the United States and help to build a railroad that would run from Chicago to Omaha, Nebraska. I've forgotten what the railroad was called originally, but it was known for years as the Chicago and Northwestern, and if you are familiar with it at all, you may have noticed that the engines all run along on the left-hand tracks and the engineers all look out of their cabs for signals through the left-hand windows just the way they do in the British Isles. They say that when the trains arrive in Omaha and have to cross over to the Union Pacific right-hand tracks, there is a fearful switching and a cursing of grandfather Douglas to this very day.

Cedar Rapids, being just about halfway between the two cities, seemed to be the best place for Grandfather to settle, especially as a cousin of his, Robert Stuart, was already living there and with his two sons had started a small cereal plant which was turning out a variety of rolled and steel-cut oats. Grandfather put some money into the company, and as a result his railroad was given the business of shipping oats East and West.

The company did well, and around the turn of the century merged with another oat mill, known as the American Cereal Company. What should they name the new company? They found that one brand of the Douglas-Stuart Mills outsold all the others (actually they were all exactly the same but were packaged differently), and it was known as the Quaker brand. The name evidently sounded solid and honest and safe for babykin's oatmeal, so they named the big new company the Quaker Oats Company, and that is what it has been called ever since.

Our little bit of Scotland included a dour Scot named Ross who kept the horses glossy and well groomed. He was also excellent with the bagpipes and he piped my father and mother into dinner every night when there was company. And while we children ate our oatmeal ·porridge and applesauce upstairs in the nursery with our Scotch nurse Miss MacDannel (known to us as Danny) the men in the family appeared for dinner in full-dress kilt. My father and his two brothers all lived near each other at this time, and it was a grand sight to behold them (I've been told), all tall and handsome, wearing the pleated kilts of the ancient Douglas plaid, the colors of soft blues and greens, and each with a short-waisted dress jacket of black or gray velvet or heavy silk twill (a material then called bombazine).

After dinner there was often a game of whist (that would be the forerunner of bridge) and I learned that gentlewomen in those time referred to the spade suit as "lily." The word "spade" or "*pique*" was considered vulgar, especially as the design started out as the fleur-de-lys. Besides whist there was music. My mother played the harp and the piano, and there was also an Aeolian pipe organ that played (when pumped furiously) rolls of music. (Several years later I remember pumping away at the thing myself while singing "Oh, Where, Tell Me Where, Has My Highland Laddie Gone" accompanied by the proper notes, thanks to the self-unwinding paper roll, with all the stops pulled out. The noise was like the dawn coming up like thunder indeed.)

Mother and her two sisters-in-law never dressed in kilts, at least not in the evening. They all three wore custom-made Parisian dresses from Paul Poiret, Worth, Patou, Callot Soeurs, Vionnet, always gowns from *La Haute Couture*.

My Uncle Walter, a handsome widower, was the most sought-after man in town and there were all sorts of scandalous things whispered about him. And sure enough, a married lady friend named Mrs. Benedict left Mr. Benedict, obtained a divorce (hard to do in those days), and she and Uncle Walter were married in Washington, D.C.

They returned to Cedar Rapids, and while the tongues wagged furiously, proceeded to enjoy every minute of each other's company. Mother told me that they were just plain in love the same as she and my father were.

The Stuart family (our Scotch cousins) were far more conservative than the Douglas clan, and were perfectly horrified when Uncle Walter married Mahala. Mrs. Robert Stuart announced that she would never have a divorcée in her house, especially one who smoked.

The Robert Stuarts were in Pinehurst at the time of this second marriage in Washington, and Uncle Walter took his bride down to North Carolina and moved into the same hotel, in fact into a suite on the same floor.

Aunt Mahala told me years later that she was scared stiff and shook in her shoes at the thought of meeting this straitlaced pair, but Uncle Walter merely said to her, "My dear Mahala, just be your natural attractive self, and you will take them into camp. Come on." And he led her down the hall, knocked on their door, and apparently cousin Maggie found her as intoxicating as Prohibition, for they became lifelong friends.

My memory of Father and kilts began shortly after I started to attend the public school in Cedar Rapids. We girls—my sister and I and the daughters of our coachman and head gardener—had brought our lunch boxes to a place under a big elm tree and sat down on the ground in a circle. Along came some older boys who began yelling at Barbara and me:

"You think you're pretty fancy and rich, doncha?" We said nothing.

"Well, you're all wrong," they shouted. "Your father is a *sissy.*"

"Yah-yah!" They all jumped up and down. Barbara started to cry.

"Your father's a sissy, just a gol-darn sissy!"

I was furious and stood up spilling cookies and hard-boiled eggs every which way.

"He's nothing of the kind!" I exclaimed firmly. "Go away and leave us alone."

"He's a sissy!" one of them shouted back, and stuck out his tongue. "He wears *skirts!*" he said, and they all started swishing around like ladies, bowing to each other and pretending to pull skirts aside.

"He does *not* wear skirts!" I stamped my foot in great anger. "He wears *kilts. All* Scots wear kilts."

"They're *skirts!*" was the answer, and they ran off.

When I got home that afternoon I was still furious and couldn't wait until my father got home from the office to tell him what those horrid little boys said about him.

He was very amused. "They are just trying to make you mad, trying to get your goat," he said. "They know that you live in a big house and most of them probably live in smaller ones. They are envious and would like to live in Brucemore." He pulled out his pipe and lit it.

"I'll tell you what you do." He chuckled and took a puff before he spoke.

"Be very polite to them from now on. Don't ever show that you are mad. Smile pleasantly. Be sure you look boys, and girls too, straight in the eye. You're their *friend*. You *like* them. You've got a job to do but I know that you can do it. And no boasting *ever* about living in a large house."

He took another puff on his pipe and added, "By the way, should they say anything further about my wearing skirts, you might ask them *politely* if they know what a Scot wears under his kilt."

"What do they wear?" I asked, round-eyed.

"I'm not saying," he replied, "but we kilt wearers are pretty masculine, and that's a fact."

I never quite understood any of this until one summer years later in Gleneagles, Scotland, when I learned that it was considered a mark of honor not to wear anything under the kilt. There was one exception: a high-stepping drummer wore a brief pair of shorts of matching plaid.

Another time, shortly after this sissy stuff, someone else at school made a remark in front of me about my father, saying that he was the president or head of a whole lot of things, and asked me if it wasn't true. I said that I didn't know and was told that I was either lying or else a dumbbell. I hurried home and asked Dad what he did at his office.

"I'm a merchant," he answered, "and furthermore there are a lot of us in town, so it is nothing to get excited or conceited about."

Shortly after this I also remember coming home from school and telling my father that I had made a new friend.

"Her name is Thelma Mahannah," I told him, "and she asked me what you did when you went to work every day and I said that you were a merchant."

He nodded. "That's right."

"Then I asked her what her father did and she said that he was a piano tuner. Then she said, 'My mother and I think that he is the Best Piano Tuner in town.' She's awfully nice."

"She sounds great to me," he said. "Someone I'd like to meet. The next time she comes here be sure to introduce me to her."

Brucemore: What was it like?

At first the property was just a big front lawn sweeping uphill to the stark three-story red-brick house standing bleakly at the top, a driveway to the left, and a sidewalk ascending to the right. That was all; behind the house it was strictly farm. There were stables and cow barns and a pond for ducks. There were fields of corn and alfalfa, chicken houses and a pigsty, and beyond was a dense woods filled with hazelnut bushes and walnut and butternut trees.

Gradually the farm receded. First the big white barn departed and an orchard with a playhouse and swings for us took its place, then a formal garden and tennis court appeared adjacent to the house, next a greenhouse and a squash court, then the pond became landscaped and a pair of white swans floated on the surface.

Today there is still a vegetable garden, which is hidden away behind the garage, and I noticed the last time that I saw it, it contained a mere three rows of sweet corn. Brucemore has become completely citified.

The house too has lost its stark Victorian look, thanks to the addition of many porches and terraces and surrounding trees. It still is a curious house both inside and outside. Each of its thirty-odd rooms contains a fireplace, and each one is different. There are two stairways to each of the three main stories and the attic, as well as the cellar, and there is also an elevator shaft. There are two basements, one with recreation rooms and laundries and a furnace room, and a lower one for storing vegetables and wine. There is a tunnel leading from the lower cellar over to the Garden House (a two-bedroom guest house) two hundred feet away. One can still crawl through it quite comfortably. It's purpose? It carried steam heat in a big pipe from Brucemore's two big coal furnaces.

Up on the third floor there is a small secret room with its own cozy little bay window looking down on the garden. Whyfore? Back in the 1920s a new and larger pipe organ was installed. The smaller pipes were all put in a third-floor guest room, the larger pipes being down in the cellar, and the bay window was walled off with an extra ten square feet, making it the smallest and most private room in the house. (The next book I write is going to be a whodunit, all laid in Brucemore, and the body will be found in the secret room. It will turn out to be the corpse of a clever little old man who lived all his life in Brucemore with no one knowing it. He came and went via the empty tunnel of course, used the elevator when we were running down the stairs, etc.)

Outside, the workmen that were brought over from Ireland to build the house also left their individual touches. The four big stone chimneys are each carved in a different design. Each side of the house bears different stone or slate inlaid areas to relieve the monotony of the brick, and the lintels over the windows and doors are each carved differently.

One last thing about Brucemore: the library is haunted (shades of the little old man). One night when I was studying algebra my father and I were sitting in the library with a fire going and the lights turned low. He was reading in his favorite armchair, his reading lamp turned on, and I was over at the desk. All of a sudden we both heard a soft swishing noise coming from above the fireplace. We looked up and to our amazement saw, in the dim light, a tall ceramic vase moving from its post at the right-hand edge of the long mantelpiece. It was moving slowly but steadily toward the other matching blue vase at the left edge. There was nothing else on the mantel.

Dad rose to his feet.

"This cannot be," he stated firmly, peering at the mantel closely. "Aha, I know," he exclaimed. "There's a mouse in it." He picked it up, turned it over and shook it but nothing fell out. The two vases, being each two feet tall and smooth, would have presented difficulties to any and all mice.

I stood up too. "What did it?" I quavered, feeling the palms of my hands turning clammy.

Dad looked bewildered. "It's not a practical joke," he announced. "There are no strings or invisible threads around." He turned to me after running his hands over and under the mantel. "It can only be that the thing is on a slant. Perhaps the house is settling. Tomorrow we'll get a carpenter's level and prove it."

With this announcement he went back to his book. The next day the mantel turned out to be perfectly level. Even a golf ball remained in stable equilibrium when perched next to the creeping vase. It made Dad so cross and puzzled that we refrained from talking about it.

A week or so later a scientist of some sort of psychology or parapsychology appeared at Brucemore. My father had sent for him from the University of Chicago and he made a special trip to Brucemore. Dad met him in the front hall and told him in a few terse words to go over the whole house, and give his scientific opinion: was there any part of it that seemed different from the rest?

To Dad's great surprise, the professor, after a careful private inspection of the whole place, announced at lunch that the only part of the house with a strange and unnatural atmosphere was the library. He couldn't explain, he said, but there was something wrong with it. He would like to stay on and conduct some experiments; perhaps it would take weeks or even months.

After lunch father marched him to the door and the car drove him to the station, and that was the end of the library's future as some kind of an official psychic phenomenon.

Later on that winter a committee that I belonged to had a meeting in the hall just outside the library. The long velvet curtains at the room's entrance had been pulled, and there were fifteen of us who sat in a circle in the hall, which when the curtains were drawn turned into a room, also with its own large fireplace.

The meeting had been called regarding a Christmas party that our club was giving. As we listened to reports about the cost of refreshments and the orchestra we suddenly heard a loud groan of agony, more bestial than human, coming clearly from the library, behind the heavy draperies.

My first thought was that one of the members had crawled in as a joke and was trying to scare us (word of the moving vase had spread).

Quickly we counted noses but everyone was there. Then we decided that sister Barbara and some of her crowd had hidden away in there, but the room was empty when we turned on the lights, and it had no hiding places or secret exits.

Some of the committee girls were so unnerved that they left at once, and we finished up the meeting around the dining-room table.

This strange groaning sound has been heard several more times since then, as well as the sound of low menacing laughter. My mother decided that it was a friendly poltergeist of some sort, pointing out that it never left the library, nor did it ever do harm to anyone, and the groans and laughter were too far away to ever wake anyone up, nor ever really disturbed anyone, and the vase never moved again.

The last time that I heard the poltergeist was several years ago. I had gone up the front stairway and had just reached the landing when I heard a semi-moan ending in a hoarse sort of cackle. Believe me, being all alone in that part of the house, I broke into a wild dash, reached the second flight of stairs and arrived in my room as if shot from a pneumatic tube.

Parties at Brucemore were different in all sorts of ways from what we have today. First of all, most big houses, instead of the present-day recreation room in the basement, had a ballroom in the attic. I even remember five or six in Cedar Rapids and they were perfectly lovely. One was in the attic of the Walter Cherry house and it had pale pink walls with crystal and gold side brackets lighting it up, there being no windows. It had a little platform for a three-piece orchestra, a smooth parquet floor, sixty-odd gold chairs around the walls, and a skylight overhead draped with artificial roses and pink ribbons. The skylight opened up to cool us off when the dance floor was crowded, and there was an adjacent sitting room where the chaperones sat, and where stood the ever-present big cut-glass punch bowl, filled with ginger ale and fruit juices.

Besides dancing, I remember playing exciting games of musical chairs, and marching grand right and left: when the music stopped you danced with the boy facing you. There was also a circle two-step that mixed up the boys and girls, and a dance where couples were eliminated if caught holding a feather duster when the music stopped.

Some of these private dancing parties were called cotillions, and that meant that there were favors. Usually they were laid out on a table and consisted of a dozen fancy paper hats and some lovely Japanese fans and perhaps a dozen tissue-paper colored boas, and so on.

The girls sat on one side of the ballroom and the boys on the opposite. The hostess would choose ten boys from the ranks and ask each of them to take a favor to a dancing partner. After they had danced a short time, they would sit down and she would pick another group. We thought a cotillion was "divine."

The private ballroom was good training for us shy young people who felt awkward and strange all dressed up and having to dance with people of the opposite sex. The girls of that period went to dancing school to learn how to waltz and fox-trot and even daringly do the tango, but we usually danced with other girls. If there *were* any boys, there were never enough to go around and they were generally shorter and rebelliously surly.

Another nonexistent party today is the tea dance, or *thé dansant* as they were called in the higher social circles. They usually took place from 5 to 7 P.M., and a private tea dance could take place in the private ballroom too. Tea or punch was served, and ice cream and cake, and the girls wore short dresses, and the boys cutaways or dark suits with white shirts and sometimes gates-ajar stiff collars.

Holidays too were special times at Brucemore, celebrated with little or no commercial help, and none of that "only 14 more shopping days" publicity, so to speak. We made out Christmas lists in the middle of December, assembled the presents soon after, and proceeded to wrap them up on the twenty-third or twenty-fourth.

Christmas gifts were always wrapped in white tissue paper, tied up with red or green cord or ribbon, and usually carried a small Christmas paper seal or two to help stick the tissue flat. Most seals were a small wreath of holly with a red bow, or a head of Santa Claus or a small Christmas tree.

The present was tagged with an equally traditional white rectangular card on a red string, and on them we wrote conventional things like "Merry Christmas to Grandmother with love from So-and-so." Girl friends exchanged all kinds of presents with each other, but boys could send only flowers or candy or a book to girls they liked or else something comical and inexpensive. Once I received an innocent-looking cardboard box, and when I opened it, out shot a yard-long rattlesnake, made of a cloth-covered coiled spring, and the boy who had sent it had pasted a photograph of his face on the front end of the snake. It was a sensation. However, if a heavy beau sent anything like a gold bracelet, back it went with a polite note of thanks for the kind thought; it could not be accepted.

Christmas at Brucemore was a glorious affair each year, as our high-ceilinged house had a three-story stairwell and standing in it tall and towering was a really huge Christmas tree, about fifty-feet high. It took the entire household to trim it with silver tinsel and red and gold ornaments and frosted white tree lights. It was always chopped down on December 24 and came in from our own woods, drawn by Maude and Dobbin, the farm horses, and when it was set up in the main entrance a few steps down from the front hall, the whole house smelled like a pine forest all through the holidays. There was only one drawback; it took up so much room that no one could come in through the front door, but luckily there was a side door that was close by, which was better than having to crawl in on all fours.

On Christmas morning when we were young we opened our stocking presents upstairs in the breakfast room, then had breakfast and got dressed, and then all descended together downstairs to the big front hall, where we all lined up in front of the tree, while Mr. Bidwell, the organist of the Presbyterian church, played Christmas carols.

All the servants came in, and everyone who lived on the place, and we all wished them Merry Christmas, and Mother and Dad gave the grown-ups shiny new gold pieces, each in a little velvet box or purse, and we sisters gave all the children big red-and-white-striped candy canes tied with red satin ribbon, and oranges and almonds in gold net bags.

After they left we opened our presents, greeted friends who dropped in and later ate a traditional Christmas dinner of turkey and flaming plum pudding, and welcomed visitors all afternoon at a traditional open house, ending the day with a cold buffet supper, deviled eggs and cold turkey and potato salad, which waited for us in the pantry.

The next day we put all the presents away, and except for the tree and the Christmas wreaths in the windows and at the doors, returned to normal.

Today the Merry Yuletide season is more beautiful than it ever used to be, what with the gorgeous lighting effects that turn our department stores into fairylands, amd our city streets into spectacles of everything from scenes right out of the *Nutcracker Suite* or *The Arabian Nights* to the town of Bethlehem itself. However, the season lasts too long.

What were other holidays like in the good old days? The Fourth of July was completely different: we had firecrackers. Girls and boys woke up at dawn's early light and sneaked outdoors, lit a long, thin brown cigar-like object called "punk," something that burned very slowly; in fact, as I remember, a stick of punk lasted perhaps an hour. After getting the punk going, then we took out a long string of little red firecrackers called "lady crackers." These were much the best because they made the most noise in the fastest amount of time.

In our case, carrying the punk in one hand and the lady crackers in the other, sister Barbara and I arrived at a spot just below the sleeping porch where my father slept during the summer. There was a brick terrace there and we lit the long fuse to the whole bunch and ran as far away as we could before they went off. It was a glorious moment.

We also had torpedoes that we hurled to the pavement and if they landed properly they made one deafening roar that was extremely satisfactory. Besides these, there was another noisemaker called a son-of-a-gun. It was a small round pellet which one tossed to the ground and then stamped on it furiously with the heel and it made loud crackling noises, smelled very brimstonish, and flashed sparks.

Thus the day passed pleasantly, and when evening came things got even better. First we lighted sparklers and sent paper balloons aloft filled with hot air, then as it grew darker we shot off Roman candles, being careful not to point them at any friends.

By this time we had moved to the tennis court where the

grown-ups took over, shooting off pinwheels and flowerpots and finally the favorite of all: a series of glorious rockets.

My special favorite, since it was mine alone, was my Halloween birthday. Long before the days of "trick or treat" my family always gave me a Witch Hunt. It was the most exciting event imaginable, for it took place outdoors through a wooded area crisscrossed by paths. Actually this was an uncultivated part of land out in the back side of Brucemore. Thirty or forty of us would start off in groups of seven or eight, each bunch of us following our own trail. One set of boys and girls followed a trail of regular yellow corn, the next a trail of white corn, another group went after candy corn, and so on. Along the way there were various exciting things to help us find the witch. A lighted jack-o-lantern apiece, a bushel basket of horns, one for each of us, and a sign that said, "Blow horns to scare witch, for she is near." At another spot there were apples in case we needed energy, and peanuts, and noisemakers appeared before us at regular intervals. As it grew dark it became more exciting, and finally there *at last* hung the witch, right in our path, tall and huge, dressed in black tar paper and tall black pointed hat with a terrible white face and gray yarn hair.

But she was always carried back near to the main house and onto a brick terrace where there was a big shallow pool, now empty of water for the winter and filled with dead leaves. In the middle stood a stake and the witch was tied to it, the fire was started, and the witch burned up most gorgeously, while we watched and ate doughnuts and drank cider. It was always a successful party, and the team that reached the witch first received a special prize. One year the winners all got black furry kittens, one apiece. How the rest of us envied them.

Once when I was very young a respectable and well-to-do bachelor cousin wrote from somewhere in Perth, Scotland, inviting himself to come and stay a month with his Iowa relatives. He was Sir Sholto Archibald Douglas-Hamilton; he was thirty-four years old, had never visited "the States," and wondered if he should bring his golf clubs or . . . were there no golf links available?

My father wrote and suggested that he spend the month of October at Brucemore, the autumn being the best season in the Middle West, and he added that there were several golf links in the vicinity, but he noted apologetically that compared to St. Andrews and Dornoch and so on, our links were new and primitive.

Sir Sholto arrived on an afternoon train in the early fall with all sorts of bags and valises and satchels, minus the golf clubs, and begged pardon for traveling with so little baggage. He was a large tweedy type with a bushy beard, a splendid Scotch brogue, and a warm smile.

When my father conducted him to our new car, a large gray open Stoddard Dayton, he was amazed. "By Jove!" he exclaimed. "You have a motah." He turned to my father. "And you have roads?" he asked.

My father nodded. The chauffeur got the luggage in somehow, cranked the motor, and off they went.

Sir Sholto seemed dumbfounded. "My word"—he pointed his finger—"you seem to have sidewalks. I say—er—it seems far more civilized than I had believed the Middle West to be." He turned to Daddy. "Cousin George, sir, are the Indians hereabouts friendly or otherwise?" He patted his bulging overcoat pocket. "I thought it best to come fully armed."

Daddy answered solemnly that there were in fact several Indian tribes in the vicinity, that on a clear night one could see the smoke from their tepees across the cornfields, and that they were friendly unless they drank too much firewater, which only happened on Saturday nights.

Sir Sholto was delighted. "They carry tommy-hawks, of course," he suggested.

"Tomahawks," my father corrected him. "And of course bows and arrows. Steel arrowheads nowadays," he added. "Cost plenty wampum."

"What sort of Indians?" Sir Sholto asked eagerly.

"The local tribes are the Tama Indians," Daddy said after a

moment of busy thinking. "I think they must be Sioux or Dakota or a mixture of both."

After they had reached Brucemore and the auto had snorted up the long elm-shaded driveway to the house, he was welcomed by Mother and the brothers, his luggage was dispatched to his room, and he was told that dinner would be at eight, with a before-dinner drink served in the library (the word "cocktail" was not yet in use), and that Daddy's valet would have his dinner jacket laid out for him.

Poor cousin Sholto turned beet-red with embarrassment. "I say." He faced them bravely. "I've nowt but apologies. I—I thought that you were all a bunch of wild and woollies. I didn't bring any proper clothes—just rough gear for stalking Indians— aye, that's about it." He turned to Daddy. "You and your savages!" And he laughed uproariously. "Aye, and I believed it all until I saw your bonnie Brucemore."

He was a delightful guest and proved to be an excellent marksman and hunter. He taught Margaret the Highland Fling and the Sword Dance, and when he returned home he sent mother a Black Angus Aberdeen bull and cow. And that is enough about Scotland in Iowa.

3
Motoring

WHEN MY PARENTS celebrated their twenty-fifth wedding anniversary, instead of giving Mother a silver water pitcher my father gave her the latest thing in automobiles: a Locomobile cabriolet. Originally, a cabriolet was a light two-seated carriage, drawn by one horse. This Locomobile 48 was what we now would call a four-door convertible sedan. However, it converted in all sorts of ways that cars no longer do. It started out as a limousine with glass windows rolled up and a black top covering everyone. Then part of the top could be removed, leaving the chauffeur out in the sunshine and the family (two in the back seat and two on small folding seats) sitting in the shade.

Or the whole top could be folded down and covered with a black canvas cover, putting everyone in the sunshine, or everything could fold away except a shell-like rear part of the top which would shade only the two people in the back seat, if you follow me.

The Locomobile differed from all other cars because perched on top of the big ordinary headlights were the dimmers, looking rather like eyebrows in their little square nickel-plated boxes. It reminded me of a hippopotamus in a way, whose eyes can look at you when the rest of him is submerged.

It was a beautiful shade of almond green inside and out, except the chauffeur's seat, which was black. The car was so low to the ground that its bottom scraped the road when a dip or gully confronted it; only a short step to reach the running board, then a step up, and there you were.

I was very proud of the fact that it had four shifts forward instead of the usual three, and Bert, Mother's chauffeur, told me that this car *averaged* thirty-five miles per hour on the open road, whereas the ordinary Apperson or Studebaker or Cadillac or Chandler averaged thirty.

These Locomobiles were six-cylinder cars, and were first manufactured in 1917 by the Locomobile Company of America in Bridgeport, Connecticut, and they were supposed to have the finest materials and workmanship in the United States. They were expensive, like the Pierce-Arrow, Stevens-Duryea, White, Chadwick, Crane-Simplex, and Peerless: all quality vehicles, and the Locomobile was more popular than every other except the Pierce-Arrow. Even in those days the price was above $10,000, but they were built to last, and ten years later they were still going strong, sleek in appearance and the only American car for a long time that had one long unbroken line from radiator cap to tail. It had another unique feature. At the very rear of the car was a flat black rectangular container-thing that looked as if it might hold a spare tire but it didn't. When it was opened up it revealed four thin black leather suitcases, handy for overnight motor trips.

What happened to the Locomobile? When my father died in 1923 I remember that Mother, Barbara, Margaret, and I all went to the cemetery in it with Bert driving, and after that Mother never used it again. It stayed in the garage, up on blocks, for several years. Then I think she gave it away, for once when I came back to Cedar Rapids from somewhere it was missing from its corner, and was never seen again, nor ever mentioned.

During this time and up through the twenties, there were so many different models that everyone in a neighborhood could have a different make. Moving around ours in Cedar Rapids, for example, Colonel Robbins, the nearest neighbor, drove a khaki-colored Kissel Kar. Next door to him the large Koch family had a Dort (which had a Rolls-Royce type of radiator) and a Jordan, and on the corner were the Dunshees, who had an Owen-Magnetic, which I think was always in the repair shop. There were people who drove Moons and Stars, plus Wintons and Durants, Metzes, Marmons, Auburns and Nashes, and on and on.

Back at Brucemore sister Margaret had her first car: a Dodge coupé with yellow wire wheels and a gear shift that was not like any other car's; the low gear was down at the left, second was up and across to the right, and third, or high, was down to the right. It was dangerous to learn how to drive in a Dodge and then drive someone else's car. I stripped the gears of a friend's Essex this way, and she was never much of a friend after that. I also ruined my father's car once. (That was in the year 1921 at age fifteen.) I had a date with a boy in the neighborhood who had walked over from his house and we daringly decided to borrow Dad's Moline Knight. This car was his pride and joy and it was made in Moline, Illinois, by a friend, a Mr. Velie, who was an automobile maker of the time.

We sneaked out to the garage, got the thing running (it must have had a self-starter) and backed it out nicely, steered it down the back driveway, took turns driving it around some country roads, and brought it back home without incident. But we couldn't maneuver it back into the garage. Instead we managed to wedge it firmly into the door post. It wouldn't go forward or backward, so we had to abandon it, and stupidly forgot to turn off the ignition.

When Bert arrived later with the Locomobile, the car was smoking away furiously. He managed to douse the red-hot wires and the next day a carpenter came to do major repair work on the garage.

In those days a chauffeur had to be an expert driver, a good mechanic, and a handyman with the sponge, chamois, and garden hose. Not only did he need to shift gears smoothly and silently; he also had to be able to change a tire smoothly and quickly (punctures occurred so frequently that one on a two-hour trip was about average), and any car that was driven on a dirt road needed a wash afterward.

Even with a chauffeur in charge of the garage it was necessary to have a general knowledge of simple mechanics. I remember knowing how to prime the engine in case it wouldn't start on a cold day, and how to crank it when the self-starter wouldn't work, and I knew how to jack up a car and pry the tire off with a tire iron, and even patch up the inner tube and pump up the tire again so that it was as good as new.

Chauffeurs led a busy life working for families like ours when each adult had his own car. As I recall, Bert had an assistant who did the car washing and filling the gasoline tanks and general maintenance.

On motor trips they were well treated. Many hotels and inns had chauffeurs' dining rooms, and even some large estates. For example, Bert was very fond of the chauffeurs' dining room at San Simeon, William Randolph Hearst's ranch. My parents were old friends of Madam Hearst, Mr. Hearst's mother (early in the century it was proper to refer to the widowed mother of prominent men as Madam) and Bert used to drive Mother and Dad up there from Santa Barbara, usually for Sunday lunch.

Bert used to save the menus, which actually had "San Simeon Ranch, Chauffeurs' Dining Room" printed at the top. The menu followed below, with a choice of chicken fricassee and rice, calves' liver and bacon, or pork tenderloin for the entrée.

The car that was a real joy was my mother's very own Rauch and Lang Electric. It was easy to drive. It had a steering bar which you pushed forward to make it go left, and pulled in toward your stomach to turn right. The brake and the accelerator were on the floor, and the bell to warn people of your approach was a pearl button in the end of the steering bar. To turn the current on was accomplished by a switch thing on the left. You pushed it forward and away you went, smoothly and silently. Going downhill you could work up a terrific head of steam, as the whole contraption was heavy as lead; the two large storage batteries fore and aft must have weighed a ton apiece.

The electric got its batteries recharged every night. I remember the charger's green flashing light in a corner of the garage, and the big black machine had a red sign on it saying DANGER: KEEP AWAY.

Mother never drove anything but her Electric, and once she was invited to a three-day meeting of the Garden Clubs of the Mid-West, or some such thing, which was going to take place in Davenport, Iowa, about eighty miles away. The road there was terrible in those days and it was too long a trip anyway without charging up the batteries along the way, so she took the car with her on the train. It went majestically along on a flatcar at the rear of the train, with some handy planks sitting beside it, and when Mother descended from her parlor car at the Davenport station, the brakeman and the station switchman set up a ramp descending to the tracks, and Mr. Velie (he and Mrs. Velie, who lived in Moline just across the Mississippi River, had met the train) graciously drove the Electric off the flatcar to solid ground, and then followed Mother and Mrs. Velie home in his own car, which was (guess what) a Velie roadster.

The flatcar was moved to a siding until Mother returned to Cedar Rapids after a rewarding visit. But on the return trip the Electric had company on the flatcar. Blowing wildly in the breeze were a dozen shrubs known to Garden Club ladies as *Taxus cuspidata* (yews to you) plus several hundred pachysandra plants and a new tree for Brucemore's front lawn: an olive tree, which I am happy to report is still alive and well but remarkably old and gnarled.

Have you ever wondered which was the largest motorcar built in the United States? It was the seven-passenger Pierce-Arrow, an open touring car. And the smallest? That would be the Crosley with its little washing-machine motor, seating four small people or two large—but this one came much later and was popular during World War II.

The Cadillac was the car with the most cylinders (sixteen) and was built as a rival to the Packard Twin-Six, the popular handsome twelve-cylinder car.

The cheapest car for us grown-ups (there were some toy cars that were cheaper) was of course Mr. Ford's famous Tin Lizzie, which cost $300 and was always black. Its competitors were the Overland, made by our friend Mr. Velie, and the Chevrolet, which was made in Detroit by Chevrolet Motors.

There were all sorts of variety to these old-time automobiles. Take the Franklin, for instance. It was made mostly of wood, and furthermore it had no radiator, which gave it an odd slanting look up front. It was air-cooled, and I'd say not too successfully. The Metz was strange (it had a disk clutch), the Cord (1929–37) had a front-wheel drive, the Stanley Steamer was driven by you-know-what, the Cole had a round chassis and looked like a big long cylinder on wheels, and so on and so on.

The best-looking car? The Duesenberg, many of us would tell you. Some raved about the Marmon as being the Dream Car (the

Kissel and the Auburn were copies of it). Others were crazy about the Stutz and the Mercer, and Wills St. Claire owners would have fought rather than switched.

The name Wills St. Claire takes me back to 1929 or 1930, when my cousin John Stuart, Jr., and a friend of his, Phelps Dunham (called Gus), were in New York City, and with them was the Stuarts' Wills St. Claire.

Gus's wife was there too, and for some reason she was going back to Chicago on the Twentieth Century Limited leaving at 6:00 P.M. Jack and Gus went with her down the red carpet that was always rolled out for Century passengers in Grand Central Station and saw her off with much waving.

Then they hurried out of the station, crossed over to the Hotel Biltmore, where the Wills St. Claire was parked, jumped into the car, and off they went, heading for Chicago. On present-day roads and interstate highways that bypass cities and towns it is about 850 miles from New York to Chicago, but it must have been close to 900 miles then, and yet when Mrs. Dunham descended the Pullman car steps the next morning at 8:40 (the train was precisely on time), there stood her husband Gus and cousin Jack to greet her.

The epilogue to the tale is that Gus was killed in an auto accident later on that summer. (I was not surprised, nor was anyone else.) Cousin Jack is still going strong, and the Wills was retired after an eventful and colorful existence.

Personally I used to think the Packard was the handsomest, but on the other hand I chose a pale pea-green Lincoln convertible roadster for my college-graduation present. My husband used to like Cadillacs and La Salles, but then one Saturday afternoon in 1939 he won, in a red-dog game, Guy Lombardo's custom-made LeBaron Lincoln and we both agreed that it was indeed the best-looking thing we'd ever driven around in. It was a dark spruce green, a convertible sedan, and when we raised its fawn-colored top for the first time we were amazed to find the canvas full of holes. Mrs. Lombardo (that would be Lily Belle) used to drive it all over Long Island, always with the top down, and when she finished a cigarette she threw it merrily over her shoulder.

The new top arrived from Detroit eventually and we loved the car dearly except for one thing. It was long before power steering, and on the winding roads of Connecticut, where we were living, it took two people holding onto the steering wheel to get the car around a curve. Lily Belle must have had muscular power like Man Mountain Dean.

And what was my very own favorite car? Besides the pea-green Lincoln with the rumble seat lined in pea-green leather ("The car sure is a dream and sure drives classy," Bert wired me when he picked it up in Detroit to deliver to me at college), which I loved madly back in 1927, I also loved even better a very strange car that I owned in the summer of 1965. It was an Amphicar, an amphibious vehicle that I purchased at Abercrombie & Fitch, the only car that I ever bought by turning to the salesman and saying, "Charge and send." And he did.

It turned up in New Jersey the next day, also painted light green and equipped with not only a spare tire but also life preservers for four, fifty feet of nylon rope, a boat hook, a bumper-fender of white canvas, and a bull horn.

I called it "The Half Nelson," for Nelson Doubleday, because Doubleday & Company sent me a check one day for the paperback rights of a book that I had written for them and I blew the whole thing on this delightful contraption.

Three of us drove it to northern Michigan, a trip that I would never take again in an Amphicar. It was too small, and with the engine in the rear it was like leaning against a red-hot radiator when a person (me) sat in the back seat. We were cramped and stiff and had to get out and stretch every half hour, and when a great big truck passed us we had to head up into the wind, so to speak, as if we were sailing on the New York Thruway.

We met the nicest people, however, and as soon as a truck driver, or anyone for that matter, noticed the two propellers just above the rear axle, they would honk their horns, wave wildly, and shout all sorts of merry remarks. Little boys and old men with white beards and everything in between gathered whenever we stopped, and if there was any water nearby we took them for a swift dip in the drink.

Once we went through a red light somewhere in Ontario and immediately we could see in the rearview mirror a police car following us. Close ahead on our right was a small lake, so we snapped shut the watertight door locks, started the propellers revolving, and splashed merrily into the lake. I loved the expressions on the faces of the two policemen as we waved goodbye to them.

Finally a word about roads: back when cars were first being built, roads were perfectly horrible. Iowa farm roads, for example, were narrow and high-crowned with a ditch on each side. In dry weather they were so dusty that visibility was difficult, and in the rain the roads were slippery mud. In the city most main roads were macadam, brick, or cobblestone, also slippery in wet weather, and there were dusty gravel roads to skid on in the small towns.

One of the best roads in the whole United States back then was the Lincoln Highway, which was known as U.S. 30. It ran across the United States from New York to San Francisco. Nowadays, U.S. 30 goes just from Chicago to Portland. However, the Lincoln Highway, for those of us who lived in Cedar Rapids (in the twenties and thirties), was the only direct road to Chicago. To get there we got up at dawn's early light and drove to Lisbon, Iowa, with the greatest ease, for the entire seventeen-mile stretch was paved. Then the Lincoln Highway turned into a wide flat road of rich brown dirt, well graded all year round and plowed free of snow in the winter, but still a road of *dirt* and therefore unpredictable. If we were lucky, there had been a gentle shower the night before and there was no dust and the road was hard. Then we could easily drive the seventy-odd miles to Clinton, Iowa, at the Mississippi River, in two hours or better. From there the rest of the highway was paved straight into the Windy City one hundred and forty miles or so east, probably a drive of only four to five hours unless a tire went flat.

If there had been bad weather it was quite different. I remember driving home from Waterloo one summer (1925, I think). Cedar Rapids was a distance of seventy miles over an unpaved road. It had been a nice day and I had been playing in a golf tournament and found myself at 4 P.M. through with the match (I lost) and off for home driving a Chrysler sedan (a venerable family car) with the golf clubs and two little caddies in the back seat. I figured that I should be at Brucemore in two hours, and that Bert could take the caddies home, as I had some sort of a date at seven and would have ample time to change clothes and freshen up.

As I was driving along wondering whether to wear the white piqué with the daring lace midriff or the silk chiffon dress with the cherries printed all over it, the skies opened and the rains came. In five minutes the road was a sea of mud and the car slid off into the ditch.

I left the boys in the car, bravely struggled out of it, and found a farmhouse not too far away. The farmer, for three dollars, agreed to hitch up his team of horses and haul us out. A half hour later we were on our way, creeping along slowly and carefully in the center of the road. However, several miles further on another car approached me, and in order to pass I had to move over to the right. Presto—into the ditch we went again and so did the other car, each into our very own ditches.

We found another farmer and his handy team and for five dollars he volunteered to pull both cars out, a group rate. By this time it was getting dark and the caddies, each nine years old, were getting hungry and plaintive, so we stopped in Vinton (population 3,000) for sodas and candy bars, and with the rain still coming down managed to get stuck right on the main street of Vinton. Luckily a farmer in a truck with chains on his tires pushed the Chrysler out of the large hole in which it was resting, and we finally reached Cedar Rapids around nine-thirty. I was so happy to see the beautiful red-brick avenue gleaming away in the gas streetlights that I felt like tossing roses out of the windows.

It took years to get a network of paved roads all over the country but it began to happen in the late 1930s, and then as automobiles multiplied travel presented other problems, involving traffic and time. There were no motels in those days, and no hotels out on the edge of large cities, and every main road took you through the center of town. The roads were badly marked, and good road maps were still rare. The following is a true example of what I mean about maps (confidentially, if someone told me this story *I* wouldn't believe a word of it but it *is* true): Mother had two cousins, rather dumb and boring, who one summer started off on a motor trip, bundled up in dustcoats and wearing goggles. The car was loaded with tire patches, a hand pump for puffing up flat tires, an extra fan belt, plus water, oil, and the essential five-gallon can of gas in case they never found a gas station (scarce on most country roads).

These cousins set off one rainy morning and their plan was to drive to Spirit Lake, Iowa, a summer resort close to the Minnesota state line about three hundred miles northwest of Cedar Rapids. They drove all day in the rain, got stuck in the mud several times, and at nightfall stopped in a little town (I forget the name) and found a nice white wooden house that rented rooms to travelers. In those days there were many of these rooms available; big farmhouses usually had a spare room for rent, which is the reason for all those Traveling Salesman-Farmer's Daughter jokes.

The cousins remembered their white house as reasonably comfortable, with inside plumbing complete with an odorous chemical toilet. Their bedroom contained a lumpy double bed, and there was a white cat asleep on the front porch in the swing. They slept fairly well, had crullers and coffee for breakfast, and drove off. The weather was better, with less rain, but the roads were worse, and they spent another exhausting day skidding along at a snail's pace. When darkness finally came again they stopped in the nearest small town and found a residential street with houses, and sure enough, one with a sign saying "Tourist Home—Rooms for Rent."

To their utter amazement and disbelief it was exactly the same white house that they had slept in the night before, and there was the white cat still snoozing away in the same swing and inside the same uncomfortable lumpy bed and precisely the same, now malodorous toilet.

Spending a second night there was a nightmare, what with their discouraging lack of progress. They hardly slept a wink, the bed was lumpier than ever, and in the morning the crullers were stale.

Besides road maps not being very good or plentiful, there were few places that served good food. Howard Johnson had only one ice-cream parlor with twenty-eight flavors, and it was on Cape Cod; Duncan Hines was as yet unpublished; there were no Dairy Queens or Pancake Houses or McDonalds anywhere; and the meals available at diners and small-town cafés, as they were usually called, were seldom finger-lickin' good.

What did we take along with us when we went on a motor trip back in those days, and what did we wear? For the actual trip we dressed for *comfort*. If it was summer and we were driving in Iowa, for example, we wore lightweight cotton sleeveless dresses and rubber-soled shoes. Nonskid shoes made safer drivers, as the clutch, accelerator and brake pedals on most cars were made of slippery shiny metal, and it was dangerous to drive with any other footgear. Men wore them too as a rule, and to keep cool wore suits of crumpled seersucker when they drove. However, remember that on a motor trip we spent each night in a downtown hotel in a large city (whenever possible), so we brought along appropriate dark city clothes for dinner and going to the movies, or whatever we did after.

If I were motoring to a party in Minneapolis, for instance, and a formal evening dress was required, what did I take along? I took my Fortuny dress. They are still practical for travel, as they don't wrinkle (they are already that way: solidly accordion-pleated). Made by one Mariano Fortuny of Venice, Italy, they were long, gossamer silk, hand-pleated dresses of classic Greek simplicity and of beautiful vibrant jewel colors that came packed each in its own little round white box which was carried just like a miniature hat box tied up with a black grosgrain ribbon bow. When it was time to put it on, out it came from the box, coiled up like a snake; it was untwisted and shaken out, put on over the head, and belted in with a matching belt. One size fitted all. They had one disadvantage: they had to go back to Venice to be repleated. Besides being easy to pack they had another advantage: they were marvelous as maternity dresses, especially when worn with a short matching poncho or jacket.

Motoring in winter, of course, we bundled up in everything from raccoon coats to fur-lined lap robes. There were heaters in cars but I don't remember any that worked efficiently, and some were extremely dangerous.

Automatic windshield wipers were a long time getting invented, so in the car we carried along things like a chamois or hunks of cotton waste to clear the windshield, and a great many drivers kept a plug of ordinary chewing tobacco in the glove compartment, which when rubbed on the windshield made visibility much longer-lasting in a rainstorm.

We also took along a whisk broom in winter to brush away the snow, a set of four chains for the tires in case of excessive snow and also for mud, a razor clamped onto a stick for combating ice on the windshield, and some red flares and a pair of red lanterns in case of a breakdown or accident.

Among the permanent equipment we also carried thermos bottles for hot coffee and cold lemonade, the standard variety with the screw top, and a stack of waxed-paper cups. If we were in muddy-road territory, most cars had a pair of rubber boots stowed away in the rear somewhere, and of course an umbrella.

What do I take with me on motor trips now? First and foremost a complete first-aid kit. Remember that people in other cars on a big interstate highway don't stop any more to see if they can help when they see a car parked along the shoulder. You're on your own, and you get to treat your own bee sting or bandage up your own scratched-up ankle all by yourself.

Next, each car should have all the equipment necessary for an emergency stop. Then too I'd have a change dispenser near the driver's seat somewhere for coping with exact-change toll booths and also for those unattended wayside food-dispensing stations where you can get a sandwich and coffee by putting quarters and dimes into various slots, and there is no one there to look after you except the machines themselves.

For spending the night in motels I have with me a sleeping mask to shut out the early-morning light, a small FM radio with an earplug to shut off any early-morning noise, and a fly swatter or some insect spray just in case there is a stray mosquito or housefly around.

Last of all, I wear only clothes that are comfortable, easy to get in and out of, and wrinkle-proof. My favorite outfit at the present moment for motel and motor wear is a light blue Qiana silk-knit dress that is printed all over with circles and swirls of various shades of blue. It has long sleeves that can be pushed up, and it washes easily and dries quickly, and if it gets spots on it they don't show at all because it is such a spotty print.

Pillows in most motels are too hard and firm. I take a little soft one of my own in its own little dark blue traveling envelope which also contains my traveling clock and some tranquilizers. I shouldn't criticize motels or anything in them, as they are generally so palatially comfortable and seem to have everything for the motorist's convenience; I apologize here and now.

I don't miss the greasy food of bygone motoring days and the narrow roads where one could get stuck behind a truck for miles and miles, and I don't miss traffic lights all turning red at once, and I don't miss tourist camps where you could rent a cabin for the night but had to bring your own sheets and towels, but there is one thing that I would love to see again: the Burma Shave signs.

There were always six of these jaunty little signs spaced along in a field on the right side of the road, far enough apart so that you had eighteen seconds going at thirty-five miles an hour to read them. At one time in the thirties there were over 7,000 sets on the public roads. Their message to man was to throw away the old badger-hair shaving brush and use the new brushless cream called Burma Shave.

For example, first there was a sign off to the right saying:
THO STIFF
Then sign number two came by saying:
THE BEARD
Sign number three:
THAT NATURE GAVE
Followed by sign number four (excitement mounting!):
IT SHAVES
(Huh?) Then sign five:
LIKE DOWN WITH
Aha! Got it! Last sign:
BURMA SHAVE

To end these motoring recollections from the past let us go back again to 1918, when some Chalmers owner could proudly call a National owner and say, "I made the Century today."

What does this mean? It was the stylish way of telling your friends that you had driven *one hundred miles* in one day.

✑ 4

Lower and Higher Learning

THERE IS A BIG yellowish-brick apartment building in New York at 24 West Fifty-fifth Street, and in the building is an excellent and popular restaurant called the Italian Pavilion. I enjoy going there more than anywhere else in New York City, and why is this? Because it is the exact spot where I went to boarding school for three long dreary years, and now when I go back there in this elegant softly lit dining room and sip a glass of Verdicchio wine with a plate of cold veal *tonnato*, or drink champagne with my hazelnut cake, I am indeed in what is an earthly paradise. The atmosphere there is for me so rewarding: to think that *here I am* and *enjoying* myself. If I'd only known that this was going to happen, those three years might not have seemed quite as hateful.

In 1920 Miss Spence's School was located in two adjoining brownstone eight-story buildings. Number 26 was where we boarders lived, and number 30 was where all the classrooms were. In my time there were about a hundred of us in the boarding school, and the day pupils numbered over three hundred. After Miss Spence died (1923) the school soon changed: it was incorporated (before that Miss Spence owned it), it had new principals, fewer boarders, its name became the Spence School, in 1930 or so, and it moved up to Ninety-first Street, where it still stands.

I arrived in New York just a month before Warren G. Harding and Calvin Coolidge became the new Republican President and Vice-President. Just before I left Cedar Rapids I remember that Mr. Harding had been campaigning in Minnesota, and my father telling me of this amazing new invention that had been used in Minnesota when he spoke at the State Fair. It was something called an amplifier, and forty of these large horn-like things were used to enlarge his voice so that a huge crowd, nearly fifty thousand people, could all hear him perfectly.

Mother and Danny and I checked into the Gotham Hotel, just a stone's throw from the school, and armed with a list of clothes allowed by the school, set off to B. Altman & Co. to buy two Spence-uniform white silk shirtwaists (for Sunday) and four white cotton Spence-style shirtwaists (the school thought this word more genteel than "blouse"). Then we bought the school's uniform nightgowns, Mother announcing to me that they seemed thicker than sailcloth. After that we looked for three simple silk or velvet dinner dresses with sleeves below the elbow and necklines above the collarbones, then two suits of dark wool, one could be fur-trimmed, and a sewing basket, a hot-water bottle, a blue or rose-colored corduroy uniform bathrobe, and so on and so on. I recall that a pair of high brown laced shoes was on the list, and slips could not have straps (too sophisticated). Sweaters were cardigans only, to be worn over the shirtwaists of course, and stocking had to be cotton lisle or wool, no silk stockings, they would be sent home at once.

I should add that on this list of required clothes was a pair of overshoes for wear in snowy weather. We girls called them "galoshes" and they went over your street shoes and fastened around each leg with four metal buckles. When fastened tightly they kept the snow out to the mid-calf, but most of us were too lazy to fasten them, and when they were worn loose they were wide and black and they flapped as we walked. Thus the word "flapper" came into being, and it was used nationwide in the twenties to designate a teen-age girl, the hoydenish type rather than the fair young maiden.

Therefore in the list appeared the following:

"Overshoes, after being put on, must be kept completely fastened at all times.

"It is forbidden to wear long hair puffed out over the ears." (The slang term for this style of coiffure was "ratting," and one could even buy a little wire cage to wear over each ear instead of ratting the hair. These cages were known as "cootie garages."

Mother and I bought all these proper things and brought them all back to the Gotham in a taxi so that Danny could start sewing on name tapes. I looked through the list of rules one more time.

Any girl who bobs her hair while attending school will be expelled at once.

Long hair must be worn hanging down the back until the age of sixteen has been reached, when it may be worn pinned up.

Any girl found smoking will be expelled at once.

Lipstick, perfume, face powder, and other cosmetics are forbidden. Rice powder and colorless lipstick are allowed and cologne is permitted *only* if it is Marie Farina's 4711.

Only two pieces of jewelry may be worn at once. Earrings are not permitted.

No birds, fish, or living plants are allowed in the girls' rooms.

Girls are not allowed to use the telephone at any time, nor are they permitted to receive any telephone calls.

It is against the rules for girls to throw money out of the windows to organ grinders.

Food and candy found in any girl's room will be confiscated.

The list went on for pages and I began to feel uneasy, but I said to myself that sister Margaret had gone there for four years and had survived, and lots of her Spence friends and roommates had come to visit her and hadn't complained about the school, therefore it must be all right.

We spent a happy evening dining at L'Aiglon, a restaurant still in the neighborhood and still going strong, then saw Fred Stone in *Tip-Top* (how I laughed), and the next day appeared at Miss Spence's School for Girls in my new brown un-fur-trimmed wool suit with matching brown felt hat and a white uniform shirtwaist.

Miss Spence, Miss Baker, and Miss MacElroy, the three Lady Principals (as they were called), were in the Lower Hall to greet us and they were charming, especially Miss Spence. Then Mother and Danny left, after we had a cup of tea up in the big living room on the second floor, at the same time meeting a few Lady Chaperones and Lady Teachers.

Then I was conducted to my room on the fourth floor, a three-girl room with two roommates already installed in it. They were both my age (fourteen), and each from Grosse Point, Michigan, and I was crazy about both of them from the start. When we retired that night (our lights were turned out at 9 P.M. by a Lady Chaperone) I was tired and happy and contented and excited (three cheers for the school, I said).

Less than a week later Connie and Helen and I had all changed our minds. We didn't like anything about the school. It was too strict. After lights out, for example, a Lady Chaperone sat all evening (one on each floor) at a desk reading, so that one could not talk in bed (they all had magnificent hearing) and none of us could go visiting without being shooed back to bed. Only one customer to the loo (as it was called) at a time, although there was room for plenty of us in the daytime.

Besides these rules there was another that drove us crazy. We had to dress, each of us, behind a little white screen. Oh, the modesty!

Worst of all to me was another rite that slowed us up. The first day of menstruation we spent flat on our backs in bed. We couldn't even be propped up by an extra pillow, and Miss Carmichael (the Lady Nurse) came around regularly to inspect. I who had been used to riding horseback and playing tennis was horrified at such pampering. The word "menstruation" itself was never used by anyone except Miss Carmichael; the other teachers and chaperones used the word "unwell" or "indisposed" or said that a schoolmate was spending the day in bed "because of a reason."

This word "reason" was in our opinion the silliest of all, and imagine our utter discomfiture when a minister came one Sunday evening, as was the custom, and spoke to us for a half hour on "The Power of Reason." Even the teachers squirmed with embarrassment, and after that the word "reason" was dropped forever and the generally well-known expression "the Curse" was substituted.

One further word about menstruation which I think is worth

telling: my mother did the most wonderful thing when I was twelve or thirteen and it's too bad that every mother doesn't do something along the same lines. She sat me down and told me that when this distressing-sounding new physical change should take place, it would be a cause of quiet celebration for me, and that as soon as it happened I should get in touch with her or Danny immediately.

"It means you are grown up," she said, "and with its arrival come some privileges that young ladies deserve. Your allowance will be doubled. Instead of it being five dollars a week, it will be fifty dollars a month.

"Then you may wear silk stockings on Sundays and to parties, and every evening that you dress for dinner."

I gasped delightedly. Silk stockings? I was dazzled.

"You may also wear perfume, powder, and pumps with heels, and give away your Mary Janes." She paused for a moment. "Oh yes, I knew there was something more. You may go to bed whenever you like, and your father and I will give you a gold wristwatch so that you can keep track of time yourself and not have to be told by your nurse."

Then she smiled at me and gave me the best news of all. "Danny will no longer be your nurse. She'll be your friend."

We received marks for Neatness, Punctuality, Accounts, and Sewing, besides marks for Latin and French and Mathematics, etc. And the punishment that fit the crime was indeed strange. For instance, under Neatness, which involved having the wrong thing in your possession, our Lady Room Inspector found that Connie had brought to the school a bottle of Golliwog perfume. It was poured down the washbowl's drain, and it didn't seem fair, as she told the teacher that she had no intention of using it.

Punctuality had the oddest punishment of all: if a girl was late for breakfast (7:30 A.M. was the deadline) or late for a class or for Morning or Afternoon Walk or Study Hall, she received a black mark. When she had three of these she had to go to Carnegie Hall on Saturday afternoon to hear the Boston Symphony Orchestra (Pierre Monteux conducting). Those who had been prompt could go shopping or to the theater or the Metropolitan

Opera or to certain School-approved moving pictures. *Having* to go to the symphony created a lot of music haters, probably some permanent ones. A *punishment* to be sent to hear Fritz Kreisler play the Tchaikovsky Violin Concerto? A *punishment* to hear Sergei Rachmaninoff play his own Second Piano Concerto? I suspect that it was a sure and easy way to fill up the Spence box, but being a symphony lover from childhood, I was horrified.

Another thing that bothered all three of us: the school was run on the Spy System, not the Honor System. If you got caught you were punished. If you were clever you could get away with murder.

If I'd only gone where sister Barbara enjoyed the free and honest life for four years—Miss Porter's School at Farmington. However, I couldn't change. Mother had set her heart on my going to college and Farmington wasn't a college preparatory school. At that time colleges didn't accept girls from Miss Porter's.

And speaking of Farmington, the boarding school that I would have loved, you may be amused to hear about their little toilets. They were each in small cubicle rooms just where the building had an adjoining wing, two wings to each floor; hence Farmington girls have always spoken of the loo or the powder room as the wing.

One day, years ago, Archibald MacLeish, the American poet, came to Farmington to lecture and read the girls some of his poetry. It was unexpected, as he hadn't been quite sure of his schedule. Therefore when Mr. Robert Keep, a nephew of Miss Porter's and the head of the school along with Mrs. Keep, introduced Mr. MacLeish, he said to the whole school:

"I cannot begin to tell all of you how fortunate we are to have with us tonight our distinguished guest. We caught him on the wing—"

That was the end of the introduction and even Mrs. Keep almost rolled on the floor with everyone else.

Back to Miss Spence's, where did I keep my perfume? Sloshing quietly around inside my hot-water bottle, where it was never discovered the whole three years that I was in residence. And

where did the forbidden face powder hide? In the Dr. Lyons
Tooth Powder can. And the lipstick? That was snuggled into a
box of crayons replacing the red one. The silk stockings? Folded
behind a photograph of my mother in a leather picture frame. (I
could go on and on.)

The worst thing of all, however, was that we didn't get
enough exercise. In the morning we went on what was called the
Short Walk. The bell rang for it at 8:30 and we lined up in the
Lower Hall rather like chain gangs, two by two in groups of six
or seven pairs of girls plus a Lady Chaperone. Then we marched
out onto Fifty-fifth Street, each group going somewhere different. Some walked up Fifth Avenue and took a short turn
through lower Central Park, others went down Fifth Avenue,
and some over to Park Avenue or Madison. We returned at 9:00
or a little after and had just enough time to hang up our hats and
coats, tidy up the room, grab up our school books, and dash to
classes.

They ended at 1:00 and lunch was informal (no punctuality
rule, and we could sit anywhere). After lunch we again gathered
in the Lower Hall for the Long Walk, the same procedure as in
the morning except that we had an hour-and-a-half walk and returned at 3:30 just in time to hang up our coats and hats again
and head for the Study Hall.

There were a few afternoons when we went to the Lexington
Avenue YWCA and played basketball or swam, but not very
often, and we had to hurry so to get back to that Study Hall that
it took the fun away. And the worst thing of all about the lack
of sports came later. In college I knew so little about field hockey
and lacrosse and all the other sports that I never even made a
team.

Everyone studied until 5:00 P.M. Then the girls who held
Rank A in their studies headed for their rooms, where they could
eat apples and pears and grapefruit, and could take baths and
write letters to boys at the Hill School or Exeter or Groton, and
could even play the piano.

Those with Rank B stayed on studying, after a brief recess,
until 6:00 P.M., and those with Rank C studied until 6:30. These

poor souls had to hurry and dress for dinner and be down in the living room before 7:00.

And what about the Rank D girls? They were sent home. I contemplated trying for Rank D after getting a Rank B for the first six weeks but decided that I couldn't do it to my parents. It would have been a dirty trick, especially as they were so very anxious to have me go to college.

So, after thinking it over carefully, I decided that I would have to study harder and get Rank A. No more writing notes to friends in Study Hall, no more drawing pictures of the teacher, no more spitballs thrown when she wasn't looking. I buckled down and worked. I also listened carefully in the classrooms to whatever any teacher said. I learned to take notes. It was hard work at first, this concentration, but *How It Paid Off!*

My marks arrived on Christmas Day (back in good old Ioway), and there was my report with *Rank A*, and with Honorable Mention (the highest mark) or Excellent in everything except Latin and Sewing.

The Latin mark (Fair) was a blot on my escutcheon and was disappointing, but not the bad mark (Poor) in Sewing. My roommates and I discovered in our keen and clever way that the Sewing Class was a hateful thing that took place on Saturday morning from 10:00 to 12:00, and it was a required course; a Spence girl couldn't graduate until she had filled a large looseleaf book with twenty-five lovely little models of various kinds of stitches and patches and mitered corners and darns. Model 25 was a baby dress, made with tiny tucks and weeny buttonholes and feather stitching, a sort of final exam. When you finished the baby dress you had graduated forever from Sewing and had free Saturday mornings in which to go shopping or do other wild things.

Therefore Connie, Helen, and I resolved to get these models completed with all possible speed, and by the time we left for Christmas vacation the baby dress was in sight, we had finished the first fifteen dismal things. Also, oddly enough, we had learned to sew, and fast, too.

As I recall, we finished the baby dresses in February, all of us delighted with a whole free Saturday apiece, and on our first free

Saturday morning we celebrated by going shopping, accompanied by the ever-present Lady Chaperone. In this case we had asked for Mrs. Lamport, the nicest of all, and we headed straight for B. Altman & Co., the department store where our families all had charge accounts.

We had a scheme that we had resolved to try. We were going to make ourselves new dresses now that we could sew a fast seam, so we went at once to the yard-goods floor. Connie bought some slate-blue silk, Helen three yards of brown or beige silk, and I picked gray. Then we bought thread to match, and many lengths of bias binding (I hope this is the right term for material that goes around necks and sleeves—trimming stuff). We bought all sorts of different colors, had a Lucullan lunch at Schrafft's, each with a "Luxuro" for dessert, all of us except Mrs. Lamport, that is. A Luxuro, in case you never had one, was a large wedge of chocolate-frosted chocolate cake, split open and filled with chocolate ice cream. Poured over the wicked thing was a thick chocolate sauce, and it was topped off with a large marshmallow complete with a maraschino cherry.

While eating these concoctions we confided our plan to Mrs. Lamport, and I'll never forget how hard she laughed. People stared. She promised she would never tell a soul, and we knew she wouldn't. She was the Trustworthy Chaperone.

We started our plan the next day. After the school's big Sunday dinner, which we had after church, all of us boarders went to our rooms for a two-hour quiet period. I think the rule was that we each had to write the weekly letter to a parent or guardian, that was all, and someone came around at 5:00 P.M. and collected all the letters. Otherwise we could do anything we wanted to as long as we were quiet.

As soon as the door was shut, we whipped out our new dress material and proceeded to make each of us a new dinner dress. They were all three of the same model: kimono sleeves, a jewel neckline with a plain straight up-and-down skirt. The seams were sewn with a simple running stitch, almost basting, if you understand sewing terms. The hems were finished in much the same way, and then we picked out a brilliant color for the trimming around the below-the-elbow sleeves and the modest necks.

My gray crepe de chine was trimmed with cerise, and I remember bright green was on Connie's blue dress, and orange on Helen's. We went demurely down to Sunday supper in our new finery, sat through evening prayers afterward, and retired as usual. The minute we were undressed we pulled all the threads out of the dresses, removed the trimming (it was easy, as the stitches were so big, just like unraveling), and folded up the separate pieces and put them in our sewing baskets, down with other scraps and under the tape measures and pins.

The following Sunday afternoon we made the dresses again, only this time my gray crepe de chine was trimmed with yellow taffeta, and Connie's slate blue had a smart plaid edging, and Helen's was bound with gold lamé.

The crosspatch Lady Room Inspector never figured out where the dresses went. Remember, we were allowed only three dinner dresses, and that is what was in our closets. She always looked baffled, as she stared at us, for the rest of the term.

Besides learning how to study and learning to sew, for which I have always been very grateful indeed, especially for the art of studying, there is one other thing for which I am grateful to the school: we *knew* New York.

Every Wednesday after lunch the whole boarding department went on an expedition. In three years' time I saw every museum and every art gallery not only in Manhattan but in Brooklyn and the other boroughs. We also paid visits to places like the Fulton Fish Market, the Telephone Exchange, the Stock Exchange, Bellevue Hospital, and the Statue of Liberty.

The best place of all was the annual trip to Huyler's Candy factory. In the spring, when we went there, I remember that even on a hot day we all wore sweaters with pockets, then a polo coat on top, also with pockets. We were allowed to sample the candy as we went through one heavenly room after another, and were each given a quarter-pound box in which to put our free samples. When no one was looking we smoothly transferred sample after sample from the little box to our various pockets. Most of us had to stand up in the subway coming home, we were bulging too much to sit.

Another nice thing about Miss Spence's was, besides getting to know the interesting places in New York, Miss Spence knew a great many interesting people. Madame Emma Calvé came to luncheon once, and to our delight got to her feet after the tapioca pudding and sang the "Habañera" from Bizet's *Carmen*. She was the biggest Carmen I have ever seen, and had long since retired from the opera, but she still had the greatest stage presence I ever saw.

There were other artists too: Clare Sheridan and Harriet Frishmuth, who were known for their beautiful sculpture; there was the British writer A. S. M. Hutchinson, and the British lecturer John Cowper Powys, and all sorts of eminent college presidents. On Sunday evenings we often had ministers from New York churches, who gave us a short sermon and a prayer. I remember Dr. Fosdick and Dr. Norwood and Bishop Darlington, and Dr. McLeod, who was my favorite (his church was the Collegiate Church of St. Nicholas, where I went every Sunday).

It was still too strict, and here is a final example: One Christmas vacation, (1921, I believe), the Chicago girls and those of us who lived in nearby territories were all taken to Grand Central Station in New York at 5:00 P.M. to travel west on the Twentieth Century Limited, which left at 6:00 P.M.

There were several taxi loads of us and two or three chaperones who conducted us and our luggage to the proper car. On overnight trips, Spence girls had a series of connecting drawing rooms and compartments. The chaperones checked our tickets carefully before entrusting them to us; they cautioned us to be on our best behavior and not speak to strangers, wished us all a pleasant trip and a Merry Christmas, and got off the train. I remember one of the chaperones, who was a black-clad widow named Mrs. Carpenter, as being particularly firm and strict. She always glared when she spoke to any girl, and I think she just plain disapproved of all Spence School girls.

After they left, the conductor shouted the familiar "All aboard!" and off we started, but not for very long. We came to a dead stop farther up the platform. The porter explained to us that at the holiday season, with so many schools and colleges letting out, the Century was leaving on this day in four different sections and that we were number three, waiting out turn, and would be off in a few minutes. The train doors were all shut and no one could get on, so at last we were free 'and almost on our way.

We all excitedly ordered things from the porter: ginger ale and lemonade and salted peanuts and cigarettes. We threw off our hats and those of us who had long hair immediately started pinning it up. We put on lipstick and powder. When the cigarettes came we all grabbed one. I remember that as I was lighting mine the flare of the match was reflected in the train window and it caught my eye, and just below the light was Mrs. Carpenter standing there on the platform glaring away at us in horror. At the same time the train began to move and away we went.

We returned to school in early January to find a new rule had been announced to all parents and guardians of the girls of the boarding department.

It read: "All girls traveling to school and home at vacations must be accompanied by a chaperone approved by the school. The expense of the chaperone will be divided equally among the individual girls."

Our parents were *enraged*, especially the ones in California. We of the Middle West were lucky, because two boarders from St. Paul, Minnesota, Elizabeth and Claire Louise Ottis, had an uncle who would be delighted to chaperone everybody and anybody who would be at the La Salle Street Station in Chicago on January 4, or whatever the date was for the return to school, in time to board the Century.

A MAN chaperoning us? Approved by the school? The answer, happily, was yes. The chaperone was U. S. Senator Frank Billings Kellogg, soon to be appointed Ambassador to the Court of St. James's.

So for two and a half more years I managed to coexist with Lady Chaperones and Lady Instructors, and at long last was admitted to Vassar College.

What a change when I arrived in Poughkeepsie as a freshman on a nice fall day in 1923. There were nine of us from Miss Spence's who had managed to pass the College Board Comprehensive Examinations and found ourselves joyfully installed in a fifth-floor section of the great big original Main Building known as the South Tower.

This tower, I believe, was the same one in which "The Group" spent its bright college years. They were a great deal more sophisticated than we were, if you remember the book by Mary McCarthy, but Vassar seemed a glorious place to our Spence group: such wonderful rules and so few, we were free as the proverbial birds. For instance, we had to be back in our dormitories at 10 P.M., but we could stay up all night if we wanted to. We could eat anything we pleased, and at any time. I remember my roommate's mother discovering a pan of ancient half-eaten scrambled eggs and a plate of fudge under a bed in our room and suggesting that perhaps this was the reason for our having so many visits from mice and squirrels.

After that we tried to be neater, but when my mother arrived she was horrified with our little attic-like room with the squirrels frisking in and out and eating walnuts on our two austere army-type cots. Happily for her, the mice were hiding in their holes.

She went back to New York and hunted up a decorator friend and sent her up to look over our room, and the result was that in less than two weeks we had wall-to-wall burnt-orange carpeting, completely shutting off the mice visits, a pair of turquoise-blue Chinese-style daybeds with orange-and-blue bedspreads and matching pillows. Furthermore, there were window screens (farewell to our squirrels) and some stylish gauzy blue curtains for the small Gothic windows.

We were ecstatic over the magnificent change and set to work ourselves. We painted the little wind-it-up-yourself Victrola turquoise blue. This little "Vic," which we had bought for three dollars from our predecessors, looked perfectly lovely painted blue, but it ran down after playing one ten-inch record. Before that it had always managed to get through our favorite record: Paul Whiteman and his orchestra playing "When Day Is Done" (and grass is wet with twilight dew, etc.). This was a twelve-inch, and the Vic now ran down just as it reached the famous tenor trombone solo. We bravely decided to play no more Paul

Whiteman, and also, it being a blue Vic, we would play only "blue" records.

Hence for the rest of the year the music from our room consisted of "Wang Wang Blues," "Memphis Blues," "Farewell Blues," and "The Blues My Naughty Sweetie Gave to Me."

There was one more, "The Empty-Bed Blues," a rival, no doubt, of "The Left-All-Alone-Again Blues," but it stayed in its little brown paper envelope.

We also put shiny black lacquer on the scratched-up desks and gilded the doorknobs and other hardware with gold radiator paint. The effect was breathtaking but we were most embarrassed to read a little squib in the Vassar *Miscellany News:* "Isn't it the height of affluence when two freshman have to import a New York Decorator to refurnish completely their quarters? Hm."

We didn't care and we loved college life. We could cut classes, there were no assigned study halls, we could wear anything to classes (pajamas under raccoon coats!), and we could even smoke in certain parts of the campus. It was heavenly, and if the food in the dormitory dining room didn't appeal to us, there was a loud scraping of chairs as we left to dine off campus.

There was one particular meal that turned up now and then which we called the Gray Dinner. It consisted of sliced pork in a cream sauce, mashed potatoes and turnips. The dessert that followed was a pearl-gray blancmange. Whenever this appeared we hurried away to the Popover Shop or the Flag Shop or the Vassar Lodge.

In the evening, if we wanted to, we could take a streetcar (no chaperones, no permission even) into Poughkeepsie to the movies, and also on weekends we could go to Yale or Princeton or even Exeter (robbing the cradle) just by announcing the fact to the housemother of the dormitory, or warden, as she was called.

One evening after I'd been in college for over a month an odd thing happened. There were about fifteen or twenty of us, all classmates, and we were walking home from some off-campus lecture or entertainment. I remember that it was a lovely mild fall evening and we had stopped for a cigarette (smoking was not allowed in the dormitories and permitted only in certain isolated parts of the campus).

We were standing around, everyone puffing away, when suddenly I had a strong conviction that there was a fire, a bad fire. It was so real to me that I broke the silence saying, "You know, there's a terrible fire burning somewhere. I have this funny feeling that it is nearby." And just as I finished the words the big fire whistle that blows at twelve noon every day began blowing violently: three short blasts and two long, then repeated, telling those of us who knew the fire signals that it was the big Vassar barn, over beyond Sunrise Lake, where the hay was stored and the farm horses stabled.

We all dashed for the lake, and sure enough there was a red glow in the sky behind the hill where the barn was. When we got there the whole barn was aflame; several horses had perished and a lot of farm wagons and machinery had been destroyed besides all the hay for the winter. Almost everyone in the entire college was there and we got home very tired after midnight.

The next day I began to feel uncomfortable about my premonition of the fire, so many people asked about it: *why* had I said that I thought there was a fire, *what* put the idea into my head? Someone even asked a Cedar Rapids upperclassman if I'd ever been called an arsonist. However, I had all those witnesses who could attest to the fact that we'd been together all evening long.

Nevertheless, schoolmates kept giving me funny sidelong looks every now and then for a week or so, but ultimately forgot all about it. Then one day in the middle of November I had another very disturbing premonition: I knew that my father was ill, that something was wrong with him. Mother's letters had mentioned nothing at all except that he was about the same or feeling pretty well. I knew better and decided that I'd better get myself home.

Into the warden's office I marched and confronted Miss MacColl; told her that I was terribly worried about my father and must go home at once. To my surprise and also to add to my apprehension, she agreed it would be a sensible thing for me to do, offered to help me pack and to find a connecting train from Poughkeepsie to Albany so that I could catch the Century to

Chicago. I reached Cedar Rapids the next afternoon and my father died just a few hours after I'd arrived.

My mother told me that she had written the college at least two weeks before, telling them that I would probably be sent for at any minute; therefore it was no surprise to Miss MacColl. When I returned to Vassar she said that as I entered her office she had just time to slide Mother's letter under the blotter, as she didn't want me to recognize the handwriting.

The only objection I had to this delightful place of learning was the required classes. Freshmen *had* to take Physics or Chemistry whether we wanted to or not. We also took another science: Zoology, Astronomy, Botany, Physiology, or Geology. I chose the last-named and disliked it intensely; it is how I caught brochial pneumonia, surveying the edge of a campus pond in zero-degree weather.

Sophomore year was better: one could elect courses like Narrative Writing, History of the English Novel, Appreciation of Art, Greek Archaeology, and so on.

I had also discovered that there were certain courses that had no final examinations, mostly writing courses and certain Music and Philosophy studies. In the second term the moment finally arrived when I had *no final examinations*, and I must say that I never received better marks. Some people should never be required to suffer through such ordeals. They acquire ulcers too (and don't I know).

At this time I discovered our college president, the eminent Dr. Henry Noble MacCracken, known to all of us as Prexy. The second term of the year he gave a course in Poetry Writing. I was anxious to have him as a teacher. He sounded so learned and interesting at occasions such as convocation, and although I knew nothing whatsoever about the writing of poetry, nor cared to become a poet, it was the only course that he gave except one on Chaucer, so I signed up for it and later found myself in a small classroom with the Great Man and fourteen poetesses, none of whom I had ever seen before. Some of these young ladies looked definitely poetic: long jade earrings and a long green flowing Hindu garment on one, another in a black velvet suit, blond and dreamy-eyed and looking rather like Edna St. Vincent Millay (expelled from Vassar years before for believing in and practicing Free Love), and there were several others with horn-rimmed glasses and mannish tweeds. I felt out of place in my saddle shoes and Brooks Brothers sweater, rather like a trap shooter among a bunch of crap shooters.

Dr. MacCracken spoke briefly of the course: we would meet twice a week and the first assignment would be to bring in any two original sonnets. I walked slowly home dumbfounded. Two sonnets of fourteen lines apiece, each with a tender poetic message, in iambic pentameter? (I shuddered, I did.) I would have to give up the course and take something easy: Analytical Geometry or Greek Life and Civilization, or even a nice-sounding course known as Masterpieces of Music. But then I'd never get to know Prexy, I reminded myself. After dragging my feet along for many minutes I finally got myself to Strong Hall, my dormitory, and had devised a way to construct two sonnets, telling myself that I was resolved to take Prexy's course.

When I got to our bookcase I found *The Oxford Book of English Verse*, picked out a nice-looking sonnet by William Shakespeare, the one beginning:

Farewell! thou art too dear for my possessing, And like enough thou know'st thy estimate—

I changed the words of the sonnet (but not the meaning) all the way through. I rewrote thus:

Goodbye! You are too sweet for my acquiring, And probably you're sure of your own worth—

It took about an hour to paraphrase it smoothly, and then I chose a sonnet by William Wordsworth, the one about Westminster Bridge, and did the same thing. That went quickly as I grew more practiced, and thank heavens I had found a rhyming dictionary among my roommate's books.

At the next session of the Poetry class I handed in my two sonnets along with the poets, enjoyed the lecture on Elizabethan lyricists, and left the class with our next assignment, which was to be any original fifty lines of blank verse. Actually I can't remember what I did about this, the blank verse; I seem to have a vague thought that I changed around the words of some battle in the Bible maybe, but I do remember distinctly our next class.

"Miss Douglas," said Dr. MacCracken the minute we were seated, "will you please copy this sonnet of yours on the blackboard." He handed me the Shakespeare "Farewell" one, sonnet LXXXVII, that I had er-re-restated, and I complied.

"Does this remind any of you of any other sonnet?" he asked the class. They all raised their hands eagerly. He nodded to one.

"Miss Lightner?"

"That is copied from Shakespeare's sonnet 'Farewell! thou art too dear for my possessing,'" she replied.

Everyone stared at me scornfully. There was nothing to do except tell it how it was.

"That's right," I said, smiling pleasantly, "that is the one I paraphrased, and for my second I did the same thing using William Wordsworth's Westminster Bridge one."

Someone mumbled something about plagiarism, and Dr. Mac-Cracken said, "See me after class, Miss Douglas," and began his lecture of the day.

After the class was over and the other students had left, I explained why I had taken the course, and that I was sorry not to be a poet, and should I leave and take something else, or what?

He couldn't have been nicer. He said that he was flattered that I wanted to take a course of his and that he wouldn't have me leave for anything. Then he invited me to come for tea that afternoon, and said that meanwhile he would think of a plan for me.

At tea he was great fun, and so was his wife, Marjorie, and his tiny little boy, Calvin, and his plan for me was perfect: he suggested that, instead of turning into a serious lady poet, I throw Lofty Culture to the winds and study the Art of Parody. I remember that he read or recited to me snatches of parodies from Chaucer (of all people) and Bret Harte, Max Beerbohm and Louis Untermeyer. I was enchanted, and went home chuckling in anticipation of the fun ahead.

It *was* great fun too, and in a way it changed my whole life. I began to enjoy the works of writers who wrote lightheartedly.

Thank heavens I lost over-seriousmindedness by stirring in a little much-needed wit and humor, and I owe it all to Dr. Mac-Cracken and I've loved parodies ever since.

One day in March 1925, about the same time that the *New Yorker* magazine made its appearance (by pure coincidence), a dozen or so of us decided to start a humorous magazine, a counterpart of *The Harvard Lampoon*, *The Princeton Tiger*, or *The Yale Record*.

We received permission from the college, named the new publication *The Vassar Vagabond*, organized an editorial board, an art department, and a business staff, and just before the end of the year, came out with the first issue. We were all so proud of it, including Dr. MacCracken, for it was really his suggesting the perusal of the parody that started the whole thing. And was there a parody in the first issue? Of course.

RECIPE

A yolk of egg, a pint of oil, and thou
Beside me, with a yellow mixing-bowl:
O Mayonnaise, to make thee, this is how!

The *Vagabond* was published every month during the school year for the next two years. Then after we of the original group graduated, it merged with a more literary college publication and didn't last much more than a year.

It was too bad, as it was such fun getting it out each month. And besides, it was a great financial success, and at our last *Vagabond* meeting during the week of commencement, the editorial staff and the business manager and the art department split several thousand dollars among the *Vagabond* board. None of us can remember the exact amount, but it was the result of advertising, especially cigarette ads.

I remember the P. Lorillard Company taking full-page ads to extol their new brand of cigarettes: Old Golds. The Philip Morris Company also wanted to interest women in their Marlboro cigarettes, which had special packages for ladies, each cigarette having a lipsticked tip.

To turn back to the Poetry course again: Dr. MacCracken was

most enthusiastic about some of the parodies that I turned out, and without telling me about it sent several off to various magazines. I forget where they appeared but distinctly recall receiving a check for twenty-eight dollars for a poem called "If Kipling Had Written Lycidas."

Last verse

Though I wanders with my buddies
Outer Lambeth to the Strand,
And wot if I seem merry, — they wouldn't
    understand.
If my eyes were red with cryin' they
    'ud label me a sissy:
They wouldn't know how sad I felt about my
    losin' Lyssie.

Here is one final parody in its entirety. Again I forget what magazine it was in but in my canny Scotch way I know that it paid twenty-two dollars.

Pies

I think that I shall never glimpse
A pie as lovely as the mince.

A pie that threatens all the living
Around the season of Thanksgiving.

A pie that one should never launch
Unless one owns a healthy paunch.

A pie that spices have perfumed
But which should rarely be consumed.

Each cook will claim the best receipt
The way to make the best mince-meat,

A minor point, but here's the question:
Which will cause no indigestion?

Poems are made by fools like I
But God alone makes safe mince-pie.

Meanwhile back to President Henry Noble MacCracken. He was not only a great and good lifelong friend but also a fine president and educator. He was Vassar's president from 1915 to 1946 and also helped to found now famous Sarah Lawrence College, which opened its doors in 1928 with only thirty pupils. This was a college with an entirely different concept of how to *enjoy* getting a *good* education.

I returned to Vassar recently as a companion to a recently widowed classmate and I was favorably impressed by it. When we were students the undergraduates were 1,200 and the tuition was $600 a term. Now there are over 2,200 and the annual tuition is $4,400. The boys and girls seemed as nice and friendly and articulate as can be, the campus was as handsome as ever, and President Alan Simpson and his wife are as intelligent and amusing as our old Prexy.

I end my college reminiscences with the last letter I received from Dr. MacCracken. It came after I sent him a book that I had written called *Wall Street Made Easy*.

> August 29, 1964
> 87 New Hackensack Road
> Poughkeepsie, New York 12603

Dear Ellen,

As an ignoramus of long standing I am highly fitted to appraise your book. Now that your gift has come I shall use no other. It is with the greatest difficulty that I suppress my mounting drive to tell you about all my mistakes and some of my lucky choices.

For over thirty years I attended, at 59 Wall Street, the monthly luncheon meetings of Vassar's Finance Committee of Trustees. All I can say is, that the stewed pears were excellent. In 1933 we were worth 50% on our bonds, and were nursing our mortgages back to convalescence.

But enough, I draw the curtain. All I can say is, I wish that you had been there, with the partners from J. P. Morgan, Brown Brothers, Bowery Savings, etc., etc.

By the way, did you know that First National of New York and Chase Manhattan were both founded by a Poughkeepsie schoolteacher?—Fact.

I love your cheerful style. Like Sir Thomas More on the way to the block. Cheerio, no matter what the barometer of custom, what?

Do drop in, we'd love to see you, and thanks again, not a million, just a hundred thou.

As ever, your
H.N.M.

I am sorry that Dr. MacCracken and my father never met; they would have enjoyed each other so much and I learned so much from both of them, in sort of equal amounts. I was very proud of that letter, but my father had been the good adviser who was indirectly responsible for my writing the book and I owed it all to him. Before I even got to college, he inspired me. One day just before I left for Vassar, he sent for me and he seemed very pleased with himself as we sat together in his "study." In those days fathers had "studies" or "dens," and either one had a big masculine desk and a fireplace and usually a leather couch (for long naps) and an "easy chair" (for short naps).

In Daddy's study he told me that instead of the regular monthly allowance of $50 that I'd been getting, he was giving me some Quaker Oats common stock: 900 shares.

"You are going to be pretty much on your own," he said. "Before this, as you know, your clothes were always paid for, everything necessary. Now you can no longer charge anything to your mother at B. Altman & Co. or Marshall Field's. You may open your own charge accounts if you like, but I advise you to pay cash."

I was thrilled and excited. "Gosh, Dad, this is wonderful," I exclaimed. "Having my own money is peachy, so much better than an allowance." I flew off the couch and gave him a bear hug.

"You won't be getting any money by the month," he continued. "I can only think of the William Wrigley Company that pays monthly dividends. The Quaker Oats Company pays quarterly dividends of a dollar a share every January, April, July, and October, on the fifteenth. As the dividend amounts to a dollar a quarter per share, obviously you will receive $900 a quarter, which is $300 a month."

I gave a rapturous sigh. "Go on," I said. "Tell me more."

"I will pay your travel expenses to and from college, and of course your tuition, school books, and medical bills," he said. "If you go to New York for a weekend or to a prom at New Haven or a football game at Harvard, you'll pay your own way. And remember that you always pay this month's bills with last month's money, so to speak, then you'll never overdraw or run behind on your bill paying. Now here are some general things you should always remember about this money of yours." He leaned forward in his chair.

"Never sell this Quaker stock unless you are dead certain that you know of one that is better. Never sell any of this stock to raise some cash. This is principal and must never be eaten into.

"Furthermore, here is a plan that I suggest you follow all your life. The October fifteenth dividend should buy clothes for the winter and pay for your general fall expenses; come January fifteenth the dividend will take care of the Christmas holiday expenses, plus your regular needs; the April fifteenth one will get your spring clothes, et cetera; but when you come to the July fifteenth dividend—" He paused.

"You shouldn't *need* it. Therefore, now's your chance to do something interesting and different with it. For instance, you could do something nice for someone else. Help a friend of yours who has much less than you, perhaps you could pay her tuition or part of it anyway, and help her through college."

I nodded. "I see what you mean."

"Or here's your chance to speculate," he went on. "Drilling an oil well or putting money into a gold-mine venture is all right when you're risking your summer-income money."

"I could even save some of it for a rainy day."

"Right you are," he agreed. "Then I have another piece of advice: Don't ever *loan* anyone money. If you like them, *give* it to them. If you don't like them, just say you're sorry and refuse. Don't be a sucker.

"One more thing, and I'm through. If I'm not around when you finish college, and I doubt if I will be, your mother will need your help, business-wise. I suggest that after you graduate from Vassar, you go somewhere: New York preferably in the financial area, and learn about investing wisely and well. There's a friend of mine, a Mr. S. Z. Mitchell, who is head of a company called Electric Bond and Share; ask him if there isn't a bank or bond house that you could work in, free of charge, and see how managing money is done. That's all."

I remember that he pulled his pipe out of his pocket and started to fill it.

"When you get settled in your college quarters send me a postcard of your dormitory. I'd like to see where you'll be living."

I said I would, gave him another hug, and went sailing out with visions of ostrich plumes and gold-brocade evening dresses dancing in my head. Upstairs I went and wrote down everything he had said.

How fortunate it was that I did, for it was the last time that I saw him alone. The next day, off I went with Mother to Poughkeepsie and Daddy died in November. He had been ill and miserable, and I don't think that he wanted to live, but besides the grief and sorrow I had the greatest regret that I'd never sent the postcard of the beautiful Main Building with an X over the South Tower. "Do it now" is right, and all these years I have tried to make up for my carelessness, and follow this rule adamantly.

Therefore, taking his advice, in the fall of 1927 after I graduated I was accepted as a "dollar a year" girl at the Guaranty Company of New York. There were thirty-five men in the class, and three of us girls, all without salaries, and I can remember that we had a splendid time, especially *dancing* at the lunch hour at the Savarin restaurant. In this era tea dancing was very popular everywhere, and here on Wall Street there was lunch dancing. The most popular place for tea dancing was the Lorraine Grill, somewhere near the Hotel Plaza.

I remember going to the theater almost every night or to the movies at the Lexington Avenue Movie Palace (that was the favorite). There were so many good plays: *Show Boat, The Front Page, Rosalie* starring Marilyn Miller (how I loved her), *Excess Baggage, Holiday, The Trial of Mary Dugan, Whoopee,* and so

on. Also there were nightclubs: The St. Regis Sea Glade, George
Oleson's, the Club Lido, the Club Richman, the Lido Venice.
George Oleson's was the favorite, and after the nightclubs closed,
usually at 3 A.M., it was stylish to go to Child's and eat pancakes.
I usually got to Wall Street around 11 A.M. or later.

Did I learn anything at the Guaranty Company's Bond School?
Well, yes, in a sketchy sort of way. I learned the general financial
lingo. When I left for the Christmas holidays I knew the difference between an equipment trust bond and a debenture bond,
and I knew vaguely what mutual funds and convertible pre-
ferreds were. I also had some knowledge of how to read the
balance sheet of a company, the difference between assets and
liabilities, what is net worth and operating revenue, that sort of
thing. I also knew what an extra dividend was. Cutting a melon,
it was also called.

On my way back to Cedar Rapids I stopped in Chicago's
Northwestern Station and bought a Chicago *Journal of Commerce*, the *Wall Street Journal*'s equivalent at the time. I thought
it would look impressive when I got off the train and would con-
vey my lofty knowledge of business.

Sitting in my parlor-car seat as the train rolled out of the station and headed west through the myriads of tracks that made
Chicago the railroad center of the country, I began reflecting
back on how well had I done with my money since my father's
death. The answer was: *only fair*.

On the plus side, for over six months I hadn't had to borrow
from my mother (borrow in this case was a stylish way of saying
to her that I was a little short of money and could she help me
out with two hundred dollars until the fifteenth when the
Quaker dividend arrived). She never asked to be paid back, so I
never did. And I had bought and sold 100 shares of National
Enamelling and Stamping common stock, thereby making a
profit that was large enough to buy me an ermine coat.

And I had also bought a large fuzzy brown chow dog for
$250, highly pedigreed and a member of the American Kennel
Club. I had entered him in a Cedar Rapids Dog Show, a charity
project that our Junior League had sponsored.

Pooch, as he was called (his real name was some long Chinese thing), went Best Dog in Show, and the man who marched him around the ring for me suggested that he take him along on some sort of a dog-show circuit, through towns in Iowa and Illinois. The dog came home fifteen dog shows later, and happily had become a champion.

I still don't know much about champion dogs, but to my utter joy Pooch turned out to be a real gold mine, (my mother was horrified about this). His stud fees were numerous and, as I remember, were $100 each, the veterinarian who handled the business getting $25 and I, his delighted owner, receiving $75. It was a lot of fun for everyone, and when Pooch started wagging his tail furiously and began moving down to the front door, we all knew that Dr. Bogart's old blue Essex would soon arrive and away he would go, sitting bolt upright in the back seat.

Last of all on the plus side, I had given my hairdresser (the girl who gave me water waves), out of the last July dividend, enough money to pay her hospital bill when she was in an automobile accident. She was a widow with two little children to support.

On the minus side were enough mistakes to cancel the good suggestions of my father. Besides getting Mother to help me out, especially during my senior year, I had never paid this month's bills with last month's money. I had had a perfectly hideous time of budgeting the $900 so that it would last through the three months and actually I never once had a cent left when dividend time came around. I had also opened charge accounts like mad, and one whole July dividend (the first one) went to Mr. Saks of Fifth Avenue. I shook my head sadly, thinking how disappointed my father would be if he knew how poorly I had managed. I was ashamed of myself, and resolved then and there that I would change my ways and do exactly as my father had advised from now on. (I'll make him proud of me yet, I told myself.)

Then, feeling very pleased with the new resolution, I rang for the porter, ordered a Coke, and opened up the Chicago *Journal of Commerce*. There in headlines on the front page was the following:

Quaker Oats Common Splitting 4–1, Dividend Remains Same

I couldn't believe my eyes, but there it was. The article said that the board of directors had voted for this at a special meeting, and that the stockholders would be asked to vote on it at the annual meeting in Newark, New Jersey, on such and such a day, etc., etc.

It looked very much as if by January 15 I would own 3,600 shares and that I would be receiving $3,600 instead of $900. It took the rest of the trip to recover from the shock, and before I descended from the train in Cedar Rapids I had made another resolution: to return to the Bond School, or its equivalent, and *work*.

It was a Merry Christmas season for all of us Douglases, as well as (I'm sure) the Stuarts and Macdonalds and Lairds and other kindred folk. The stock of the company was closely held within the family at this time. Actually it was traded on the Chicago Exchange, but the weekly pattern seldom ran to more than two or three trades, and scarcely ever more than a ten-share lot.

I went back to Wall Street and worked in earnest. I took a course in Security Analysis at the New York Stock Exchange Institute, another in Accounting and Double-Entry Bookkeeping, and a wonderful one called Industry Analysis.

I remember I had a horrid time with Accounting and that Double-Entry Bookkeeping (and still do), but eventually returned home and helped my mother as much as possible with the running of Brucemore, as well as the tender loving care of Mother's investments. I enjoyed it and she did too, and I am proud that we were a good team.

Traveling by Rail

5

ALL ABOARD!

It was 2:30 in the morning, Tuesday, January 15, 1918, and the Douglas family, as usual, was leaving Cedar Rapids to spend the rest of the winter in California. The Overland Limited had left Chicago at 8 P.M. Monday for Omaha and points west but was to make a special stop in Cedar Rapids to pick us up.

The trunks had gone the day before, and the most exciting moment of all had arrived. Here we were with several friends to see us off, presents in our arms, luggage piled up on a cart beside us, standing in the freezing cold at this startlingly late hour of the night, and suddenly we heard the familiar far-off cry of the arriving train. It thundered into the center of town, stopped with steam and snow swirling about it, the porter of our assigned car descended, put down his familiar little yellow step, and up we climbed: Barbara and I scrambling up first, then sister Margaret and Mother and Danny, finally Rosie, cousin Aleck Douglas, my father, and of course the porter, who, after getting all the luggage on, slammed down the steel door covering over the steps we had climbed. The conductor, still on the ground, shouted his familiar "All aboard," the brakeman waved a red lantern signaling the engineer to start, and they swung aboard somewhere up ahead as the train gathered speed.

Inside our car it was warm and the narrow hallway leading past the men's smoking room-washroom was dimly lit. However, our two connecting drawing rooms and compartment were blazing with light and the berths were waiting for us with snowy-white sheets, some even covering the windows, extra Pullman blankets folded neatly at the foot of the berths. It was so cozy and familiar and pleasant that we squealed with delight.

Danny shared a drawing room with me and Barbara, and as she was much the largest she always had the lower berth. Barbara and I drew lots to see who got to sleep in the magnificent upper berth where one could look loftily down on everyone. The loser got the hard little narrow sofa to sleep on, which was most uninteresting, especially as it had no hammock. The upper and lower berths always had small green string hammocks each stretched between the two little wall lights of the berth, into which one could put valuable things such as presents and handkerchiefs and books.

The first day on the train was just as exciting as getting on it. After we had taken turns getting dressed in our narrow floor space, and getting washed up in our small washroom with the shiny nickel-plated washbowl, and its toilet with a sign on it,* a waiter arrived all the way from the dining car, bringing us breakfast on a huge silver tray.

He and George, our porter, set up a table in the adjacent compartment. In case you aren't familiar with Pullman-car travel, a compartment is smaller than a drawing room, has no sofa and only an upper and lower berth. In the daytime the mattresses are locked up in the upper berth, and the lower becomes a place where four people can sit facing each other. There is also a washbowl in a corner next to the door, and a toilet in the other corner by the door. It is discreetly hidden from view by a green plush-upholstered wooden cover, and can be used as a fifth seat if a poker game or party is taking place.

Another curious thing is that all Pullman porters were called George, unless you knew them personally from former trips. They were also always black, as were the dining-car waiters, and a nicer, more courteous and pleasant group of men never existed. I don't ever remember one who wasn't cheerful and polite, and nothing was too much trouble for them.

The waiter spread a white tablecloth, unloaded his tray, and soon we were peeking into one covered silver dish after another and filling our plates with hot corn muffins, bacon, and jam. Be-

* This sign was in all train washrooms for many years. It could be sung to the tune of Dvořák's *Humoresque:* "Passengers will please refrain/From flushing toilet while the train/Is standing in the station." ("I love you"— added by the passenger.)

sides that we poured hot cocoa from thermos jugs into our cups, and topped them off with whipped cream. Through the windows we could see flat snow-covered Nebraska. We were on our way!

Meanwhile George was busy "making up" our drawing room for the day. Away went all the sheets and blankets, and by the time we were through with breakfast we could move back into what was now our living room. There were two or three plump pillows on the sofa, our hats had been put away in paper bags, the luggage was all stowed away under the seats and in the overhead racks. It was our home, and we happily proceeded to open our going-away presents, and unpack our books and games and knitting. The presents were mostly candy and cookies, which we put aside. While sister Margaret read aloud to us we knitted our squares for the Red Cross. Our whole school in Cedar Rapids had volunteered to send one hundred baby blankets to Belgian orphans, and each of us had promised to knit ten bright-colored woolen squares. When thirty were sewn together they made a blanket. Knitting was the vogue, even for *men*, and it was permitted in church.

The train stopped for a few minutes at Grand Island, so we put on our coats and ran down the whole station platform and back. It was freezing cold, and we were out of breath when we got aboard the train. By this time our parents were up, and cousin Aleck (who had a lower berth in the next car) joined us.

A word about Cousin Aleck that might interest you: he was unusually tall for those days, over six feet, so he had arranged to have lower berth No. 11 or 12, one of the two nearest the men's room. Why was this? These two lowers were always six inches longer than the others, and tall men could sleep without being squeezed between the headboard and footboard.

He was a great addition to our party, a bachelor in his twenties, who worked for Daddy's corn-starch company in Cedar Rapids, and who was a terrible tease and a practical joker and who taught us all sorts of strange and wonderful things: how to play mumblety-peg and how to palm cards and shoot craps.

How is it that after over sixty years I am able to remember all these details of our trip so well? Because for a Christmas present on December 25, 1917, I received from some older relative (my grandmother, I think) a handsome gilt-edged leather-bound diary for the year 1918. I wrote in it faithfully every day, line after line, page after page, for just about six months. Then it evidently proved too much for me, for I began filling up space with an occasional place card from a luncheon that Margaret went to, and a postcard of the Busch Gardens in Pasadena that someone had sent Danny. Then in July, menus from hotels began to appear, church notices, and by August it was bulging with comic strips. By October it was filled to overflowing, and the rest of the pages remained blank, but I am happy that I kept it and I especially treasure the postcards of the Overland Limited.

The Overland Limited was an all-Pullman-car train, the word "Limited" meaning no coaches. Each Pullman car had a name painted on it in four different places; Lake Wales, for example, might be its name, and in large letters it always appeared on each side, and on each door just above the doorknob as you entered, front or rear. The Pullman cars were named after rivers, mountains, lakes, and I think national parks, and perhaps canyons, deserts, and maybe geysers. Anyway the name signified the kind of a Pullman car it was. If the name was Lake Wales or Lake Okeechobee it meant that it had two drawing rooms, two compartments, and twelve sections (each with a lower and upper). And if it said Cedar River or Elk River it had all drawing rooms and compartments, and so on. I never knew which meant which, but it must have been handy for the railroad men.

During the morning my father went to the barbershop, located up in the front of the train in the men's club car, a car full of tobacco smoke and overstuffed leather chairs and brass spittoons (a horrid place, I thought), and eventually it was time for lunch. In our frugal Scotch way we had brought along a picnic basket filled with sandwiches wrapped in waxed paper, and there were hard-boiled eggs and apples.

After that it was more games, a fifteen-minute stop in North Platte (still in Nebraska but close to Colorado). Here another engine was hitched onto the long train to help us ascend the Rockies, and after we had freshened up, it was time for dinner in the sumptuous dining car, and by now the train was going around curves. Water was sloshing in the drinking glasses and the soup was spilling out of the soup plates unless one kept a spoon there, as a sort of anchor to windward (something one could *never* do at home).

By bedtime we were in Wyoming, and by the next morning we were over the Continental Divide, and coasting merrily downhill all the way to Ogden, Utah. After a long stop there in the midafternoon (after another now dried-out picnic lunch) came the most exciting part of the trip. We crossed Salt Lake! It was huge, and the Union Pacific tracks went straight across the lake so close to the water that the train seemed to be riding along on the lake itself.

Before we reached the lake, however, we were prepared for it. We had our winter coats and mittens on, and walked back to the observation car (a kind of recreation car, in case you've never seen one, complete with bar, card tables, swivel chairs, and magazine racks). We hurried through this car to the end of the train and out onto the rear platform, and there we seated ourselves on green folding chairs, the porter covering our knees with steamer rugs, just as if we were in deck chairs on a ship.

When the train pulled out we got a wonderful backward view of everything, including the trip across the lake. We also got cinders all over us and in our eyes, but it was a splendid experience, and the clackety-clack of the train rattling over the rails and the whistle blowing and (after leaving the lake) the people to wave at as the train rushed through small villages were unforgettable.

We reached San Francisco the next day in time to have a late lunch at the St. Francis Hotel, all of us delighted to be off the train after such a long trip, and I remember that Mother took me to a perfectly fascinating oriental store called S. & G. Gump, on Post Street near the hotel. Mr. Solomon Gump took us upstairs into a strange red-lacquered room with straw matting all over the floor which smelled deliciously of sandalwood. It was full of oriental statues and fountains, and while Mother talked to Mr. Gump I wandered around looking at everything, especially the price tags. I couldn't believe my eyes when I found that a dark-green jade birdbath (just about my size) was priced at $70,000. It was the largest amount that I'd ever seen on any price tag by at least $69,500. I was very impressed with Mr. Gump and still am: while now generally less expensive, the store is in the same spot, and still full of beautiful things.

Late in the afternoon the family met at the Market Street ferry, went back to Oakland, and took the Southern Pacific train known as the Lark to Santa Barbara, getting there the next morning at 6:30.

An overnight train trip such as the one on the Lark was humdrum indeed after the three-day voyage of the Overland Limited, and the procedure was entirely different. All the luggage except one little suitcase apiece was checked in the baggage car, not to be seen until we reached the Santa Barbara station.

These small overnight bags were called "dressing cases" and some were expensive and elaborate beyond belief, others simple and makeshift, and all were necessary for spending the night sleeping in a berth on a train. The dressing case is nonexistent today, but when night train travel was the easiest way to get somewhere almost everyone owned one. It was a little fitted suitcase (some heavy as lead) and it contained toilet articles such as brushes, comb, and mirror, and bottles and jars for cosmetics and lotions.

There was room for a dressing gown and slippers and pajamas or nightgown, and they were usually kept ready and fully equipped at all times, which made packing easy.

Did we ever have any unpleasant accidents or incidents on all these train trips? The answer is seldom indeed. We made the same round trip to California every year (getting away from the Iowa winters) and another summer trip to northern Michigan or the Atlantic seacoast (getting away from the Iowa summers), and the safety records for passenger trains were excellent.

Train travel was generally great fun, but now and then it could also present problems. I remember one trip when I was 10 and we were again on our way West. Barbara and I had jumped off the train to watch it get washed. It was a thirty-minute stop at North Platte or Cheyenne maybe, and it was fun to see the men with water hoses standing on the roofs of the cars letting streams of water cascade over the windows while men on the ground holding long-handled brushes reached up and scrubbed off the dirt and soot.

Another long train of Pullman cars pulled in alongside of our train and a lot of their passengers got off and mingled with us. It was confusing, but Barbara and I walked around enjoying ourselves, feeling like seasoned travelers.

Suddenly the familiar cry of "All aboard!" rang out. By this time we were a long way from our own car, and there wouldn't be time to walk to it outside, so we jumped on the train up at the club car and started back. The train began to move as we hurried back to our car, and we had trouble pushing the heavy doors open as we went through each one. Finally to our horror we arrived at the observation car, the end of the train. Our family wasn't there!

What did we do? We panicked. We began to weep and wail in loud tones: it was life's darkest moment.

Apparently we had climbed on the wrong train. The porter and some sympathetic passengers tried to comfort us, and soon the conductor appeared and informed us that we had jumped on the second section of the train instead of the first section, that it was an easy mistake to make, and that we were all going in the same direction. As soon as we reached the next stop he would personally deliver us to our parents in our own car on our own train, and meanwhile he would like to offer us an orangeade.

Years later, when Barbara and I were in our early twenties, the same thing happened to us. It was Christmastime in New York and we were taking the Twentieth Century Limited from New York to Chicago with Mother. She had the tickets and the luggage and we were supposed to meet her at the Century's gate in Grand Central Station.

At that time of year, with colleges and schools having Christmas vacations, the train traffic was perfectly terrible, and the Century was running in five sections, each waiting at a different gate. Barbara and I were a little late arriving at the station and by the time we got to the gate where we were supposed to meet Mother, we found that it was the first section and that it had already left. By the time we found a conductor to whom we could present our problem the second and third sections had also pulled out. However, he put us on section number four and told us what to do in order to get to Drawing Room A in Car I-327, First Section.

We sat in the club car sipping Coca-Colas until we reached Harmon, New York, the place up the Hudson River where the New York Central Railroad changed from electric engines to steam locomotives. It wasn't an official stop for the Century, but a brakeman helped us down to the ground and rushed us up a stairway and down another to a different track and different train, and swung us aboard section three.

At Albany we made section two and finally at Syracuse we arrived triumphantly on section one, just in time for a late dinner with Mother, who had been so busy reading *If Winter Comes* that she hadn't missed us a bit.

Several years after this, probably in 1931 or 1932, a most attractive bachelor cousin of ours came up from Chicago to northern Michigan to spend a weekend with us at our cottage in Charlevoix. After a busy two days of golf and sailing and tennis, he found himself on the Resort Special, the Pere Marquette Railroad's finest train, homeward-bound.

He left his coat and luggage in his lower berth, and headed for the club car, feeling that a nightcap was in order, it still being early in the evening. To his delight he found himself sitting next to an extraordinarily pretty girl (in those days he was called a wolf) and the two had a merry time together, so much so that she suggested that he join her in her compartment for a further rendezvous.

To this he heartily agreed, returned to his berth, changed into pajamas and dressing gown, and presented himself a few minutes later at the door of her compartment, which fortunately was the first one in the car, so his move was undetected by anyone on the train. Shortly after this the train pulled into Traverse City, and there was a mighty switching of cars going on for what seemed like hours. However, it was not until morning that our wolf-boy discovered that the Resort Special had split into two trains, one going to Chicago and the other, which he was on, heading for Detroit.

What happened if a strange man tried to get into your berth uninvited? It happened to me once in 1935 on the way to Florida. The railroads took this sort of thing very seriously indeed, and handled it most efficiently.

My husband and I left Chicago one February evening in a drawing room aboard an Illinois Central Railroad train, and arrived in Jacksonville, Florida, late the following night after an uneventful trip. We had an hour and a half in Jacksonville before "the sleeper" (as night trains were usually called) left for Tampa. I remember that we took a taxi ride around downtown Jacksonville just to enjoy the balmy tropical air, came back to the station, collected the luggage, and with a red cap helping us boarded the Flagler Railroad train. As we got on I noticed a seemingly drunken man in a light-green overcoat making his way toward the train.

The train had no private rooms, so GW (that would be my husband Gregory Williamson) and I found ourselves in lower berths opposite each other in the middle of the car. This was considered the best spot in the Pullman car: to ride over the wheels was noisier and bumpier.

We said good night to each other and I undressed and tucked myself in bed with the latest copy of *Time* magazine, and just as I opened it up the train started off for Tampa. As it clanked out of the station with switches creaking and grade-crossing signals ringing, I recall reading about Hauptmann and his trial, and that he had been convicted for kidnapping the Lindbergh baby, and then read an article about the possibility of personal income taxes being made public.

Suddenly I had the feeling that someone was looking at me. It was creepy because I'd never felt that way before, but there was no one else in the snug little berth and I even peered out into the corridor and there was nothing in sight except all the green Pullman curtains swaying gently with the motion of the train. I told myself to forget it, that I was just not used to lowers, having spent the night before in that drawing room.

I turned off my little reading light around twelve-thirty and tried to go to sleep when I distinctly felt something touch my feet. Quick as a fox, I jumped out of the berth and into GW's, waking him out of a sound sleep.

"My berth is haunted!" I exclaimed. "There's a spook in it. I felt it!"

"All right, all right," he said sleepily. "I'll trade with you. This berth is fine. No spooks at all." He kissed me on the cheek and moved across the aisle.

A few minutes later I heard a furious ringing for the porter. I looked out, and what should I see but my husband sitting on top of a nude man lying prone in my berth. It was the same drunken fellow that we'd seen in the station and he had been assigned to the lower next to mine.

The porter came, the conductor came, and the brakeman, and a few extra porters from other cars, plus a few curious passengers, all staring at the incongruous sight.

It was very difficult to climb into one berth from another after the long green curtains were up for the night. They were thick and heavy and closely woven, besides being fastened inside each berth with straps that were buttoned tight. This wily man had slit the straps with a sharp razor, and had slithered in, completely unnoticed from the outside: a real inside job, as the porter said. He had been sitting in his customary little porter's seat at the end of the car and had seen the two of us change berths, but nothing else.

The next thing that happened was the man's instant removal from the train. The train was stopped at Silver Springs, the next town, and our porter and an assistant porter bundled him hastily into his pea-green topcoat, put his feet into his shoes, threw his clothes into his luggage, and shoved him off the train. The scent of orange blossoms filled the air as, shouting and protesting, he was escorted off onto the platform. He was even suggesting to GW that we shake hands and forget the whole thing.

The next morning we were both awakened early and led to a section complete with a table at which were seated two officials representing the Flagler Railroad. They asked all manner of questions, had I cohabited with the man, had I ever seen him before, why had I switched berths with my husband, and so on. Then they asked if I would sign a paper, a legal sort of document that I believe promised them that I wouldn't sue the railroad for a million dollars' damages.

After I'd agreeably signed it they shook hands and asked where we were staying in Tampa. We explained that we were sailing for Jamaica that afternoon on a freighter of the Aluminum Line called the *Austvengen*. They wished us a good trip, shook hands some more, and departed.

We arrived in Tampa, and after an early lunch at the Tampa Terrace Hotel, took ourselves and baggage down to the harbor and hired a motor launch to take us out to our little ship. After getting settled in our cabin we were standing on deck surveying the busy harbor and enjoying the sunshine and sparkling blue water when we saw a strange sight. It was a small gray rowboat heading straight for our ship. A large black man was rowing it and perched in the bow was an enormous basket of flowers, all red and yellow and orange, and draped across it was a broad red satin ribbon saying "Bon Voyage" in big gold letters. In the stern rode a case of champagne, and when it was delivered to the *Austvengen* it turned out that it was for us. The card that came with it said that the Flagler Railroad sent its warmest good wishes.

There was one very annoying thing about railroad travel that normal people who like a cocktail before dinner often discovered: the Dry State. A few still exist in the South, and while the train is chuffing along through South Carolina, for example, the bar is locked up by the porter and not until the train has reached Georgia can it be opened.

The Wolverine was the Michigan Central's crack train, the

Michigan Central being a part of the New York Central System, and it ran daily between New York and Chicago, with special cars for Grand Rapids and Kalamazoo. I remember taking the Wolverine many times from Grand Rapids to Detroit, Michigan. It left Grand Rapids with only a day coach, a baggage car, and one Pullman car, departing around four in the afternoon. When it arrived in Detroit, it joined up with the Chicago Wolverine cars and as soon as the whole train was switched together and the new Detroit passengers had found their proper seats, the train left the station and descended into a tunnel that went under the Detroit River (actually a part of Lake Erie), and crossed the border into Canada after less than five minutes in the tunnel. Then it arrived shortly after in Windsor, Ontario, where it stopped for more passengers.

However, the Wolverine was not allowed to serve any alcoholic drinks while in Canada. Buffalo was where the bar would be opened again, but we didn't get there until after midnight. What could we do in the meantime?

The first order of business was to dash to the club car as soon as we could locate it among all the cars being switched together. Then we found seats and rounded up the porter as fast as possible, trying to figure out how many drinks would be needed to make for a pleasant evening. Two cocktails was safe and sane before dinner, but what about afterward? One highball? Two? Three? Maybe you were planning to go to bed early and wanted only one short drink, but what if you by chance should run into some old friends, or meet congenial people? (I met Norman Rockwell on this train once, and Henry Luce another time, and never enjoyed the evenings more.)

It was better to order a little extra. Consequently, the drink orders were huge; usually two or even three porters took the orders, poured liquor into rows and rows of glasses (I don't recall any of those nice little bottles at this point in history), and by working furiously managed to accomplish the job just as the train was well into the tunnel. Then along came the Canadian customs officials and slammed the liquor supply closet shut, and locked it tight. It was exciting as could be, and to come out even was the neatest trick of the season. (I don't think it ever happened to me.)

Besides the two-hundred-foot yacht and the summer cottage at Newport and the stable of racehorses, what else was a splendid established symbol of prestige and untold wealth? It was the private railroad car, of course. It was better than a titled son-in-law or an old master, and also less expensive. A private Pullman car, unless it was paneled in gold leaf or *capo di monte* ceramics, could be ordered for about $150,000, and in the 1920s Pullman had built about five hundred of these, and another company, American Car and Foundry, had built another hundred or so.

Each one was named the way a yacht is. I remember Mr. Andrew Mellon's was called the Vagabondia and Mr. George Pullman's was just Pullman, and Mrs. Charles Schwab's was Loretto II. They were almost all built along the same lines. There was a dining room for eight to ten, a master stateroom with adjoining private bath, three or four more staterooms for guests, and a living room with its observation platform. Besides these there was a galley and quarters for the crew, which usually consisted of a black cook and a waiter-porter.

To travel in one's private car cost eighteen first-class tickets to its destination, plus all taxes. There was also a demurrage charge if the car spent the night on a siding, and there were sanitation charges along the way.

There were three different kinds of private cars. First, cars owned by individuals for their own private use. Cissie Patterson, for example, had one called Ranger, in which she traveled constantly all over the country. She had seven different sets of slipcovers for the furniture and had them changed every day of the week.

Second were the official cars of railroad executives. They were owned by the railroad itself and could only be used when on railroad business. I remember Mr. Fred Sargent, the president of the Chicago and Northwestern Railroad, coming out to Cedar Rapids in his private car, and I saw it sitting in the broiling sun down on the tracks in the middle of town while he was sitting cool and comfortable by the Brucemore pond discussing business with my father.

The third kind of private car was also owned by the railroad, or sometimes by the Pullman company, and could be rented by the day or the week or the year, or maybe even for a lifetime.

At the present time there are only two or three privately owned cars left in the whole United States.

There are two train trips that I regret most of all no longer exist. One was the trip of the California Zephyr from Denver on the Denver, Rio Grande and Western, which took us to San Francisco via Aspen, Colorado, and then through the Feather River Canyon. The comfortable and luxurious train had Vistadome cars, and the view of the towering mountain peaks and then the deep canyon with its steep sides and hairpin curves and then coming suddenly out of the narrow canyon into the whole state of California spread out below was breathtakingly beautiful. It was the best sightseeing trip in the United States.

The other trip was the old Orient Express in Europe. The train was all black, sinister indeed, and used to leave Paris every evening at 7:28. One dined sumptuously the first night in a French *wagon restaurant*, ate Italian the following day in an equally excellent Italian *vagone ristorante* while whirling across the plains of Lombardy and along the seacoast before and after Trieste, on to Zagreb and getting to Belgrade in Yugoslavia late that evening. The following day was Greek all day long, with a long stop at Salonika and lots of delicious grapes to eat in the Greek restaurant car, plus glasses of St. Helena (ahh) wine. One reached Athens early in the morning of the third day, the end of the trip. When I took this trip it was in the fall of 1961, but in the years before World War II it was a far more romantic one. The Orient Express went all the way to Baghdad. It had special cars for Sofia, for Tirana and Bucharest, and stopped at Istanbul and Damascus before pulling into Baghdad.

Once in Damascus (in 1928) I saw the Orient Express leaving the station. I was too far away to see any people, but I'll never forget how romantic it looked, and I pictured it filled with ladies swathed in veils à la Mata Hari, smoking cigarettes in yard-long jeweled holders, and being followed by mustachioed *boulevardiers* and *espions* of every nationality.

Train travel is making a comeback in this country, although it is not as stately or luxurious as before. What special suggestions or advice do I have for the present-day rail traveler besides a flask for the Dry States and a dressing case or "overnight" for the sleeping berth? First of all, take along only as much luggage as you yourself can comfortably carry. In some situations porters and red caps are almost nonexistent. Traveling in knitted things that won't wrinkle is sensible, and pants are really the best for curling up in coaches or climbing into berths. Bring along an inflatable pillow for extra comfort, a bed jacket or sweater for reading in bed, and bed socks for chilly feet. People on trains should always have a flashlight with them, and Dramamine pills if they are winding through the Alps or the Sierra Nevadas.

Finally, don't forget to carry plenty of small change for vending machines in stations and even on trains, and pack both an alarm clock and some sleeping pills.

Food on trains today (in what used to be a parlor car) is unfortunately very much like the food served on planes. It comes on individual trays, one for each passenger, and has been thawed out or heated up in a radar range by the car's attendant. No longer does the dining car serve fresh Colorado brook trout after the train leaves Denver.

↻ 6

Santa Barbara Winters, Michigan Summers, Sometimes Hither and Yon

EVEN THOUGH WE tried all kinds of summer spots, we always wintered in Santa Barbara, with never an exception, leaving Cedar Rapids by train after New Year's Day and thereby avoiding the worst part of the bitterly cold Iowa winters.

For Barbara and me the change was terrific in all ways and it was very pleasant to be in the warm sunshine. But upon arriving in Santa Barbara we had to work hard for weeks catching up to our schoolmates. We had left public school and here we were in a private school that had French and Latin and "Nature Study," subjects unknown to Cedar Rapids, and consequently every afternoon for three or four weeks, while our schoolmates rode horseback, played basketball and tennis, we stayed inside and were tutored.

It was worth it, however, for we were *back*, in Santa Barbara and in our beloved house, Glendessary.

It was, and is, a comfortable brown rambling house, up in the foothills of the Santa Barbara Mountains behind the Mission, a beautiful Spanish adobe church, at present the seat of the Franciscan order in the United States. The Santa Barbara Mission was built in 1786 by Father Junípero Serra, and the land around is still cultivated by the Franciscan monks.

In 1918, to take a typical winter, Santa Barbara was a small town, its population about 10,000. There were only a few paved roads besides State Street, which ran from the Mission down to the ocean, and the paved road north to San Luis Obispo and San Francisco and south to Los Angeles. The town had no roads whatsoever over the mountains that ring it, only a few trails, and the ocean has no harbor even now. It was quiet and peaceful and beautiful.

How delighted we always were to be in Glendessary with the cool mountain air, the warm sunshine, the smell of the eucalyptus trees and the calla lilies growing close to the front terrace. Barbara and I would run through the garden, and around the whole place, greeting our gardener and his family and even the Indian vegetable man.

After three months of applesauce and canned white cherries and canned creamed corn, and turnips and potatoes from our own root cellar, his fresh green vegetables were a heavenly sight. Incidentally, the Indian vegetable man's name was Mr. Take-a-Pee, which amused my father, but Mother and Rosie and Danny were all embarrassed greatly, and the first year that he came they avoided calling him by name. He was a cheerful, pleasant man and we all liked him, so ultimately they took to mispronouncing his name. He was always Mr. Toe-Kah-py after that.

Our house, Glendessary, belonged originally to the poet Robert Cameron Rogers, who died in 1912 at the age of 50. I don't remember ever seeing him, but I remember his wife and son. However, he was famous the world over because of a piece of pure luck.

As I understand (my father told me all this), he was from Buffalo, and because he had inherited a lot of money, he gave up a law career and moved to Santa Barbara. A friend of his, an author named David Gray, said of him, "He loved living and sitting in the sun better than working, so he never developed his mind but, at that, he has written some of the best poetry in the language."

He wrote a poem called "The Rosary," among other things,

and it was published in some lesser-known magazine. By chance, a woman who was a personal friend of the composer Ethelbert Nevin saw it and liked it, so she cut it out and mailed it on. Mr. Nevin liked the poem instantly, and the next day set it to music. It was written in 1894, but for some reason was never sung publicly until 1898, whereupon it was an instant hit. It was sung everywhere for years and years, by everyone from Madame Schumann-Heink and John Charles Thomas to sweet girl graduates at commencement exercises and hired sopranos singing (accompanied by harps) behind banks of ferns at weddings. By 1913 the *annual* sales of "The Rosary" in the United States reached 287,267, and even in the 1930s the yearly sales were still in the thousands.

In the garden at Glendessary there was a low stone bench built against a wall covered with a veritable blanket of yellow roses, and overhead was a pergola from which hung big clusters of lavender wisteria. Barbara and I decided that undoubtedly Mr. Rogers must have composed his famous poem while sitting at this very spot, so we proudly pointed it out to anyone who came to see us. The word got around all right: for a while postcards of the flowery nook sold at the newsstands of the Potter Hotel and the Arlington and also at the railroad station. We were proud indeed to have put Mission Canyon on the map, so to speak.

We got ourselves unpacked and settled in Glendessary in no time at all, and the following Monday appeared in the Santa Barbara Girls' School, the same as the year before, each of us up one grade, to be greeted by many of the same friends and teachers.

In 1918 Santa Barbara seemed far more war-conscious to us than Cedar Rapids was. There were American flags and Red Cross flags everywhere, and most of the girls arrived in school wearing khaki "trench caps," narrow brimless caps perched over the right ear. These were worn only by soldiers who had done overseas duty; the soldiers who had never left the United States wore khaki hats with brims. Also lots of girls wore khaki capes. We could hardly wait to get some too.

Santa Barbara was also highly rationed. There were two "Meatless Days" each week, two "Wheatless Days," and one "Sweetless Day," which sounded the worst of all, with no sugar anywhere except in things like grapes. In addition to these restrictions, everyone in the school not only belonged to the Girl Scouts but also collected things for them. They went from door to door collecting old empty, flattened toothpaste tubes and used tinfoil.

Both Barbara and I felt as if we were a pair of slackers. We hadn't even bought any Thrift Stamps (I was ashamed of us). Thrift Stamps cost 25¢ each, and got pasted into a book until there were twenty of them. You turned them in and received a large fancy $5 stamp, which you pasted into a larger booklet. When filled you owned $100 worth of Thrift Stamps. Then you got to turn that in and you received a Liberty Bond.

We rushed home and I remember I asked Daddy if he would get us a few Thrift Stamps and he said certainly not, that he had already subscribed heavily to the third Liberty Loan Drive, and to go away and leave him alone.

How could we make some money fast? It took quite a little thought, but I finally devised a splendid way of supplementing our meager allowances. The asphalt driveway leading into Glendessary was long and on a down grade. It was the kind of driveway that the British refer to as an "avenue," and it was flanked by two rows of tall eucalyptus trees. On a hot sunny day around noontime a great many snakes loved to slither out and warm themselves on the driveway.

(Although Barbara shared in the profits she never knew the source; it is better not to tell secrets to nine-year-olds.)

Mr. Peterson, the gardener, had two sons about my age, and I hired them to help me. My father had a real phobia for snakes and the rest of the family was scared of them, so I had to wait until no one was around before pushing the big heavy roller from the tennis court down the driveway and over all the snakes as they lay stretched at full length snoozing peacefully in the sunshine. My family would not have approved of this at all.

After they were all thoroughly flattened, Walter and Allen would scrape them up, skin them neatly, and we would dry the snakeskins by tacking them up on the sunny back wall of the garage, completely out of sight.

Later Mrs. Peterson, their mother, who happened to be a dressmaker, would stitch the skins onto stiff belting and add a buckle to each. She also added the rattles as a final decoration (most of the snakes were rattlesnakes), and I took them to school and sold them for $3, $4, and $5 apiece, depending on the size of the snake and the number of rattles.

It was delightfully lucrative. The snakes were so popular that brothers began to want them too, and therefore the Cate School in Carpinteria and the Thatcher School in the Ojai Valley began to send in orders. Barbara was mystified and delighted. We filled up books of Thrift Stamps by the dozen, and the Peterson boys, who had the hardest job of all, pulling the heavy roller back uphill every time and to its home by the tennis court, were very pleased with the money they made, as well as Mrs. Peterson.

It was a wonderful sinister secret racket but after weeks of prosperity I was finally caught, alas, and in the oddest way. Not all of the snakes who came to sun themselves were rattlers, and one day among the squashed snakes was a fascinating jade-green one with a rose-colored belly. It made a most unusual belt; in fact, I sold it for $7.50 to a senior at my school.

Several days later a large man with a bushy red beard came to call on my father. He was wildly excited over his daughter's new snakeskin belt—it was one of California's rarest snakes, he'd never seen one before in all of his forty years as a herpetologist, and he wanted to know exactly where on the driveway it had been lying when flattened by the roller, so that he could locate its mate, if by chance there was one.

My father was very amused by the whole project, and forgave me with the solemn understanding that he would supply us with Thrift Stamps if we would allow him to have the roller locked up forever.

While I was busy with my snake activities, sister Margaret had been busy working at the Canteen, a Red Cross project which passed out coffee and doughnuts to all the troop trains that constantly went through Santa Barbara at all hours of the day and night.

She and the other young ladies who worked there so devotedly had the most wonderful thing happen to them—they danced with the Prince of Wales.

For some reason he appeared in Santa Barbara, coming from Canada, where I imagine he had been royally received at army training camps and military stations. At any rate, he arrived in Santa Barbara one afternoon on behalf of some sort of a Charity Drive for the Fatherless Children of France, and all of us schoolgirls saw him standing on the steps of the flag-draped San Marco Building downtown, surrounded by bodyguards and generals and the Mayor.

He was the best-looking thing I have ever seen, ever. Dressed in the uniform of a British cavalry officer with highly polished boots and ribbons galore on his chest, his blond hair golden in the sunshine, he took my breath away, especially when he smiled at all of us. Even later as King Edward VIII and Duke of Windsor he was handsome, but in Santa Barbara, to all of us giggling girls he was too good to be true. He became our idol and we could talk of nothing else for the rest of the year.

Meanwhile sister Margaret went that evening to Montecito (the suburb of Santa Barbara that is on the ocean) to a small party given by a Mrs. William Miller Graham, who had a daughter, Geraldine, in her early twenties, as was Margaret. Margaret wore a floaty pale-yellow chiffon dress purchased at I. Magnin and Company, with a bunch of blue forget-me-nots at the waist and a matching blue velvet sash. She looked very dashing with a matching hair ribbon holding back her curly red hair.

The party turned out to be a small dance, about thirty young people present. There was a small orchestra in a corner playing fox-trots and a punch bowl close by, big standing vases of roses and lilies everywhere.

And suddenly there he was, His Royal Highness, in his impeccable cavalry officer uniform, shaking hands informally with Mrs. Graham, and introducing her and Geraldine to his three or four equerries. These young men, also wearing cavalry uniforms, immediately turned to the young ladies, looked them over, and each one bowed low before the girl of his choice and began to dance.

The Prince of Wales stayed talking to his hostess while every one else joined in the dancing. The dances were very short, just a circling around the room and then the music stopped and everyone changed partners. Margaret danced with two of the equerries and found them most agreeable.

Then after a glass of punch, His Royal Highness began to dance. The girls present figured it out. The Prince's escorts tested the girls, and signaled to him in some secret way who were the good dancers, as well as who were the girls of a proper height for him, for he unhesitatingly picked out the shorter and more graceful ones.

Margaret (thank heavens she was short) came home with stars in her eyes and a slight but noticeable British accent. She had danced with him three times. None of the other young ladies had done any better, and she said he not only was great fun to dance with but was also perfectly charming and amusing.

And I developed stars in my eyes too, later on, when she gave me the yellow chiffon dress. For years I thought it was the most beautiful and sophisticated gown in the world, and I think that I may still have it somewhere in an attic trunk, as I would never have parted with it.

The teacher of the seventh-graders of the Santa Barbara Girls' School when I was there in the winter of 1918 was a plump blond lady who had a red face and wore starchy high-necked cotton dresses, and her name was Miss Plenderleith. One morning she was teaching us English, droning along in her methodical authoritative way, and for some reason she read us the verse by Gelett Burgess:

> I've never seen a purple cow,
> I never hope to see one,
> But I can tell you anyhow
> I'd rather see than be one.

I had heard this ditty many times; my father had been very amused by it and I believe was a good friend of Mr. Burgess besides. As Miss Plenderleith read I had an inspiration. When she finished I raised my hand and waved it wildly.

"Yes, Ellen," she said, "what is it?"

"I've never seen a purple cow either," I stated, "but I have seen a purple dog. In fact, we have one at home."

Miss Plenderleith looked at the class and shook her head

woefully. "There are no purple cows, there are no purple dogs in this world either, and furthermore it is a pity that we have a classmate who cannot always seem to tell the truth."

"I'll bring him to school tomorrow and you can see for yourself, Miss Plenderleith," I volunteered. There was much delighted giggling among my co-workers.

"That will do," Miss Plenderleith said. "Live purple animals do not exist. We will now stop being silly. Please open your grammars to page thirty-four."

I hurried home from school with the speed of a racehorse and found Rosie.

"Rosie!" I panted. "Do you remember the day you washed Squiffy and put too much bluing in the water when you rinsed him and he turned almost purple?"

"But of course!" she exclaimed. "It was an accident, the whole bluing bottle fell into the washbowl instead of a few drops. *Tiens!*"

I told her my plan, asked for her help, and before it was time for supper Squiffy, Mother's highly pedigreed snow-white West Highland terrier had been tinted a magnificent shade of heliotrope. He looked rather like a beautiful shaggy purple Chinese chrysanthemum.

The next morning I led him carefully down the winding Mission Canyon Road to the school, a purple satin ribbon for a leash. My mother had donated it from one of her best evening gowns and had watched our departure with great amusement.

Squiffy made me late to school. I had forgotten that dogs, especially independent tough little terriers, take their time sniffing at various trees and fence posts along the way, so by the time I reached the school the bell had rung, and all the girls were in their classrooms. I didn't mind a bit, for I would therefore make a spectacular solo entrance with my purple dog, who was now trotting along obediently by my side.

The corridors were empty, and I opened the door to the seventh-grade room unseen by anyone. Miss Plenderleith was standing on her little platform in front of her desk reading from the Book of Psalms, her usual way of starting the day. All heads turned to look at me and when the girls saw Squiffy on his purple leash they all stood up laughing and pointing and shouting.

I stood in the doorway, Squiffy giving several short barks and wagging his short purple tail happily. Miss Plenderleith turned a violent purple herself.

"Be seated, all of you!" she commanded in a thundering voice. She stepped heavily down from the platform and marched toward me, shaking a finger.

"Dogs are not allowed in this school, as you very well know, especially *dyed* dogs. Come with me." Over her shoulder as she marched me firmly out the door she ordered the class to wait in complete silence for her return.

Also in silence Squiffy and I were taken to Miss Chamberlain's office, our principal. She gave both me and the dog a reproving glance, told me to take him at once to the tennis court, which was completely fenced in, leave him there, and return to the seventh-grade room. As a punishment, I had to stay in the room at recess and copy a poem by Heinrich Heine, Miss Plenderleith's favorite poet. Squiffy was never mentioned.

When school was over at last at 1 P.M. the whole class dashed with me to the tennis court to liberate Squiffy, every little girl angry at Miss Plenderleith and each one wanting to hug and admire the dog.

Half the class accompanied me home, and I felt rather like Joan of Arc or Robert Bruce or both. My mother and Rosie greeted us sympathetically, fed us milk and oranges and jelly sandwiches, and pointed out that Miss Plenderleith was sadly lacking in a sense of humor and told us not to plan any revenges or tricks, as she wouldn't understand things like that anyway, being the kind of person she was. Then she took back her lavender sash, told Squiffy to go outside and sit in the sun, hoping he would fade, and told us to go and play games by ourselves.

The next day, word of the purple dog had spread around through the school and several teachers were laughing about it and Miss Leadbetter, our athletic director whom we all adored, said what a pity that we were seventh-graders because Miss Plenderleith was a wonderful teacher but always serious and wouldn't understand such an interruption or ever allow a little fun in her classroom. And she never changed. Barbara had Miss P. when she reached that grade three years later and found her just as imperious and strict. None of us ever had a good time with her around.

The next excitement during 1918 occurred in the late spring when a movie company known as The Flying A came to Glendessary and shot several scenes in the garden for a silent film called *Hearts or Diamonds*. I can still remember the director in riding breeches and boots waving his megaphone wildly, shouting and swearing at the actors while the cameras (hand-cranked by the cameramen) were grinding noisily away. The garden was filled with heavily-made-up actors and actresses everywhere one looked.

My father was charmed with the proceedings and always when the shooting was through for the day, invited the director and the stars and most of the company into the house for a drink. There was a pretty blond star by the name of Mary Miles Minter who wore lavender make-up that Mother took a great dislike to, and I remember a sultry brunette who kept calling Dad "Georgie," and the leading man, William Russell, with patent-leather hair who gave Barbara and me each an autographed photograph. Alas, soon after that it was time to pack up, and we returned to Cedar Rapids as soon as school was over.

That was the last winter spent at Glendessary. After that we rented different houses each winter, none of which seemed like home.

Meanwhile, Iowa summers being even more notorious than their winters, each year we escaped to the lake in Charlevoix, Michigan. As you might surmise, fifty years ago when we went somewhere for the summer it was a Major Move. The year 1928 was typical of most. We went in a motorcade of four cars and left Cedar Rapids at 8:15 A.M. Sister Barbara and cousin John Hamilton went in her black Chrysler roadster with the yellow wire wheels, Mother and Danny driven by Bert in Mother's big blue Lincoln limousine, our cousins the Hamiltons in their Packard driven by their chauffeur, Bob, and me with cousin Anne driving my pea-green Lincoln coupe (my graduation present from the year before).

We all stopped for a picnic lunch by the roadside somewhere beyond Dixon, Illinois, and reached Chicago just after four in the afternoon. We drove the cars straight to a pier just east of the old Michigan Avenue Bridge on Lake Michigan where the lake steamer *Manitou* (of the Michigan Transit Company) was waiting. We took out the luggage needed for overnight, and then the cars were driven down into the hold of the ship by waiting crewmen, while we walked up the gangplank, found our cabins, and set sail north on Lake Michigan promptly at 5:30 P.M. The gleaming white *Manitou* seemed as large as the *Berengaria* compared to the other yachts and small craft on Lake Michigan (exception: the huge ore boats), and it even had a narrow promenade deck, and a big open quarterdeck at the stern that contained comfortable wicker chairs, and was edged with many pots of red geraniums and white petunias that shook violently with the ship's vibration.

There were probably two hundred of us passengers. We ate dinner in two shifts, while a small orchestra played as we ate and for dancing after, and there were two slot machines and some pinball contraptions in a small game room. It wasn't exactly oceanic travel, but we were out of sight of land almost all the way north. We reached the Charlevoix channel shortly after the noon whistle blew a blast from the single black smokestack with the big white "M" on it. There ahead of us was the tall red wooden water tower with "Charlevoix" painted on it, and there was the long narrow channel leading to Round Lake, where among the reels of fishing nets and moored fishing tugs stood the *Manitou*'s long pier awaiting our arrival.

Lake gulls flew around the ship as we sailed slowly into the channel and up ahead we could see the familiar black iron bridge already opening to let us through. As we went by the main street people waved and auto horns greeted us, and there we were at last turning into Round Lake. Across it stood the beautiful new green-and-white boathouse with our sailboats riding at anchor, and beyond it we could see the pine trees and birches of our club, the Chicago Club.

And down below on the *Manitou*'s dock stood Mr. Gaskin, the club's superintendent, who was waiting with the club's baggage wagon to transport our trunks. Thirty minutes later we were all ashore and climbing into our cars, and the *Manitou* was already blowing its whistle to open the bridge again, as it headed next for Petoskey, then Harbor Springs, and then its final port, Mackinac Island.

We drove our four cars happily around Round Lake and into the club grounds through the familiar white picket fence, down a sandy hill to the lower terrace, and pulled up at cottage 4, our own brown-shingled, white-trimmed, rambling summer home. There we left everything and all hurried along the path and up the green wooden steps to the big white ivy-covered clubhouse and marched into the dining room, getting to our table just before the dining room doors closed at one-thirty.

And thus began our summer, a way of life that we led at least every other year, and most of us who still go back there today look forward to doing the same things with the same people in a spot that hasn't changed very much since it was organized and built almost one hundred years ago.

There are twenty-five cottages on the club grounds, most of them built between 1900 and 1905, and there are five or six newer houses owned by members that are just outside the property.

The tennis courts have changed from real grass to fake grass, the old bathing beach's gravel has been replaced by fine white sand hauled over from Lake Michigan, and the fleet of sailboats which used to be of the international six-meters class is now a flock of easy-to-maintain Sunfishes, with nylon sails and fiberglass hulls, but the white birch trees and the cool dry air and the marigolds and petunias and daisies that last ten days after they have been cut, are still the same as they always were.

Also there is a corner of the grounds where cottages seven, eight, and nine are grouped together. This is known as Scotchman's Corner, and our cousins, the Stuarts and Macdonalds and their offspring, are still living there. Several years ago at a cocktail party the Stuarts gave, we were all standing around on their terrace with drinks in hand, when what should we hear far in the distance but the skirling of bagpipes. The sound grew louder and louder, and ultimately a line of twenty-five or thirty pairs of pipers in full Highland regalia and playing "Men of Harlech" came marching toward us all the way from the boathouse. It was a glorious occasion and the pipers came by bus from Detroit, where they were pipers for the Chrysler Corporation.

There have been other changes too. Dinner was always the main meal of the day and was served at noon, with our mothers wearing flowery hats and flouncy dresses, and the men in jackets and ties. When there was a sailboat race, we tore from the dining room, changed into sailor pants and middies, and sped to the boathouse, and before dinner most of us had also changed from tennis shorts or bathing suits.

Gradually dinner moved to evening except on Sundays, and Sunday evening after a supper of cornmeal mush and stewed pears we all went next door to the Casino and sang hymns. We still sing hymns, but now after a buffet supper of roast beef and broiled whitefish and assorted fruit and pastries.

The hearty breakfast has also slowly vanished, and now members sip their coffee and orange juice at home.

To get away from this formal summer resort life, many of the members began buying woodsy land or country property farther up Lake Charlevoix or over on the Lake Michigan shore among the sand dunes. They all carried names that made them sound unpretentious. The King family's was called the Shack, the Wallers' was known as the Bungalow, the Wilsons' was the House in the Woods, the Stuarts' was simply the Farm, and ours was the Cabin.

Eventually we became so fond of the Cabin that we gave our cottage to the club and moved to the Cabin permanently. It is still called the Cabin although there are now five large separate log cabins scattered along the lake on a hundred acres of property.

In Charlevoix there is another club, older than ours and considerably larger, and we have always had pleasant rivalries with them: sailing races, baseball matches, golf and tennis tournaments.

The high point of the year was a costume party given late in August, to which the Chicago Club always went en masse in the same costume. The first time that we thought of going alike was back in the late twenties. We all dressed up as Alpine climbers, old and young and fat and thin, all roped together by one long rope. It was a great moment when we all marched single-file into the Belvedere Casino, so the following year we appeared (again with a rope) as the Volga Boatmen, all of us wearing black beards and wigs, and boots and tunics.

There followed a succession of everything from fan dancers to Ethiopians, gangsters, firemen, and Olympic teams. The last one was when we all came dressed in anything we pleased, but just before our grand entrance we all went down and submerged in the lake. We ruined the dance floor and the furniture and no one danced with us. Now they charge admission, I believe, when we come, and we come as individuals.

Somewhat surprisingly the little town of Petoskey, seventeen miles north of Charlevoix, has been known for many years as one of the best shopping centers in the country. Besides Indian trading posts and genuine leather gloves and moccasins, it has stores to suit every need, from interior decorating places to Maus & Hoffman (men's haberdashery) to Lilly Pulitzer, to places where one can buy linens from France, pillows from Ecuador, jewelry from Italy, and needlepoint from London. When I was in San Remo on the Italian Riviera for the first time, and was overjoyed with the lovely shops, I sent each of my sisters a postcard from there saying "Greetings from the Petoskey of Italy."

During the summers that we didn't go to Charlevoix, where did we go instead? The answer straight off is nowhere as nice as northern Michigan.

The year I was eight and Barbara was five, my parents rented a large yellow-brick house known as Goring Hall in a little spot known as Goring-by-the-Sea, which is near the town of Worthing, England. It was a large place, and an uncle and aunt and their three-year-old son and our grandmother came too, plus Danny and Rosie and Hedwig (cousin Carl's nurse). We were met in Southampton by Perrin, the Goring Hall butler, and as our ship docked I remember seeing him standing by the gangplank wearing a huge pink carnation in the buttonhole of his sober black suit.

We drove fifty-odd miles in a big open gray Panhard car driven by a chauffeur with the remarkable name of Horn, and when we drove up to the main gates they were opened by the gatekeeper and his wife, who stood by bowing and curtsying as we drove through and down the long avenue to the house.

When we reached the front entrance, all the servants (who came with the house) were standing on the steps waiting to greet us, and Perrin presented each one. I can't remember how many, but there was one who was introduced as a "tweeny," apparently something between a kitchen maid and a chambermaid, I believe. The cook was a Mrs. Slopp and she rated second to Perrin himself.

I remember little about the house except there were only two bathrooms, and each was a long distance from Barbara's and my room. The beach too was a long trip from Goring Hall, too far to walk, and when we got there (by a pony and cart) there was no sand, just gravel and sharp stones, and the water was cold and gray. It rained almost every day, or perhaps every other day. We visited Brighton and Chichester and saw the Downs, hundreds of treeless hills, all exactly alike. We played some of the time with Percy and Stanley, who were the sons of Mr. Everett, the chief gardener, and we learned all sorts of funny words from them. Needles were "egg-eyed sharps," and spools of thread were "reels of cotton," and "lorries" were trucks. They had "drapers" instead of dry-goods stores, and we laughed our heads off at their quaint words. Mr. Everett was very proud of his "hothouse," which to us was a greenhouse, and a very disappointing one at that. The peaches that grew there didn't taste like the Charlevoix ones. We hated them, and the grapes too. Our Catawba ones in Michigan were much better, so were Iowa's Concords. They were very disappointing. However, we made the best of it, and finally the time came for us to leave for Paris, and soon after that we'd be homeward-bound.

Paris, however, I remember well indeed. The Tuileries Gardens just across the Rue de Rivoli from the Meurice was the most wonderful park in which to play—*cerceaux* (hoops) to roll, Punch and Judy shows in exotic French, balloons in nets—and our *salon* in the Meurice had not only a purple rug, something I'd never seen before, but also a gorgeous white-and-gold piano. And next door to our hotel was a restaurant, Rumpelmeyer's, where Danny took us every day for lunch and we were allowed to choose our very own pastry. (Oh, those *napoleons*, oh, those *éclairs*.)

One day, things were different. Barbara was sick and I think sister Margaret too. Anyway I recall much confusion of doctors arriving and French being shouted about and everybody busy. I think the idea occurred to Mother and Danny at the same time: Let's get rid of Ellen. How?

The result was that I found myself alone with my father on a splendid Sunday afternoon. Hand in hand we walked to a carriage stand, and took a hack to the Trocadero, and to my utter delight he invited me to go to the top of the Eiffel Tower with him.

It was too good to be true, and the ride up to the main platform in the big glass-enclosed, creaking, upward-curving elevator with all of us sightseers sitting around the four sides was thrilling, to say nothing of the changing there into the smaller elevator that went straight up to the top.

Daddy pointed out Notre Dame and the river Seine and Sacré Coeur and told me about Mr. Eiffel and said that it was the highest edifice in the world, and then bought me a little gold replica of the tower on a gold chain. I was in seventh heaven as we waited for the elevator and decided that I had the best father in the world. I remember that we were standing next to three or four fashionably dressed French couples, the ladies all wearing big flower-trimmed straw hats tied down with veils and ankle-length rustly dresses. The men were elegantly mustachioed and wearing their best Sunday suits and top hats.

The elevator never came.

"*Il ne marche pas, Il ne marche plus. Il est fini,*" the attendant announced to us and pointed to a narrow iron fire escape. "*Il faut descendre à pied.*"

"French machinery is always breaking down," my father said with exasperation, "but we don't want to spend the day here, and the man says it is done for." He gave me a brave smile. "Come on," he said. "Follow me, and hang on to my hand. Keep your other hand on the railing, and don't look down. Just keep your eyes on the railing."

Some agile young men darted off ahead of us, shouting and laughing to each other as they ran nimbly down the steps. They weren't really steps, they just were three iron rods, round and difficult to walk on. Also there were no back treads, and the whole thing was so narrow that a big man like my father had to turn sideways in order to descend. He must have hated every step.

We started off, the French couples first, Daddy and I next, and some quiet older people after us whom we left far behind. It was horrible from beginning to end, and the worst thing about it was the French ladies. They went hysterical as they clattered down the dirty steps with all of Paris spread out below them and nothing but fresh air surrounding us except for the flimsy little railing.

At first they whimpered things like "*J'ai peur*" and "*Je déteste*" and "*Quel voyage épouvantable,*" but then they began to scream and shriek. Some of them prayed at the top of their lungs. "*Notre Père Qui est aux Cieux,*" and so on. Then they also would yell about how we were all going to fall or jump. "*Mon Dieu, nous allons mourir,*" one lady kept repeating at the top of her lungs.

I was so frightend by it all that my knees shook, and this made the descent harder work. And my father began to swear and said awful things that I knew he shouldn't be saying. "God damn," he would mutter, and then "Damnation," which sounded perfectly dreadful to me, worse than his frequent "Hell" and "Godalmighty."

It seemed to go on forever, and although I tried desperately not to look down, I couldn't help but see little tiny horses and carriages and wee small people far, far down below. And I also noticed that one of the French ladies, always just a turn below us, had started off in a pair of high-button white kid shoes with black patent-leather toes. As she kept descending the shoes turned into all-black ones, but the longer that we went down and down, the less noisy the French ladies became. However, at long last, when we finally reached the main platform, the ladies all began to scream and caterwaul all over again.

Daddy led me away, but not very far. We limped into the

nearest bar, where he ordered a double whiskey straight up. I can't say that I blame him in the least, but I was miserable as I sat, dirty and crumpled from head to toe, blisters on my little black hands, and prayed under my breath that I would soon be sitting in Danny's lap, eating strawberries and vanilla ice cream, and she would massage my legs, which were still shaking uncontrollably.

Eventually this happened, and after a hot bath and a night of sound sleep I was as good as new. I remember that Daddy was so stiff and sore from the ordeal that he stayed in bed the whole next day.

However, because of those French women I developed a fear of high places that stayed with me for about fifty years. Unlike the cat family, who all prefer to slink around the edge of a room, I, whenever above the second floor of a building, stayed away from the windows. I couldn't go above the sixth or seventh floor *anywhere* for years, and hated being alone in any elevator even if it was going down to the basement. I couldn't go out on people's balconies or enjoy a view of the Grand Canyon or any view from a nice high mountain.

I have finally improved to a great extent. I no longer need a brandy before going to a cocktail party in the Waldorf Towers or the Top of the Mark, and we now have a little apartment in New York on the eighteenth floor, but I still prefer an aisle seat on planes and never lean out of open windows or sit on their ledges. My life would have been better if my father and I had struggled down the Eiffel Tower by ourselves.

As we grew older European summers began to improve. One memorable year we rented a house called the Villa des Mouettes in Biarritz. As you no doubt know, Biarritz is in the Basque country, close to the Pyrenees and also to the Spanish border, and the villa was right on the Atlantic Ocean; in fact, at high tide the door to our concierge's quarters (that would be the superintendent) had to be closed with a special watertight door. The waves really thundered in and the spray shot up to our living-room terrace two stories above. At low tide the front side of the house was surrounded by gritty yellow sand: a crummy beach compared to the one at home, but the big crescent-shaped public beach (*la plage*) with its wide yellow-brick walk and gay little dressing tents and warm yellow sand was fun.

Our cousins the Hamiltons were there too, staying nearby at the Hôtel Palais (formerly the summer palace of Napoleon III and the Empress Eugénie) and cousin Anne and I, being fifteen or sixteen years of age at this point, were Boy Crazy. We had both been brokenhearted to have had to leave Cedar Rapids and John and Don and Chuck and Ted and all the other boys that we danced with at the Country Club, but it wasn't two days before we had become acquainted with an eager group of boys our age, thanks to cousin Anne's being a glamour girl, and thanks to our being able to speak French.

The Hamiltons and my mother and father graciously permitted us to go tea dancing every afternoon, if we were invited. There were to be no evening dates, and we had to be home before sunset, otherwise we were unchaperoned.

There was only one thing wrong with the summer: all the boys that we knew were too short. Most of them were from rich South American families, particularly those who came to Biarritz from Venezuela, although we did know a few Spanish youths from San Sebastián, and one or two young Frenchmen, but we towered over all of them. In fact, there wasn't one single boy there whose head we couldn't see over the top of. But we gradually became used to being giantesses, and we became expert at the tango, and something called the schottische, which was sort of a polka in waltz time, and actually I think it was a forerunner of the samba.

When we weren't dancing or eating ice cream at Dodin's we were over in San Sebastián. One of our tiny boy friends by the name of Pepito was a nephew or a cousin of King Alfonso XIII of Spain and we went to a good many bullfights, sitting splendidly in the Royal Box. Pepito was the only member of the royal family ever there, but we lunched several times at the sumptuous summer palace, and became pretty casual eating off the royal china, and drinking diluted wine in goblets encrusted with gold coronets.

At first we were squeamish about the bullfights, and when

the matador killed the bull we would hide behind our fans, but gradually we began to find it more exciting and more exciting, like watching Bobby Jones winning the U. S. Open, or Bill Tilden and Jean Borotra (the Bounding Basque) playing a tennis match. We even knew some of the toreadors and matadors, and yelled *Olé* and threw flowers at them.

As we were beginning to enjoy ourselves hugely, the summer ended abruptly for me. An art teacher from Cedar Rapids' Coe College turned up to visit Mother, a Miss Wolfe, and it was decided that sister Margaret and Miss Wolfe and I should proceed at once to Florence and Rome, where Miss Wolfe would take us through the museums, churches, and galleries of the two cities. Danny would go with us too, and Mother, Dad, Barbara, and Rosie would motor with Bert in a large brown Renault that we had acquired for the summer. We would meet at the Hotel Excelsior in three weeks.

Rome and Florence were hot and dusty and full of tourists, and Margaret and I saw enough Botticellis and Giorgiones and Raphaels to last us a lifetime, and Danny was very helpful each evening when we tottered into our *pensione,* she made us each a delightful footbath.

The week before the family was to arrive, in some way we were granted an audience with the Pope. It was not a private audience, you understand, there would be some three hundred of us, but I was absolutely delighted: not only would I see the Pope and the Vatican, but I couldn't go in anything but a black dress, something that I had never owned and had always wanted but girls my age were not allowed to wear; black was too sophisticated.

We found an elegant black silk dress at La Rinascente (the Altman's of Rome), and with black patent-leather pumps and a black straw hat I felt as *femme fatale* as Pola Negri, or a vamp very like Theda Bara.

We all knelt as His Holiness Pius XI and some attending cardinals arrived in a huge room near St. Peter's, and he swept down past the long line of us holding out his hand to each supplicant in turn, so that we could kiss his ring. He murmured nice things as he went along, but there was no delay until he came to Danny.

Instead of kissing his great big ring, an intaglio set in gold, Danny kissed his hand. He stopped dead in his tracks and asked Danny in Italian what was her religion.

I replied politely that she was "*scozzese*" (that is, Scotch) and that she was "*una protestante.*" He smiled at me and asked where we lived. I told him that we were Americans, from the United States, and our state was Iowa.

He nodded and said in perfect English that he knew of it and had heard that it was very fertile. Then he wanted to know how I happened to speak Italian, and I told him that I learned from Signora Cafagna, my Italian teacher in boarding school. Then I complimented him on his excellent English and he said that he spoke thirteen languages, then proceeded on his way after saying, "God bless you, my child."

After the audience was over, we were mobbed. Everyone pushed and shoved and wanted to know what he had said to us. If it hadn't been for the guards getting us out a private door, that black silk dress would have been torn, and the black straw hat squashed to pieces.

7

Traveling by Ship

ON THE QUARTERDECK of the Cunard Line's flagship, the *Queen Elizabeth II*, there is a large restaurant called the Columbia, and in it, conspicuously displayed, is a large silver cup which was presented in 1840 to a Captain Woodruff, who sailed the first Cunard ocean liner, *Britannia*, from Liverpool to Halifax and Boston. In those days the company was called the British and Northern American Royal Mail Steam Packet Company, and Samuel Cunard, a shipowner from Nova Scotia, received a contract to establish a regular monthly shipping service between Britain and North America, the first service of its kind. The name was shortened to the Cunard Line, and the company's motto was (and still is) "Speed, Comfort, and Safety."

The word "liner" was comparatively new when Mr. Cunard started his company. Before this, ships would usually wait in port until the hold was filled with cargo. Sometimes the mail and passengers had to wait around for days, or even weeks, but a "liner" sailed on a certain announced date for a specific port.

Mr. Cunard's ships eventually had another new feature: they had screw propellers instead of the old steam-driven salt-encrusted paddle wheels and their hulls were of iron instead of wood. Mr. Cunard made a fortune, and before he died in 1865 he had not only been knighted but had left to the Atlantic Ocean the most distinguished line of all time, and to the sorrow of many of us who never crossed the ocean any other way the *QE II* (as of this writing) is the only large ship that still sails across the North Atlantic.

It is hard to imagine what transatlantic travel was like in the days of the *Britannia* and her sister ships. The first Cunard liners were strictly *no frills*. With a tonnage of just over 1,500 tons, they carried 124 passengers. They were hideously uncomfortable, the food was poor and cooked in a galley one deck above, so that it almost always arrived cold and sometimes wet and salty as the stewards crossed an open deck. The trip took fifteen days at best and there was no hot water. There were primitive unsanitary loos, and most of the passengers slept on upholstered benches that lined the walls of the main saloon, and were curtained off at night and converted into private bunks.

There was one stewardess, and two or three stewards, lone candles lit the rooms, and a live cow in a padded pen on the deck gave fresh milk.

Competition and know-how increased rapidly, and by the early 1900s there were a great many ships sailing under names like White Star Line and Red Star Line, North German Lloyd, Holland-America, French Line, and so on. The Cunard Line built the *Mauretania* about sixty years after the *Britannia,* and the change in style is nothing short of unbelievable.

The engines were turbine, there were four screws, and her tonnage was 31,938, making her in 1907 the world's largest liner. She had four smokestacks (the only others to ever have four were the sister ship *Lusitania,* the *Aquitania,* and the White Star Line's *Olympic, Titanic,* and *Britannic*). On her main deck forward, the series of public first-class rooms started with a conventional pattern that most passenger ships still use: library, writing room, and drawing room (or main lounge or grand saloon), then a men's bar and smoking room, followed by the grand staircase leading down to the large embarkation entrance hall and dining room.

The *Mauretania* also had telephones in the best cabins, some private baths, and two electric elevators. Back before World War I, most large ocean liners like the *Mauretania* also had at least two other classes for passengers besides first. Second class, which cost less, had smaller cabins, no private baths, and simpler food with less choice. Then sometimes there was a sort of lower-class second class called second intermediate. It had still smaller cabins with more bunks and less space, very *no frills.*

Last came steerage, or third class, and that part of the ship was usually crowded beyond belief, with as many as eight bunks to a cabin. This steerage sometimes had a lower class in it too, where the passengers (usually Asians) cooked their own food in a certain closed-off special area of a deck far down to the stern on the leeward side of the ship.

The *Mauretania* was so fast that on her second voyage she captured the famous Blue Riband from the German *Kaiser Wilhelm II*, until then the fastest ship on the North Atlantic run; she was known as the Greyhound of the Atlantic, and held the Blue Riband for twenty-two out of her whole twenty-eight years of service.

Noël Coward said that she was most appropriately called the Greyhound because she galloped up and down with every wave. However, she and the *Aquitania* were both long and narrow, and in a heavy sea this makes for rougher travel than on boats of broader beam. The old *Rotterdam*, on which I sailed once in 1924, was so short and wide that she seemed safe, slow, steady, and rather like a raft.

Why was the *Mauretania* scrapped in 1935? Because of the increasing demand for cabins with private baths, and unfortunately there was no way to accomplish such a remodeling job, it would be cheaper to build a whole new ship.

Among these new ships was the famous *Titanic,* and the story of its sinking was actually the first sad thing that I can remember. In 1912 my Aunt Mahala and Uncle Walter had been in Europe buying furniture for their new house on Lake Minnetonka, a suburb of Minneapolis. They boarded the *Titanic* at Cherbourg just as it was getting dark, and were taken out to the ship by tender. Then an odd thing happened.

My aunt was tired from the boat-train trip from Paris and because they had been up late the night before at a farewell party at Maxim's or some such spot, so she and her personal maid, Berthe, had found a little bench in a corner of the big flat deck and were sitting there quietly when a shabbily dressed small gray-haired Frenchman appeared in front of them. He leaned forward and spoke in French. His voice was so low that they had trouble hearing him.

"Excuse me, madame," he addressed Aunt Mahala, and his accent was that of *le Pays Basque.* "This ship, she is not safe. *Je vous en prie* [I beg of you] not to sail on her." He bowed and vanished. They looked around; in fact, Berthe walked all around the tender but never saw him again.

When told about it, Uncle Walter merely laughed and told her that he had just been talking to some friends of theirs who had embarked at Southampton, where many of the passengers had seen a black-faced stoker peering at them through a hole in a smokestack of an adjacent ship, and had made faces at them. Several *Titanic* passengers took it as bad luck and were upset. The rest thought it was silly.

They went on board at 8:30 P.M., and the ship sailed immediately. It was Wednesday, April 10, and this maiden voyage was uneventful until Sunday. Much later Aunt Mahala wrote of that last Sunday night:

> On the Titanic. We dined the last night in the Ritz restaurant. It was the last word in luxury. The tables were gay with pink roses and white daisies, the women in their beautiful shimmering gowns of satin and silk, the men immaculate and well-groomed, the stringed orchestra playing music from Puccini and Tchaikowsky. The food was superb: caviar, lobster, quail from Egypt, plover's eggs, and hothouse grapes and fresh peaches. The night was cold and clear, the sea like glass.

> But in a few short hours every man in that room was dead except J. Bruce Ismay, Gordon Duff, and a Mr. Carter.

In 1912, the *Titanic* was newly launched, "practically unsinkable," and the largest ship afloat. She was not designed to break the speed records (26 knots) of the *Mauretania*, but designed to go 21 knots in luxury and comfort and with greater capacity. Imagine, then, a ship almost as large as the modern S. S. *France* (66,000 tons) sailing across the Atlantic with 2,212 persons aboard and carrying only sixteen regular lifeboats. Forty-eight would have saved every soul on board. Imagine, also, a ship of that size with no searchlights, no trained crew to launch the lifeboats, no organization or boat drills of any sort, no loudspeaker system, not even an officer shouting orders through a megaphone. Furthermore, the lifeboats carried no lights, no food or water, and regrettably not even a single chamber pot.

Aunt Mahala and Uncle Walter had gone to their cabin that

Sunday evening a little after eleven, and started undressing. As he was taking off his shoes, the iceberg sideswiped the entire starboard flank of the ship below the waterline, slicing the double-plated hull open. It was hardly noticeable to them, perhaps a very slight tremor. However, Uncle Walter noticed that the screws were no longer turning and decided to go up on deck to see if anything was wrong.

He came down in a few minutes and told her that although he could see nothing to disturb him nor could he obtain any information, nevertheless the ship was standing still, and that she'd better put on her fur coat, for it was bitterly cold, and come along.

They roused Berthe, who was sleeping in an inside cabin just opposite theirs, and the three of them went up to the main deck, where by this time lifeboats were being lowered and rockets were being shot off up at the bow.

Auntie said there was no panic of any sort and everyone was quiet. She and Berthe were assigned to Lifeboat 4, and Uncle Walter and a ship's officer helped them in, her husband assuring them that he would join them later. When she begged him to come with her he shook his head and said, "I would be less than a man if I left before every woman was in a boat." At this point no one realized that there weren't enough boats.

Before they were lowered to the water, the same officer who had helped them in put in some candles and some sort of lamp. It was the only lifeboat with any lights, and eventually most of the other boats formed a chain behind Lifeboat 4.

The trip down to the cold black water was precarious and terrifying, as they were lowered by hand, tipping this way and that, and for a time it seemed as if the lifeboat itself might buckle. However, they made it, with a splash at the end, all full of women and children except one large crewman. He had a terrible time trying to row with his one heavy oar, and couldn't seem to get away from the big ship looming up high above them.

Two women tried to help with another oar, in fact Auntie and Berthe rowed for a while when the others got tired, but the oars were unwieldy as could be, and even the crewman lacked rowing experience. Consequently, they never got more than a few hundred feet away from the *Titanic*. (Actually there was one more pair of oars in the boat, but they were still lashed together with the builder's heavy twine and no one could get them apart.)

To view the ship, even from where they were, was a most fearful sight, as they could see that the long line of round brightly lit portholes slanted downward, so much so that up near the bow the lights were shining up through the cold still dark water. In fact it was all too plain to those in the lifeboats that the *Titanic* was sinking.

Besides the rockets going off and the ship's orchestra playing continuously, they could hear men on the boat deck shouting to each other as they tried to launch the last two collapsible lifeboats, made of wood with folding canvas sides. The other only noise was the steady blowing of escaping steam from the boilers, which had been going on ever since the ship had stopped. Suddenly the lights on the ship all flared up with a strange reddish glow. Some bulkhead down below must have given way, for the ship lurched forward and then all the lights went out. Apparently everything inside the ship broke loose at this point; the noise of boilers and machinery thundering down into the bow was unbelievable. Aunt Mahala said her lifeboat was near enough even to hear things like china crashing as well as deeper rumbles of all the machinery. Then, silhouetted against the stars, the whole stern of the *Titanic* rose up perpendicularly. One eyewitness said that it had reminded him of New York's Flatiron Building. Then slowly and steadily the great thing sank down and down and vanished.

The suction that had worried the people in the lifeboats turned out to be totally nonexistent. Lots of people stepped into the water from the stern railing as it reached the water, and then swam away. One crewman, a young man who worked in the bakery, drank down a quart of scotch in the first-class bar, then stepped off into the 27-degree water and paddled over to a raft of some sort. It was already filled, so he spent the rest of the night in the water, and lived through the experience.

My aunt said that the most terrible thing of all was the cries of the people in the water, and this dreadful chorus went on and on, always getting fainter and fainter, for over an hour. Of the 2,212 on board, there was room for only 950 in lifeboats, and in the end only 705 were saved. Some of the partially filled boats did return and save some, but many of them didn't dare for fear that the suction would have pulled them down.

My aunt remembered that as the lifeboats began to tie up to their lighted boat, eleven of them together finally in a long chain, one officer who had swum to safety told them that, thanks to the radio wireless operator, an SOS message had been picked up by the Cunard Line's *Carpathia* and that she was coming to their rescue at full speed. She said that when they heard about the radio message that had been picked up by the *Carpathia* they all gave a prayer of thanks to Guglielmo Marconi, to whom they owed their lives. The rest of the time they sat mostly in silence, stiff and cold and uncomfortable. The lack of a chamber pot added terrifically to their discomfort; every woman in her boat could have used one. As it was, the only thing they had was some sort of a rolled-up cotton knitted underskirt that they used, rinsed out in the icy water after each use, and passed on to the next sufferer.

They had passed candles back to the lifeboats behind them, and when the *Carpathia* finally arrived, ablaze with light, firing rockets to announce her arrival, the chain of lifeboats waved their tiny lights in return. Just then a breeze sprang up, putting out most of the candles, but it was beginning to get light. By the time they pulled up alongside the *Carpathia* the sun came up, revealing big and little icebergs as far as they could see, all tinged pink in the sunlight.

Aunt Mahala said that, tired and stiff though they were, she and Berthe climbed up the big rope landing net on the ship's lee side without assistance (some of the women had to be hauled up in slings), and they were wonderfully treated by everyone on board. The most amazing thing was that not one of the rescued passengers died, nor was anyone really ill. Outside of a few cases of mild frostbite and of course shock, there was no illness at all from exposure, and this included all the people who had swum to the lifeboats and had then spent the night in wet clothes, in some cases with the sea water washing partly over them the whole time. (Four of the crew died, however, two in lifeboats and two more on the *Carpathia*.)

As you probably know, several days after the *Carpathia* landed in New York the White Star Line sent two small cable-repair ships to the area where the *Titanic* had gone down. There, with a priest assisting, the crews retrieved over three hundred bodies that they were able to identify, as well as many more.

Uncle Walter's body was the first one to be identified, and it was of some comfort for the family to know that he had not drowned, for there was no water in his lungs, and he apparently had been instantly killed by a crushing blow at the base of his head.

His body came to Cedar Rapids by a special train, and I remember all the ladies and gentlemen in black, speaking in whispers, while a large closed coffin rested in the library surrounded by tall vases of white flowers.

And that was the last of the *Titanic*, but what about those other new luxurious British ships? I never sailed on the *Mauretania* myself, but I crossed twice on the *Aquitania*, twice on the *Queen Mary*, and once apiece on each *Queen Elizabeth*, and found them all to be excellent in every way.

The *Queen Elizabeth II* is completely different from the other Cunard liners, so first let's take a look at the way they were back in 1957, for example.

"All ashore that's going ashore" was the cry over the loudspeakers, accompanied by page boys calling the same words as they walked through the corridors, sounding a gong as well. Ships often sailed from New York at ten or eleven in the evening because there was little traffic at that time of day, and it was easier to get a taxi to or from the pier.

The visitors took their last swallows of champagne when they heard the "all ashore," bade their traveler friends goodbye and left the cabins, and hurried out to the covered gangplank waiting for them at the embarkation hall.

Meanwhile the stewards were busy still delivering flowers, Bon Voyage telegrams, and traditional steamer baskets tied with ribbons and containing fruit and candy. There were also notes saying that Clara and Charles were treating you to a bottle of champagne anytime you would like to have it served in the bar or dining room. There were "steamer letters," some containing notes to be read the first day, second, and so on.

As soon as possible after you arrived on board, your husband, let's say, after being conducted to your cabin and having it unlocked by your steward, went back to the main hall, found the chief dining steward, and asked for a table for two at the second sitting. Then he went to the chief deck steward and reserved two deck chairs on the sunny side and sheltered from the wind. Remember the word "posh"? It's an old British word standing for "Portside Out, Starboardside Home," referring to the old British Empire days when viceroys and diplomats went out to India and Singapore via P & O, and preferred the shady side for their cabins and deck chairs.

Of course, another important thing was checking the luggage: had it all arrived and was there a trunk "not wanted on board" which could be sent down to the baggage room? The nicest invention on board a luxury liner was an individual trunk room, a big bare closet, preferably with an outside door as well, so the luggage could be delivered to it direct. The steward when given the keys would open the wardrobe trunks and he and the stewardess would take away the dinner jackets and evening dresses that needed to be pressed.

The first night at sea no one dressed up, just dark traveling clothes; this custom always prevailed on Sunday nights too. All other nights, in first class, men wore black ties or even white ties, and ladies were in evening dresses, usually very elaborate.

On the Cunard Line the Captain, the Staff Captain in charge of the Social Activities, the Chief Engineer, the Chief Purser, and the Doctor had tables of eight to ten, and passengers were invited by written invitation. To sit at the Captain's table was, of course, the prize spot, and white tie there was *de rigueur*. However, if you really didn't want to sit there you could politely refuse. You could *never*, however, *ask* to sit at the Captain's table.

I only sat with the Captain once; it was Captain Visser on the *Nieuw Amsterdam*, and I was traveling alone. Consequently, it was great fun, the people at his table were all interesting and attractive. It does have one drawback: the guests all have to wait until the Captain arrives, they cannot be late, and they all eat what the Captain orders.

The Captain at sea traditionally exercised authority under God alone, and he still can. A master, under English maritime law, is a magistrate at sea. He has the power to put the President or Director of the Line into irons, he can send a woman passenger of suspicious appearance to her cabin for the rest of the trip, and he has the power to perform marriages at sea that are exactly as binding as on land.

A college friend of mine was married in New York at an elaborate wedding in June 1924, shortly after her graduation from Vassar. The ceremony took place in St. Bartholomew's Chapel and the bride, who was a beautiful blonde and a Vassar ex-daisy-chain-carrier, wore a glorious wedding gown of white lace, and was preceded down the aisle by eight bridesmaids in pink lace carrying pink roses, and a handsome dark-haired maid of honor in a similar lace dress of an American Beauty shade, carrying American Beauty roses. There were also eight ushers and a best man, and after Dr. Norwood, the rector, had pronounced the bride and groom man and wife, there was a customary reception at the Colony Club.

No one knew where the happy couple were spending their honeymoon except Cy and Charlotte, the best man and maid of honor, and the two of them, knowing that they were sailing at 7:00 P.M. on the *Aquitania* in a certain suite, decided that they would sneak off quietly during the reception, go down to Pier 56, and take along her roses and some of the wedding champagne to give the bridal suite an air of charm and welcome. They even took some candy rose leaves and a dish of salted nuts and a few slices of the groom's cake to add a further homelike touch, and off they went while the bride and groom were just leaving the party and going off to dress.

Charlotte and Cy, still in their wedding attire, boarded the *Aquitania* and were admitted to the suite, where Charlotte put her American Beauty roses in a big vase on the center table; Cy put the champagne bottles in a big cooler (there were three), turned to go, and left a little note saying "Bon Voyage and love," etc.

Just as they were tiptoeing out, Cy looked longingly at the champagne and said that there was plenty of time and lots of champagne, and why didn't they stay and have one drink? Charlotte agreed, but suggested that they would do better to take the third bottle of champagne with them, and find a quiet place to enjoy it where they wouldn't disturb the newlyweds.

They went up to the deserted Garden Verandah, high up on the top deck, where they had a magic view of New York and the river, golden in the setting sun. As they sipped the champagne, they fell in love. Before the ship sailed they hid themselves away behind the thickest of the Verandah's ferns, and emerged only after the *Aquitania* had dropped the pilot at Ambrose Light.

Then they alerted the bride and groom and asked them to accompany them, and presented themselves to Sir James Charles, the Commodore of the Fleet, who married them straightway, with the newlyweds acting as their attendants.

Every one of the ship's cabins was taken, so the honeymooners gave Cy and Charlotte their sitting room, the steward set up two little cots, and they proceeded to share the trousseaux all the way to Cherbourg.

The odd thing about this curious wedding trip *à quatre* is that Cy and Charlotte are still happily married, as far as I know, whereas the original pair broke up by the end of the summer.

A more typical day aboard a British ship at sea started whenever you rang for the steward or stewardess. If you were a lone female, or two females or even four, the stewardess was always summoned. If you were a married couple, you rang for the steward.

Breakfast came (some passengers, I am told, ate in the dining room, but I don't think I ever met one), which you ate in bed, reading along with your tea and eggs a printed sheet of the world news in brief plus another sheet listing the day's activities. There were always exercises and workouts in the gymnasium, and shuffleboard and Ping-Pong in the morning with hot bouillon and crackers at 11:00 A.M.

After lunch there was usually a bridge tournament in the card room, a movie in the theater, a concert and tea in the main lounge, and possibly a lecture on something worthwhile in the library.

After dinner there was another concert somewhere, bingo or a game of wooden horses who raced when dice were thrown in another public room, a movie in the theater, and dancing afterward in the main lounge, with a cold buffet supper served at midnight. When the dancing stopped and the lobster salad and cold roast beef were taken away, if you wanted further merry making, you went to the Cabin Class (or Second Class, as it was called earlier). There was usually a nightclub there going strong until very late.

To sneak from one class to another sometimes took a great deal of ingenuity, as the stewards kept the doors locked tight especially at night. It was usually easy to get from First to Cabin Class, but to know some Princeton college students in Tourist Class and get them up to First or Cabin Class for a little dancing was accomplished by going, for example, to the chapel. The Tourist student would kneel there quietly for a minute or two, then walk reverently out the entrance to Cabin Class. I've forgotten now which ship this was, but next he proceeded to the infirmary and from there when no one was looking he could whip across to a stairway and arrive in First Class, snug as a bug.

When I was boy-crazy that summer in Biarritz, we came home on the *Aquitania*, and I remember some college boys getting up to First Class to see us by a narrow iron ladder that ran up the side of the ship just inside its outer plates. Apparently it was a fast crawlway for crew members to get two or three decks up or down, almost like a one-man vertical tunnel.

That same trip I also met Sir James Charles, the Commodore. He was one of the largest men I've ever seen in my life and one of the handsomest. At the Captain's dinner (always the next-to-the-last night before landing) he had the most gold braid on his uniform and the most ribbons (for medals) that I ever saw on any one person. He came over to our table and shook hands with all of us, and told sister Barbara and me that we were going to enjoy *excessively* the special dessert of the evening. And we did: it was a soufflé served by a chef in a two-foot-high chef's hat, and the soufflé was the same height and surrounded by glacéed strawberries and pink spun sugar.

Lucius Beebe wrote the following about him in his book *The Big Spenders:* "Sir James' tastes at table were vaguely those of Emil Jannings playing Henry VIII. Stewards wheeled in carcasses of whole roasted oxen one night and the next evening small herds of grilled antelope surrounded a hilltop of Strasbourg *foie gras* surmounted with peacock fans. Electrically illuminated *pièces montées* representing the Battle of Waterloo and other patriotic moments made an appearance while the ship's orchestra played Elgar."

What did I like best of all on the Cunard Line ships? One of the nicest things of all was the Terrace Restaurant on the *Queen Mary*. It was small, perhaps a dozen tables, and it was located high up somewhere near the bridge. Elegantly decorated with gold-and-white Louis XVI chairs and tables and rose-colored rugs and draperies, it was bright and cheerful even on the grayest day, it had a view of the whole ocean from every direction, and at night with the curtains drawn it was cozy and warm.

The food was excellent, as it had its own kitchen with a French chef inside creating continental dishes, and the *sommelier* had a dazzling array of wines. To eat there for the trip cost eleven dollars a day extra, but it was well worth it.

The other two *Queens* also had these upper extra-fare restaurants, but the *QE I*'s seemed more formal and cold, and the food was as British as the food in the huge dining salon down below. The *QE II*'s Queen's Restaurant is the restaurant for *all* first-class passengers, and is attractive and the food is good, but it is large and impersonal.

Then I remember how much I liked the big smoking room on the first *Queen Elizabeth*. It was not only frightfully British, but also most tastefully elegant. It was filled with comfortable black leather armchairs, each with a little table for the cocktail and a saucer of cheese biscuits or something. It was where the ship's pool was auctioned off every night before dinner, and this event and the beautiful room made it the high point of the day.

The ship's pool? It is *money*, and the money bet on how many miles the ship will go in one twenty-four-hour day. Let us say that the *Queen Elizabeth* on an average run-of-the-mill day went about 620 miles from twelve noon to twelve noon. The smoking-room steward before the end of the cocktail hour would appear and announce that bids were open for numbers 600, 601, and upward through number 640, each sold to the highest bidder.

The auction would start, the first numbers going for as little as a pound or two, or a few dollars (the currency being pounds eastbound, dollars westbound), and, as the numbers approached the 620 mark, increasing to sometimes several hundred dollars.

It was extremely exciting, and of course a lot depended on the weather, for if it grew rough and the stabilizers had to be turned on they slowed up the ship's speed by several knots. Conversely, with a calm sea and a following wind the ship might exceed the 620 norm by forty miles or more. Consequently there were bidders for the high field, and also the low.

Perhaps you have read the short story by John Collier in which the young man traveling first class had no money left to pay his bar bill aboard ship and all the tips and other expenses? He bought the low field in the ship's pool, talked to a nice motherly lady on an upper deck, and in full view of her calmly jumped overboard, figuring that she would alert the first deck steward she saw with a cry of "Man overboard!"

Unfortunately, however, the motherly lady's nurse appeared instead and the tale ends with the nurse saying, "Now, now, we aren't going to run away again are we, that was very naughty," etc. etc. And the motherly lady kept saying, "But I had the nicest chat with a young man and then he jumped overboard," and the nurse said patiently, "Yes, yes, and now we'll go down to our cabin and I'll read to you, won't that be nice?"

What about the new *Queen Elizabeth*, the Second? She isn't really a ship the way the other Cunarders were, she is run like a seagoing hotel, rather like the kind you'd find in Las Vegas.

When you want breakfast in the morning you don't ring for the steward, you call room service. There is no purser, there is the hotel manager instead. The privileges of traveling first class come with the price of your room. If you pay for an outside cabin with dressing room and bath (no matter where it is located on the vast ship) you may drink and dine in the first-class

Queen's Grill, which is hidden away on the boat deck just behind the shopping center. Inside it is surprisingly like the old Cunard ships: there are uniformed stewards, serving excellent food from the Grill's own kitchen, and the atmosphere is similar to the Terrace Restaurant on the *Queen Mary*.

Downstairs, after dinner you can go to the gaming tables and try your hand at roulette and blackjack and the *croupiers*, beg your pardon, I mean *croupières*, are pretty and dressed as if they came from a San Francisco Gaslight Café. There are rows and rows of slot machines too.

Summing it up, it is still possible to experience leisurely travel on the *QE II*, but gone is the formality, gone is much of the tradition, and gone is all of the elegance. One can wear anything from the orange pants suit to the trailing sequin-trimmed yellow chiffon gown at almost any time of the day or night, and in nearly any part of the ship.

Due to an unusual number of threats and bomb scares, no passengers are allowed on the Captain's bridge at any time, and the customary tour of the ship's engine room and kitchens is nonexistent.

There is no Captain's table any more and I can't remember a Captain's dinner or a Captain's gala of any sort. Perhaps they save this sort of thing for their occasional Round-the-World and Mediterranean Cruises.

What was my favorite ship? It is a toss-up between the *Cristoforo Colombo* and the *Raffaello*, both of the Italian Line. The *Colombo* was small, but I would say a sort of optimum size. For example, it could sail through some narrow channels in the Azores that larger craft couldn't manage, and it could even tie up in Venice on the Grand Canal close to Santa Maria della Salute.

Another gorgeous thing about the *Colombo:* it had a great big curving room with windows on three sides (including a little bar called the Bamboo Bar) just under the Captain's bridge. It was wonderful to sit there with the sea all around, and in a storm it was spectacular. At dusk it was closed up with lightproof curtains so that its lights wouldn't bother the boys up above on the bridge.

The *Raffaello* was bigger and more elegant, but had just as nice people aboard, just as good bridge players among the officers, and both had horse races, but of a spectacular nature. They were called Cinemaraces, and instead of stewards moving six little wooden horses down a felt racetrack while various lady passengers shook dice to see which horses would be moved, a Cinemarace was a real live movie of a real live racetrack. You were each given a regular racetrack folder, and the horses had phony names, and you bet just as if you were at Santa Anita or Belmont.

Another thing that I liked about the Italian Line: the officers all ate together in an adjacent dining room. Lots of them joined the passengers for dancing and conversation later on and it seemed like a better way to run things. I still remember a polite forced conversation every night for a week with a Chief Purser on some American Export Lines ship, the *Constitution* or the *Independence*. He was a dour man, and it was hard work.

Another advantage of the Italian ships was that they set sail from New York heading immediately south and stayed in warmer parts of the Atlantic until they reached the Straits of Gibraltar, the entrance to the even warmer waters of the Mediterranean. I remember coming home once on the *Cristoforo Colombo* and landing in New York on the sixteenth of December. It was sunny and warm all the way home until almost the last day, and it was fun sitting in a sheltered spot on the top deck addressing Christmas cards.

Then too they had more things to do than on other ships. There were, besides all the Ping-Pong tournaments and movies and weight-reducing classes, a lot of exotic entertainment that seldom occurred anywhere else. On the *Raffaello* one westbound trip I recall a magician who pulled white doves from behind ladies' ears at a performance in the first-class lounge; and later, in the children's playroom, he made every boy and girl a special animal all out of colored balloons.

There were puzzles to be solved. Nicknames, for example: Who was the Manassa Mauler? The Sultan of Swat? These were delivered to the cabin every day, and when completed were handed in to the library steward. The prizes were all worth having, so everyone tried to win.

There were also various games at night: everything from obstacle courses on the dance floor to competitions for the most remarkable headdress. And for those passengers who liked to sit and watch, the Italian ships had fashion shows (usually at tea time) and full-fledged symphony concerts (usually after dinner).

All in all, these ships were more pleasant to sail on, and I think it is partly because as a *people* the Italians are naturally so pleasant. Their food seemed better too. The beds with their smooth linen sheets and their warm light blankets seemed more comfortable, and the cabins and the public rooms with their soft carpeting and harmonious colors and beautiful lighting seemed more elegant.

One last high point of the *Raffaello* and I am through. GW and I felt very well-to-do one trip to Italy back in the 1960s, and instead of booking our two little adjoining single cabins each with bath that we usually took, we splurged and found ourselves in a very large and elaborate suite known as La Rosatea. It had a bedroom and sitting room all together, the bedroom really being a large alcove and curtained off lightly during the day. It had two bathrooms, each with a little dressing room, and a lot of closets scattered about. We enjoyed the whole thing very much. The last day of the trip came, and just before we tied up at Naples we checked all the closets to see that nothing was left behind, and found to our surprise a third bathroom that we'd never noticed before.

I could go on and on, and tell about the wonderful caviar every night on the *France* of the Compagnie Générale Transatlantique, and of the biggest and brightest and most comfortable cabins of all, to be found on our very own *United States*, which the Duke and Duchess of Windsor always sailed on, and how frightened we all were on the maiden voyage of the *Ile de France* when the big lacquer-red grand piano broke loose from its moorings in the Grand Salon after dinner one evening when the ship was pitching terribly (no stabilizers in those days), but I think I've said enough, and here's what the Italian loudspeaker says when the passengers must go ashore:

Attenzione! Attenzione! Scendi a terra, la nave è in partenza.

8
Gangsters and Debutantes

ONE PLEASANT FALL day in the early thirties found me watching a baseball game in Chicago. It was the World Series, the Chicago Cubs in their very own ball park, Wrigley Field, were playing against the New York Yankees. I remember that Guy Bush was pitching for the Cubs, and that Babe Ruth was batting for the Yankees, the place was packed, and there was much booing and shouting when Guy Bush struck out the Sultan of Swat.

Along about the top of the eighth inning a big man in a pearl-gray suit and wearing a large white fedora hat stood up. He was about three rows in front of where I was sitting. Without a single glance anywhere he turned and started moving toward the nearest exit. One second after he got up, several dozen different men stood up all over the park, and also moved to their exits.

I got a good look at the big dark-haired, black-eyed, cigar-smoking man as he left. It was Al Capone, with his many body-guards. Gangsters in those days, while not exactly in the social swim, were seen in public and were stared at, the same as we used to stare at movie stars.

Gangsters gunned down each other and grabbed headlines, but left the rest of us alone. However, there were holdup men in Chicago, most of whom were amazingly polite. The only time that I was held up, the man who was pointing the sawed-off shotgun at me said, "Sorry to do this, lady, but just hand me the money in your bag. That's all I need." Naturally I gave it to him, he tipped his hat, and then jumped into a waiting sedan and was driven off.

This sort of holdup occurred now and then. A dark inconspicuous car with three or four men in it would wait outside some nightclub or dancing spot and then follow you home, jump out of their car, and rob you at your own doorstep.

The way to avoid this was simple. You made sure when you were two or three blocks from your house or apartment that you were not being followed. If you were, then you drove to the nearest brightly lit hotel, told the doorman that you were being followed, and he would let you stay there until the other car had left.

The hoodlum's car had to drive off or the doorman would call the police. And once a whole carload of us had been to a debutante ball and were driving out to Lake Forest when we discovered that we were being followed. One of the men, who had quite a buzz on (that would be drunk), rolled down the window and shouted at them, "Go and follow someone else, we're going all the way to Lake Forest and we have spent all our money anyway."

They tooted their horn and, waving merrily, turned left.

There is one more incident about gangsters that I would like to mention, and that takes us first to London, England. I was there in 1931, in July I believe, and my husband and I were lunching at the Ranelagh Club with our friend from Chicago Ogden Ketting.

Over the martinis he told us that, several years before, a British member of this Ranelagh Club had approached him, and after introducing himself as Sir George Mosscrop-Smythe, had asked him for advice about a trip across the States.

"I shall be going on my way to India," he said, "and I am taking my entire family: my wife and five youngsters, two nannies, my valet and my wife's maid. Now if I were traveling alone I shouldn't hesitate to go through Chicago, but with my family accompanying me, tell me truthfully, do you think it is quite safe? I hear these gangsters are all over Chicago, perhaps it would be a bit wiser to go across Canada instead?"

Ogden explained in a polite and sober manner that he and his family should be perfectly safe.

"You will arrive at the La Salle Street Station first thing in the morning," he said. "Take some taxis to the Drake Hotel. Get a sitting room on the lake side of the hotel, have breakfast there. Then the children might like to see the Chicago Field Museum of Natural History, where the wonderful Carl Ackley exhibits are: life-size gorillas in darkest Africa, very interesting. Then you could lunch at the Blackstone or return to the Drake, and then go back to the station in time to catch the westbound Santa Fe Chief."

He suggested several other points of interest. Sir George made a few notes and thanked him profoundly.

"Very good of you, old boy, I shan't forget this," he said, and off he went, following Ogden's suggestions to the letter.

Five gangsters invaded the Drake Hotel lobby at 3:30 P.M., just as Sir George was paying his bill and his whole retinue were standing by and about to leave for the station. The cashier was held up, and was killed after the bandits took between $5,000 and $10,000. "Then came, in the attempted flight of the gunmen, more than an hour of guerrilla warfare over North Side boulevards and streets in which pistols kept up an intermittent rattle. [I quote the Chicago *Tribune*.]

"When the affair was over it was found that two of the bandits were dead, three were in custody, three persons were wounded, two women had been injured, and as a finality one of the captured bandits confessed fully."

The money was never recovered, and it was the only time the Drake was ever held up (until very recently) in all of gangland's history.

Sir George took his retinue to the Santa Fe Station as quickly as possible, luckily uninjured, and they sat there, shivering with fright, huddled together in a corner of the waiting room, until their train was announced.

When they finally reached India, Sir George sent a letter to the Ranelagh Club demanding Mr. Ketting's instant resignation.

Debutantes, that is what we were in those days. After graduation from boarding school, or "finishing school" as it was sometimes called, parents introduced their eligible daughters to society by giving a party. Sister Margaret "came out" at an afternoon garden party at Brucemore. She wore a pale-green tulle dress with matching green picture hat and carried a bouquet of yellow roses. She and Mother "received" together, while a small orchestra, hiding in the grape arbor behind the two, played excerpts from *La Bohème* and *The Chocolate Soldier*.

Sister Barbara and I came out at Christmastime after she and I graduated, respectively, from Farmington and Vassar. Ours was a Silver Ball, and it took place in the Crystal Room of the Hotel Montrose in downtown Cedar Rapids. Mother, who loved planning and giving parties, had transformed the ballroom into what looked like a clearing in a silver forest. There were tall Christmas trees sprayed with something called "diamond dust" that made everything sparkle madly, the men in the orchestra wore gray sequin-trimmed jackets as they played sitting on a platform draped in silver cloth, and Barbara and I wore dresses of silver lamé trimmed with silver lace.

As was customary, there were dinner parties beforehand at various houses. I know that we had twenty or so guests at Brucemore, then proceeded to the hotel at 10:30, where Mother and the two of us, standing at the entrance to the ballroom, received the three hundred-odd guests. The men for the most part wore full dress: white tie and tails. Some of the younger boys, seniors at Exeter and freshmen at Yale, for instance, were dressed in what used to be called tuxedos or dinner jackets; now they are better known, of course, as "black tie."

There were two orchestras which took turns playing. One was big and brassy and played fox-trots: numbers like "You Gotta See Mama Every Night" (or she won't be home when you call) and "I'm Going South" (taste that sugarcane right in my mouth) and "Ja-Da" (the lyrics to this were an inspiration: Ja-Da, Ja-Da, Ja-Da Ja-Da, Jing, Jing, Jing).

The other orchestra was smaller, and played what was known as "schmaltzy" music. They had a solo violinist and an accordion and played a waltz called "Beautiful Ohio" and another called "Girl of My Dreams" (that would be "The Gorilla Song"). Also they played "Rio Rita" (life is sweetah, Rita, when you are neah) and "I'm the Sheik of Araby" (your love belongs to me, at night when you're asleep, into your tent I'll creep—ooh, so *daring* for those times).

At midnight there was a "lap" supper served outside the ballroom in the mezzanine lounge. There were scrambled eggs and little sausages, followed by ice cream and cake and coffee. Some of us pulled up chairs and formed a group, others sat in twos on the big wide stairways leading down to the lobby below.

Was there drinking at this Silver Ball? Indeed there was, but surreptitiously. No one during Prohibition drank publicly. Most of us girls did not drink, but many of the men did, and as was the custom, various men guests of ours had reserved rooms for the evening in the hotel as near as possible to the ballroom, and all during the evening many couples were tripping up the stairs to the floor above, where we were invited into Henry Hamilton and Harry O'Donnell's bedroom or across the hall to one that belonged to the Witwers and the Killians.

Bellboys went to and fro with setups, the men produced flasks, and we all sat on the beds or the floor, and our parents would have been shocked beyond words. No chaperones? *Bedrooms?* Mixed company? However, this same thing went on all over the United States until December 5, 1933, at every hotel that had a ballroom. In Chicago at the Congress Hotel or the Blackstone, for example, a group of men would reserve a sitting room or a suite, but it was different in Cedar Rapids, there weren't any.

And what did these people drink? What was in all these flasks? There was bathtub gin, first of all, made at home with bootleg alcohol, distilled water, and a few drops of "essence of juniper," which could be purchased at any drugstore.

Other flasks contained bootleg scotch or Bourbon or gin. Bourbon was more popular on the West Coast, and scotch on the East Coast. In the South a corn liquor called "Sweet Lucy" was prevalent. Distilled corn liquor was also known as "Jersey Lightning," and came from bootleg stills hidden away in New Jersey.

The boys in Cedar Rapids drank, among other things, "spiked beer." It was legal beer (3.2 percent alcohol) and came in glass bottles (cans were nonexistent). When opened, a little beer was poured out and in went some bootleg alcohol. It packed quite a wallop, I am told.

In nightclubs one ordered setups, and then proceeded to pour the booze into the glass from one's own flask while holding it quietly under the table. We drank orange blossoms: bootleg gin and orange juice. In a magazine called *Vanity Fair* there was a poem called "An Alphabet for Ushers." It started off:

> *A* is for Dear Aunt Augusta
> Who, highly indignant, recoiled
> When some usher who must have been drinking
> Said "Gussie, old dear, let's get boiled."
>
> *B* is the Bride who is blushing
> As you give her a kiss on her cheek
> It recalls, don't you see, certain evenings
> Of which tact now forbids you to speak.

It went on in this general way until it came to *O*:

> *O* is for sweet Orange blossoms
> Which are worn in the hair by the bride
> The groom thinks they're essential to weddings
> For he has six Orange blossoms inside.

We also drank alexanders, which were usually made of gin shook up with crème de cacao and cream; we drank bronx cocktails, which were orange blossoms with vermouth added, and old-fashioneds, which were a concoction of Bourbon, sugar, bitters, maraschino cherries, and slices of orange and lemon. I also remember the horror of them all: an angel wing, which contained gin blended into melting vanilla ice cream.

Today, among all the Harvey wallbangers and bull shots and bloody marys and grasshoppers, about the only survivors of the past are the martini and the manhattan. And even these are different actually, because in ours there was much more vermouth and they were always "straight up," never "on the rocks."

Was it difficult to find gin or whiskey during Prohibition? It was *easy*. Everyone had a bootlegger and men boasted about what excellent bootleggers they had just the way women tell each other what wonderful hairdressers or obstetricians they have.

Every man knew his bootlegger well, usually saw him once or twice a week, and paid him a great deal of money over the months. The booze or hooch, as it was usually called, was delivered surreptitiously at night as a rule, to a prearranged spot or just brought to one's house by the bootlegger himself or his son or brother, innocuously dressed and driving a dark inconspicuous two-door sedan. This was the delivery car; the bootlegger's own car was undoubtedly a Packard or a Cadillac.

Once during this era, our whole family was in Rome for a week or so, and staying at the Hotel Excelsior. My father on arrival went down to the hotel's barbershop to get a shave. The barber, very proud of his English, at once said, "Signor Douglas, where you from?"

Dad, knowing that Cedar Rapids would be *terra incognita*, said, "Near Chicago" (225 miles isn't too far at that).

"Good!" the barber exclaimed as he stropped his razor, "then you know my brother maybe, yes?"

Politely Dad asked the brother's name, and it turned out to be his very own bootlegger, Joe (Giovanni) Eppafanio, the efficient man who got excellent and genuine scotch whiskey for him straight from Canada, case after case, year after year, and delivered direct to Cedar Rapids regularly every month.

He delighted the barber by telling him all the latest news about the Eppafanio family in the United States; daughter Rosa had just had her first child and brother Tony (Antonio) had moved from Toledo to Monroe, Michigan, and had bought a new super-high-powered motorboat that could outrun any revenue agent's on Lake Erie.

Brother Tony was the rumrunner of the family, and his business was to cross Lake Erie, always at night, arrive at a port on the Canadian side in Ontario, pick up his order of so many cases of this and that liquor, and return, keeping a sharp eye out for any "revenooers," as they were called. He made the run on moonless nights only, with no running lights, and, as I recall, was caught with a load of booze only two or three times.

The revenue boys, in their slower boats, caught rumrunners by lying in wait for them with their lights and engines off, then suddenly they would catch them by turning on a huge searchlight.

However, the rumrunners were as clever as pack rats. Straightway they jettisoned their contraband cargo as quickly as possible, and most of the time the federal boys couldn't arrest them, there being no evidence. And the cleverest rumrunners of all had some sort of a secret marker, showing where the sunken evidence was located, and then they could return later and haul it up.

I heard about one enterprising entrepreneur who found another way of smuggling booze across the Canadian border and into Buffalo. It was late at night and a big ambulance came roaring up to the U.S. customs, sirens wailing and red lights flashing. Inside was a patient lying prone, covered with bandages, some with fresh blood seeping through. Bending over the patient were two ambulance attendants with stethoscopes and an oxygen inhalator.

"Emergency!" cried the ambulance driver. "Automobile accident near Welland, specialist at Buffalo General Hospital will try to save him."

The customs boys waved them through at once. It was a complete hoax. The whole car was filled with whiskey. (You can't do this often, I say.)

Besides rumrunners crossing Lake Erie, there were thousands more, busily delivering delicious spirits from Cuba to Florida, Mexico to California, Nova Scotia to Maine, and so on. Also there were any number of crew members of ocean liners and freighters who delivered liquor to bootleggers while in port. In the dark of the night a rowboat or launch would glide alongside a ship (and on the side away from the pier) at a prearranged time, and receive its regular shipment.

According to law, when Prohibition went into effect, no alcoholic beverages could be bought or sold (except for medicinal purposes) in the United States and also within twelve miles of the United States at sea. This "twelve-mile limit" fixed it so that friends who came to see someone off couldn't drink on board unless they brought their own hip flasks.

There was a bright spot about the arrival of these big ocean liners. Often before turning around and sailing right back to Southampton they would go on a fast weekend cruise to Bermuda or Nova Scotia and back. Hundreds of people went on

these, and as soon as the twelve-mile limit was reached everyone
aboard proceeded to "tie one on." These drinking cruises had a
very bad reputation, as you can imagine.

The town in the United States that was the most "wide open,"
meaning the town where it was easiest to get an illegal drink, was
Key West, Florida. It had saloons and even liquor stores scattered
about. I remember arriving there on sister Margaret's yacht and
walking around buying some crème de menthe in one place and
some cognac in another, just the way you could in Paris or London. It was so exciting, so *devilish*. How come?

Key West in those days could be reached only by the Flagler
Railroad. There were no roads leading south from Homestead,
Florida, but the railroad tracks came down through the Florida
Keys over a series of bridges, and over a hundred miles south
stood the Key West station. Therefore if there were any revenue
officers aboard someone in Homestead would telephone down to
the Key West Chamber of Commerce and all the liquor would
disappear from sight. If a raid ever took place by boat, the same
thing would happen.

Besides bootleggers, there were three other ways to acquire
liquor: first and second, from your friendly family physician,
and your equally friendly pharmacist. From either it was possible
to get prescriptions for pure grain alcohol. To this was added
distilled water and juniper juice and, presto, there was your
"bathtub gin."

The third way to get liquor was to become a moonshiner or
know a handy moonshiner. There were many more of these in
the South than in the North, but I know that in Princeton, New
Jersey, during Prohibition there were six stills operating in the
town limits, all turning out a delicious form of drink known as
"Sweet Lucy."

There were big stills and little stills, some ten and twelve feet
high turning out twenty or thirty gallons a day, and some small
ones that were made out of a car radiator with copper tubing
attached that turned out a whole gallon a day. They made distilled liquor from any grain—corn, oats, rye, wheat, and even
potatoes—then the sour mash (fermented grain) was soaked,

boiled, then distilled, and finally bottled in thick glass gallon jugs.

The men who operated these stills were known as ridgerunners or hillbillies, and in states that are still dry, North and South Carolina, for example, business is going on as usual.

Ridgerunners were and are as clever as rumrunners. When the revenooers, or nowadays the police, come looking for an operating still, they are hard to find. Generally they are buried underground with the smokestack hidden in a clump of tall thick pine trees. Some of them are portable and can be rolled to another part of the pine woods, others exist underneath something else, a glue factory or a shoe store.

A friend of mine who used to live in Tennessee tells me that both his grandfather and father operated a still all during Prohibition. It was carefully hidden in a secret room in their barn, and the gallons of "corn likker" that the still turned out were buried in the front lawn, just under the grass, a place that was never detected. The still's smokestack was piped underground to a deserted mill pond two hundred yards away.

And in addition to all this commercial smuggling of liquor, what about private citizens? Did we bring in contraband whiskey when we returned from a foreign land? Of course we did, many of us, and in all sorts of ingenious ways. I remember while in college coming back from a spring vacation in Bermuda. We had landed in New York and were going through customs, and two Princeton friends of mine were on the pier too, each wearing a derby hat, very much in style in those days. They apologized for not taking their hats off when we said goodbye, but each derby, or bowler as the British called them, was filled with little bottles of whiskey and brandy.

Another friend of mine had a special spare tire on his car that held a huge rubber tube that was in reality a flask. It held several quarts of scotch every time he came back from Canada, and he was never caught.

Once back in the 1920s Mother, sister Barbara, and I sailed back to New York on the Cunard Line's H.M.S. (His Majesty's Ship) *Aquitania*, after having spent the summer motoring around France. For the last two weeks Barbara and I had been on a shopping spree in Paris and our trunks when we left on the boat-train for Cherbourg were positively stuffed with dresses from Molyneux, Madeleine & Madeleine, and Vionnet. The hat trunk that we shared was full of glorious chapeaux from Réboux and Agnès, and the shoe trunk bristled with satin slippers from Pinet and Madame Daunou. We were also flat broke.

The trip home was uneventful, for I don't remember much about it except for one thing. The last night on board when Mother and Barbara and I were dining together at our cozy little table for three, in the large beautiful dining saloon Mother said, "Isn't it *nice*, I had tea with Frank and Clara Kellogg this afternoon, and he has invited us to go off the ship with him, in fact it is all arranged, and we won't have to go through customs."

Frank Billings Kellogg at that time was our British Ambassador, the Ambassador to the Court of St. James's, to be correct, and they were old friends of Mother's from Santa Barbara.

"What does it mean not to go through customs?" we asked eagerly.

"When we go off the ship at the Pier," Mother replied, "we go and stand under the letter 'X' instead of the way we usually do, under 'D.' As soon as our luggage arrives as well as that of the Kelloggs, it is put on luggage carts and porters push them down to where the limousines are, and away we go to the Plaza Hotel, and away go the Kelloggs to the Ritz."

She looked very pleased. "There is no delay, and also there is no duty to pay. We have freedom of the port."

"You mean that no customs officers will open our bags and paw around?" I quavered.

"That's right," Mother said. Barbara and I kept very quiet. We knew that Mother wouldn't approve of bringing in anything illegal, but here was a chance that was too good to be true. After dinner, and after coffee and a crème de menthe frappé with Mother in the main lounge, we dashed to the smoking room, which had the biggest bar on the ship. We sat down and counted what money we had left. By pooling *everything*, including my lucky silver dollar and a handful of French centimes and a dirty ten-lira note and a stray Swiss franc, we managed to scrape together almost seventy dollars. With this we proceeded to buy dozens of small bottles of scotch and brandy.

Although, as I said before, we drank very little ourselves, these bottles would make wonderful presents when people took us to restaurants and nightclubs. We also stocked up on Cointreau and Bénédictine and exotic Pernod (absinthe) and lugged it all down to our cabin. Seventy dollars bought a surprising amount of liquor in those days, and we immediately found that we had no room at all in our trunks for this addition.

Fortunately our cabin adjoined Mother's, and happily she was all packed and luckily playing bridge up in the card room, and most luckily of all we found two empty drawers in a standing wardrobe-trunk of hers. We wrapped our contraband goods and put them in these drawers, using a Kotex between each as padding, and after all the bottles were safely and snugly settled, we covered the top of each drawer with a souvenir flag saying "*Aquitania*" on it that we'd received at the Captain's farewell dinner.

The next morning we speedily left the ship with polite bows from the customs men, said fond goodbyes to the Kelloggs, and soon found ourselves at the Plaza, and when the trunks arrived shortly after lunch we unpacked the assortment of bottles and lined them up on a big table in our sitting room. Mother was astonished and horrified at what she saw, but most amused.

That evening I went off dancing with Newby Murray, a bachelor friend from Yonkers, and he had chosen some Courvoisier brandy from our collection. When we reached the Joseph Urban Room on the St. Regis roof he ordered a ginger ale for me and a setup for himself. He poured a shot of the brandy into his glass, took a sip, and a look of wonder and surprise came over his face.

"Good Lord," he exclaimed, "my bootlegger's been selling me what he claims is genuine French brandy, but it doesn't taste like this—I've been robbed!"

There is one last observation that I'd like to make about revenue and customs officers during Prohibition: they weren't *all* mean. Once my husband and I were in Quebec somewhere, skiing in the Laurentian Mountains, I guess, and we took a night train to Chicago. We had a drawing room and we told the porter not to wake us up when we crossed the border; we said that we would leave our suitcases unlocked and open for inspection on the long narrow sofa and the customs boys could tiptoe in, search for smuggled goods, and only wake us if they found anything.

The porter wished us a good night and we got ready for bed. However, we *did* have two bottles of fine Canadian whiskey in our possession, but we stood them neatly up between the suitcases, tied them together with a big red ribbon, pinned a ten-dollar bill on the ribbon and a card saying, "Be a Good Fellow."

We slept soundly all night and actually never heard a sound, but the next morning when the porter called us, we were unspeakably delighted to find that the ten-spot had disappeared, and instead of the two bottles of whiskey there were four bottles.

And going back, where was I on December 5, 1933, the night of the Repeal of Prohibition? (Accurately, it was the Repeal of the Eighteenth Amendment, an unsuccessful experiment that lasted exactly thirteen years, ten months, and eighteen days plus a few hours.)

I was in Chicago on that delightful and eventful night, at a dinner party given by some friends, Margie and Wirt Morton. We were at the Tavern Club, which is high up on the top of 333 North Michigan Avenue, and there were ten or twelve of us. I remember the dress I was wearing: a honey-colored satin which had short sleeves that were trimmed with dark mink, and I had daringly added a *femme fatale* touch to my make-up: a healthy coating of brown mascara on the eyelashes.

It was so *exciting* to be able to order anything at all (at half the price or less compared to the old speakeasy) and perfectly *legal*. We all felt like children let out of boarding school, and our host ordered champagne cocktails for everybody. I very seldom drank in those days, a little wine with dinner when we were in Europe or on shipboard, a little champagne at weddings and bridal dinners, but that was about all. This evening, however, I drank several of those delicious cocktails before dinner and had a most marvelous time. Sitting next to me was a very funny man who kept us all in roars of laughter. I remember laughing hysterically in between sipping the drinks.

Just before it was time to go into dinner, several of us girls prudently stole off to the ladies' room, and I caught a glimpse of myself in the mirror. I gasped at what I saw. I looked entirely different—that is, I hardly recognized myself. It was a horrible feeling.

"Dear Lord," I whispered to myself, "you're drunk."

Then as I moved closer to the mirror I discovered the trouble. I had laughed so hard at the funny man that my mascara had run down my cheeks, making me look like the Witch of Endor.

It was a grand party, but it took me a long time to recover from the shock; in fact, I can still see that face.

But back to our Silver Ball again, it had another thing that doesn't exist any more: the stag line. At all big parties there were almost always 30 per cent more boys than girls, sometimes more. They stood around the ballroom watching the couples whirling by, and when a stag saw a girl that he liked he stepped out on the dance floor and put his hand on the partner's shoulder, usually saying, "May I cut in, please," or something of the sort. The partner bowed and walked off, and the stag danced away with the girl until someone else cut in on him.

It was considered rude to cut in on the same girl until someone else had cut in first. And what happened if no one cut in at all? Then the partner dancing with the girl was said to be "stuck." Sometimes the girl's brother or a pal would rescue the man, other times the girl might say she was tired or would like to go and "powder her nose" (the polite way of getting to the ladies' room) and would leave him. Another way of getting unstuck: the partner could hold a dollar bill in his right hand behind the girl's back.

However, at most parties where there was a chance of this lurking danger, the debutante herself would ask a few of her best men friends to keep an eye out for a dancing wallflower, and see that she had a turnover of partners. These young men were referred to as "ushers," and they usually wore fresh white gardenias in their lapels.

What were the reasons for girls getting stuck, as if you didn't know? The main one was not knowing enough men. I went to a dance in Scarsdale once and knew only one man in the whole place. I danced with him all evening long and no one came to the rescue, and I was too shy to tell him to introduce me to some of his friends, and he was too dumb to think of it.

However, I got over being too shy and months later found myself hopelessly stuck at the Dartmouth Winter Carnival. The man who had invited me (the word "date" was considered slangy in those days) had passed out cold, and I was on my own. So what did I do?

I'm only too happy to tell you. Spanish shawls were very fashionable at this point, and I had a gorgeous one of golden yellow, covered with hand-embroidered red roses, and edged with yards and yards of long yellow fringe.

As I danced past the stag line I would swirl the Spanish shawl gracefully out and around, like a flamenco dancer, and presto! the fringe would catch on the buttons of some stag's dinner jacket, and he would be hooked, so I would disengage myself from my partner and unfasten the new catch and dance merrily off with him. It worked perfectly, and I had a splendid time.

A girl got stuck also for being a bad dancer, or being too fat or too tall, or being so different-looking from the other girls that she was a freak. And that was just what happened at our Silver Ball. A good friend of ours, a senior at the University of Chicago, telephoned a week before the event and asked my mother if he could bring his fiancée, and of course Mother said it would be a pleasure, and what was the lucky young lady's name? It turned out to be Vasilka Petrova, which should have warned us perhaps, but we certainly weren't prepared for the vision that arrived with friend Don.

Miss Petrova came dressed rather as if she were going to dance the leading role in the ballet *Swan Lake*, only she was not dressed as a white swan, or a black swan, she was half black and half white. The effect was startling. On her head was a close-fitting cap of feathers, white on the right half of her head, black on the left. Her short low-cut silk dress was the same, a white sleeve and blouse and skirt all on the right, black to the left.

A white silk stocking and white satin slipper covered the right leg, the other leg was black. She also wore a lot of black mascara on the eyelashes of both eyes, her lips had dark red lipstick on them, and she looked like the silent-movie star Pola Negri, who always had heavier make-up on her face than anyone else in Hollywood. Young ladies of this era wore only a little face powder, lipstick that was pink, and perhaps a little rouge on the cheeks and a dash of mascara, but nothing theatrical.

Miss Petrova wasn't cut in on until after the supper had been served, and the lights in the ballroom had been turned down low, but I don't imagine that she minded, what with being engaged. However, when her beau Don was standing in the stag line Mother went up to him, took him outside, and scolded him for bringing her to the party; said she was too sophisticated for Cedar Rapids, and not to bring her again. Don went and cut in on her, and they meekly left, Miss Petrova, as I recall, wearing a long black cape made of monkey fur.

As was customary, our Silver Ball ended at 3:00 A.M. and the orchestra told everyone the news by playing the waltz "Three O'Clock in the Morning." This was the usual sign-off number, although "Good Night Sweetheart" was also popular as well as "Show Me the Way to Go Home" (I'm tired and I wanna go to bed) plus "Sleepy-Time Gal" and (I almost forgot) "Good Night Ladies."

Two or three nights later found me in Chicago at another party, a dinner dance this time, and it took place at the Saddle and Cycle Club. It was given by Mr. Barrett Wendell, who was a most charming old gentleman, and it was in honor of Bertha Palmer, who I think had just announced her engagement to Oakleigh Thorne.

Going to this dance changed my whole life. It started out perfectly normally, tables of ten, delicious food, and we danced between courses, with plenty of stags cutting in briskly. Besides the regular bachelors and single girls, there were several young married couples at the party. One of these husbands, his first name was Steve, cut in on me when I was dancing with a knockout man, someone that I wanted to *know better*, and it was disappointing to have to bother with somebody's husband.

This went on all during dinner. Every time that someone cut

in on him, he would wait until another cut, then back he came. I tried to be merry and bright and I *was* flattered by his attention, but it was annoying, and I kept wishing that he'd go and dance with his pretty blond wife and leave me alone.

After dinner was over and the dancing was without interruption, there he was again and as soon as he had cut in he steered me over to a big glassed-in porch. It was empty and chilly, and I didn't feel very enthusiastic about missing all the fun on the dance floor.

"Sit down," he said. "I want to talk to you." He lit a cigarette and took a puff. "I've been trailing you all evening because I think you are doing things all wrong and I want to give you some advice."

I wiggled uncomfortably, feeling gauche.

"As you know," he continued, "you're not a beauty queen nor a Wampus Baby Star [that would be a young movie starlet]. Yet you have the kind of silly line that dumb blondes use. That sort of 'You chase me and I'll run slow' stuff. Earlier you asked me if I liked Indians and I asked you why, and you said that you did, but with reservations, and you knew sailors. Gobs and gobs.

"It sounds to me as if you were copying some line of chatter that doesn't suit you at all. Why don't you be yourself, say what you *really* think?"

I felt like crying. To be so critical was unkind, and I'd been having such a good time.

I stood up, and he courteously got to his feet too.

"Now don't be mad," he said. "Think it over. You could be a real stem-winder if you just stayed natural." He took my arm, and we returned to the festivities. He smiled down at me.

"At least you're a good dancer," he murmured. Then someone else cut in, to my relief. Married men, I snorted to myself, and resolved to forget him forever.

When I got back to my little apartment at the Hotel Drake, I found that I couldn't get to sleep, and his words of wisdom came back to haunt me. *Why don't you be yourself, say what you really think?*

The more I thought about it, the more I was inclined to agree with him. I had been silly and coy and out of character; from now on I would try to be natural and pleasant and *interesting*.

It took a long time to drop the oh-you-kid stuff, but I found that it paid off, and I am still grateful to Mr. Stephen Y. Hord for his advice. I've never seen him since, only in the far distance, and he never cut in on me again.

Years after, I was lunching one day in New York with Kathleen Norris, who was GW's godmother. She had learned the same lesson as I had, and knowing her, I imagine much faster, and she commented that not being a glamour girl hadn't fazed her in the least.

"I always give a pretty girl twenty minutes," she said. "Then I move in. The men have had time enough to admire the girl's looks and she isn't in awe of me, and thinks that I am a harmless mouse-like type. She becomes fond of me. However, she finds out that I am not only friendly but fun too, and so do the men."

9

Keeping Clean and Cool: Life Style of the Twenties and Thirties

ONE VERY HOT summer evening in 1930 found me walking along the station platform of Clinton, Iowa, with a bachelor friend of mine named John Carey. He and I were by chance both going to Chicago from Cedar Rapids or else coming from Chicago, I forget which, and were out getting a breath of fresh air while the big steam locomotive took on a load of coal and a few hundred gallons of water.

It was actually just as hot out as it was inside the train, but at least the hot muggy air was moving a bit and it was pleasant to stretch the legs after sitting for a long time in the club car. It was just before dinner, and I remember that we were hungry as wolves, and the waiter had already gone through the train playing his musical chimes and calling, "Dinner is now being served in the dining car forward."

We walked up to the engine and watched it snorting away, then back past the baggage cars and the coaches, and finally returned to alongside the diner. Up above us was the kitchen, and we stood there watching the hectic activity going on. There were three chefs, all black, as was the custom. They wore white pants and white jackets. However, the white jackets were all open, and you could see their black chests glistening with sweat.

Suddenly one of them opened the door of the refrigerator, or icebox, as it was usually called, and drew out a large raw frost-coated steak. Before he put it on the broiler he leaned back and joyfully rested the whole thing on his chest, rolling his eyes in ecstasy as it lay there.

We looked at each other in horror, our appetites vanishing with the speed of light. We went back to the club car and each sipped a ginger ale, then I think we finally went to the diner and ordered two baked potatoes and two oranges, washing the fruit in our finger bowls.

Most of all, air conditioning has changed the life style of the civilized world. Up to the early 1930s everyone who could afford it sent his family to a summer resort. That is, unless you lived in something of the sort to begin with. Offices in the summertime had every window open whenever possible, and every desk had to have a dozen paperweights to keep papers from flying away.

Summers in Washington, D.C., were almost the worst of all, what with the humidity added to the heat, and lots of people still think that the Congress was affected by it. Tempers grew short and filibusters longer. There should be a summer session for our senators and representatives in Maine or New Hampshire or Colorado, were the constant suggestions.

The first summer that I spent in Chicago (1932) almost killed me after all those cool dry summers in northern Michigan and Biarritz and Gleneagles, Scotland. However, I learned that the Northern Trust Company of Chicago was the first and only fully air-conditioned building in town, and immediately went down there and got a job opening savings accounts. It kept me comfortable all day, and at night, by pouring cologne all over myself and then sleeping under an electric fan's breeze, I managed to survive.

There were all sorts of tricks to keep cool. One was an attic fan which sucked cool evening air into the house, while pushing the hot air out at the top. This worked well at night, and during the day the windows were kept closed, the shades drawn.

Theaters on stifling days used to have huge cakes of ice sitting on each side of the stage, each with a big fan blowing away on it. At curtain time the fans were turned off until the end of the act. They *did* help. And I remember a summer in a rented house in Gibson Island, Maryland, where it was so hot that several times we dressed for cocktail parties in the cellar, the only cool place in the whole cottage.

And what was the status symbol of this un-air-conditioned era? The swimming pool is the answer. At this point there were only three private swimming pools in Cedar Rapids. One belonged to the Dows family, who were cousins of ours, and to reach it from Brucemore was easy: through a gate, up a brick pathway to the top of a hill, and there it was, a small dark pool shaded completely by three vast elm trees.

Its water was always cool or just plain cold, the diving board was dangerous when it got wet, as it was a plain wooden plank, and I'm sure that frogs and eels swam below us in the deep dark waters. However, we had many a good time there, and it was perfect for picnics, as there was a little house by the pool (nowadays this would be known as a cabana or a pool house) which had a big fireplace where we roasted weenies and marshmallows.

The other two pools weren't used by us much; one was far away on the other side of town across the Cedar River, and the other was very small, and always crowded with screaming little kids.

And that brings me to the Quaker Oats Company, of which I was still a stockholder, and the stock market crash in 1929. As people lost their jobs they began eating cheaper foods, wearing old clothes instead of buying new ones, and smoking their cigars until there was hardly a butt left to throw away. However, what did people eat to save money and fill themselves up? Something cheaper than meat, that would stick to the ribs? You're right, they ate oatmeal. Consequently, we stockholders on April 15 each received a five-dollar extra dividend per share of common stock.

On April 16, the day after the extra dividend arrived, workmen also arrived at Brucemore, and by the time the roses were abloom, we and all our friends were splashing away in our big white pool and the same thing has been going on all summer long ever since.

Being in full sunlight until late in the afternoon, the water often managed to get hot and soupy, but we had a solution for that. Ice, in those days, was still being delivered by an ice wagon, a big wooden closed contraption drawn by two huge gray Percherons. From the new pool, which was built on a terrace close to the house, we could hear the ice wagon's bell clanging as it came slowly up the long front driveway. When it came even with the pool, we would run out and order two large rectangular slabs of ice, and the iceman and his assistant would take their tongs and haul the ice to the pool's steps, and in would go the ice with a splash. It was great sport trying to stay upright on one of these, rather like a log-rolling contest, and it made the pool delightfully cool for a short time.

The pool is shadier now, and a cabana has been added, and I wonder how many people altogether have enjoyed it. Thousands have certainly, and it was a great way to spend the extra dividend. I'm sure that my father would have approved.

Air conditioning, besides keeping us cool, also keeps us clean. In cities before its invention, imagine how dirty windowsills always were and how fast white curtains turned black, and how often woodwork and walls had to be washed. A terrace or a cool balcony was perpetually sooty.

Ladies who lived in town in the summer, or those who came in just for the day, always wore dark silk dresses with small forget-me-nots or polka dots printed on them, the kind of thing that wouldn't show the dirt. Our mothers carried fans and smelling salts. Nobody wore white shoes, as they were made of white buckskin or kid and had to be cleaned all the time. The men who worked in town during the summer, especially the commuters, wore easily rumpled seersucker suits, the coolest material to be had.

Automobiles like trains have also benefited terrifically from air conditioning. Picture yourself about to cross the Mojave Desert in a 1930 Buick. You would stock up on enough dry ice to last two hours, put it on the floor of the car, roll up the windows over halfway, pray that you would get there before this carbon dioxide would evaporate away. The temperature in the desert is still sometimes 169 degrees.

And I remember my Bostonian correct modest grandmother telling me how she managed to cross the desert (at about this same time) on the Santa Fe Chief. She had been visiting friends in Pasadena, the month was April, and it had suddenly turned very hot. The Arizona desert was like a furnace.

Grandmother first locked the door of her compartment, removed all her clothes except a small cotton chemise, pinned a Pullman towel around her hair, covered herself with "4711" cologne, and alternately eating peppermints and sipping lukewarm water from the faucet marked "ice water," proudly survived.

Air conditioning has contributed something else to us; we are now more attractive. We not only keep cleaner, and live in cleaner houses, but we don't perspire much any more.

There is a saying that "Women glow, Men perspire, and Horses sweat." I have news for you; women before the 1930s perspired dreadfully. Athletic young girls (that's me and my friends) worried about this embarrassing problem at dances, and all sports except swimming. There were so few things that helped. We could wear dress shields (rubberized-silk pieces of cloth sewn into our dresses under the arms), but these contraptions made our underarms hotter than ever, whereupon we perspired even more.

There *were* a few antiperspirants, but they were so strong that if they were used we broke out in a rash, and furthermore the stuff destroyed the material of the dress in due course of time. Deodorants were pretty bad too. There was a hygienic-smelling powder called Amolin, I recall, that destroyed offensive odors when sprinkled around, but also made the wearer smell like a pharmacy, or the way a doctor's medicine bag smelled when he opened it while making a house call.

What could we do about this problem? Well, it was difficult. The best thing was to wear dresses that were cut low and not too tight under the arms. Black and white dresses never showed perspiration, and those made of chiffon were generally surefire, so was lace, especially delicate lace, the cobwebby type.

When playing tennis white sharkskin dresses made us look

crisp and neat even when we were dripping wet. It is difficult with all the present-day detergents, spot removers, spray-away stains, and wrinkle removers and drip-dry material to imagine how hard we had to work to achieve the same thing. Most dyes were mediocre, dresses faded easily, cotton dresses shrank when washed in hot water, almost everything except knitted things wrinkled and needed to be pressed every time they were worn. Home pressing often resulted in scorched clothes until the steam iron made its bow, and dry cleaning was poor compared to modern methods. Besides that there were moths with magnificent appetites that ate nothing but woolen things, and they were everywhere. Winter woolens had to be sealed up airtight with camphor (mothballs) inside or they would turn into shreds.

We wore hats everywhere. They were part of our costume. There were such lovely ones too. Easter bonnets with big brims and trimmed with flowers (I even had one with real Easter lilies on it once), gorgeous bright-colored twisted turbans that were made stylish by the singer Carmen Miranda, velvet hats with ostrich feathers floating along one side copied after the Empress Eugénie's beautiful headgear, Scotch tam-o'-shanters for golf, *berets basques* for tennis, trench caps along with waterproofed trench coats for rainy days, and even stocking caps for skating and bobsledding. The last-named were, in case you've never seen one, yard-long knitted woolen caps of bright colors that could be wound around the neck, acting as a scarf as well as a cap.

One last thing about hats: in the 1930s hats got crazier and crazier. I remember having a close-fitting black hat with tiny little clocks all over it, and another of blue velvet with a silver fox's head perched on top. GW used to bark at me when I put that one on.

The New Yorker magazine had a story in it about zany hats that I've always remembered. Luncheon at the Colony restaurant was the most stylish place for women to go in those days, and the article described all the wacky hats at the different tables. One lady had a bird's nest on the brim of hers, another dripped purple tassels, and so on. Then Gloria Swanson sailed in and eclipsed everyone. Hers was shaped rather like a volcano, and smoke came out the top.

"Gloria's hat smokes," commented one lady to her tablemates.

"Tell me, my dear," said another languidly, "can it blow rings?"

And why did hats get scarce? Hair spray is the answer, as if you didn't know.

And in those same days, what about clothes? Were they different from what we wear now? Not very different, really. We even wore the equivalent of the miniskirt when we danced the Charleston. For example, I remember a favorite dress of mine was very short (above the knees) and cut straight up and down with no belt and no sleeves. It was pretty and feminine, nonetheless, as it was made of pale-pink satin, and it was beaded all around the hem with big roses all made of little frosty beads of darker pink and leaves of green beads.

For those who didn't care to Charleston or do the Black Bottom, another strenuous dance, there were long dresses with tight waists and full skirts referred to as bouffants. I had one which I wore to a Yale prom, and it also went to the Quadrangle Club at Princeton and a debut in New York, and the interesting thing about it is that my daughter has also worn it to a dance in Princeton, and I think she still wears it. It came from a shop in New York called Mary Walls, and is a bouffant with a full skirt, is sleeveless, and has a cowl neckline. The whole dress is in three shades of blue, the top being a pale gray-blue satin. At the waistline the color changes to a deeper blue, and the bottom third is a darker sapphire blue. And the whole skirt is made of petals, all sewn together. It stays in style, maybe because it is simple and elegant.

There is one difference in dressing customs between then and now. We dressed precisely for the occasion. We played tennis in a uniform: a short white dress, white tennis shoes and socks, and usually a white cap with a visor.

When we went racing in yachts it was white sailor pants and white middies, plus slickers (oilskin hat and jacket) if the weather required them.

When we went to church we always wore our best daytime

clothes, not too bright-colored, with our best hat and white gloves.

Sunday dinner was always at noon, and even if we didn't go to church, we still dressed up for dinner. Sunday night we dressed for the traditional Sunday-night supper by wearing an informal outfit. For example, a black velvet dress with a street-length skirt.

And we never never wore pants except for certain sports. We wore them almost always for fishing, hunting, horseback riding, and always wore them for mountain climbing and skiing. The first pants suit that I ever had was made of gray whipcord, it came from Abercombie & Fitch, and I wore it when skeet shooting. The year was 1939.

There is another difference that affected our clothes, and that was modesty. We never wore low-necked things, our bathing suits had skirts, and we wore bras that flattened us rather than uplifted us.

It was our Victorian-era parents who were really the modest ones, but a lot of it rubbed off on us. Philip Claflin, who has been a friend of mine since Harvard and Vassar days, told me once that his mother would arise in the morning clothed in a long, billowing, lace-trimmed white nightdress (they lived in Massachusetts).

She would kiss Philip good morning, and then proceed to ask him questions for his geography lesson, or hear him recite poetry, and all of this time she was getting dressed. She kept all of her undergarments behind her on a chaise longue, all neatly laid out under a coverlet, and while she listened to him, he in turn could hear a constant sort of rustling going on inside the voluminous nightdress. Then all of a sudden the little noises would stop, she would throw the garment off over her head, and there she was, standing fully dressed in a gray tailored suit with a frilled white blouse and a fresh handkerchief in the pocket.

Actually, I never even saw my mother in a nightdress except once in Paris when the Mercedes Hotel caught fire. She always appeared in beautiful lace and satin negligees. She was also extremely modest, and she was very strict about two things: all dirty words, off-color stories, profanity, that sort of thing, and the other (most hateful) the chaperone.

There was a beau who lived in Evanston, Illinois, a perfectly respectable Princeton graduate whom I'd met in Michigan during the summer. In the fall of 1930 he invited me for a weekend, to come Friday, play golf on Saturday, and go to a football game and leave on Sunday. I couldn't go, Mother said, unless his mother wrote to her direct.

His mother did write mine, but mine still didn't feel that it was quite proper. However, the young man solved the problem by arranging to have me stay nearby, at the house of his married sister. It was ridiculous, really, as he lived in a house with guest rooms, and maids running all over the place.

In Cedar Rapids we were unchaperoned; that is, when we went to a party, some escort took us in his car and brought us home, and some of the boys daringly kissed us good night. When they kissed several times, it was known as "necking," especially if they began breathing hard. If they did more than kissing and hugging, then it was known as "petting," and if it turned into just plain sexual intercourse, it was known daringly as "going the limit."

It seems to me that almost all of my close friends were as virginal as I was, and we all blushed at off-color jokes and didn't understand the meanings of most four-letter words. For instance, we never even used the word "breast"—it was referred to as "front" or "bosom." Salesladies, when we bought bras, asked for our "bust" size, and the word "bra" wasn't used until later. In the Middle West it was a "brassiere," pronounced *bruh-zeer*. The change of all this in fifty years is most remarkable, and that is a fact.

In 1928 Alice Babst, a New York friend of ours, made her debut at the Colony Club, and for the small debut dinner that took place before the ball, Mr. Babst, Alice's father, had signed up the Yacht Club Boys to entertain while we ate. They were a quartet, very up-to-date indeed, and proceeded to sing the latest Cole Porter song, "Let's Do It." Mr. and Mrs. Babst were so shocked by the song that they stopped the Yacht Boys right in the middle of the song and sent them on their way.

Chaperones, as I said, weren't required in Cedar Rapids when going to a party, or going home, but there was always a chaperone or two keeping an eye on us at the festivity. Chicago and New York were entirely different, especially New York, where a maid or housekeeper went along to the ball or whatever, and sat with the other chaperones all evening long, in the coat room of the Colony Club, or the one near the old Ritz Hotel ballroom, or the one off the Hotel Plaza's Terrace Room. Some of us girls would team up and share one of these poor ladies; once a limousine stopped and picked up six of us, and the last girl had to sit on the chaperone's lap.

There were other things besides air conditioning that changed our way of life, and actually a friend of ours who lived in Lisbon, Iowa (seventeen miles from Cedar Rapids), just by chance helped cause one of these. Her name was Elizabeth Stuckslager, and she was known to her friends as Eke, and the year is 1933.

This was the year that Franklin D. Roosevelt was elected President for the first time, defeating Herbert Hoover by a large majority, Fiorello H. La Guardia became the Mayor of New York City, and Chicago's World Fair, "The Century of Progress," opened on May 27 and closed for the rest of the year on November 12. Prohibition was repealed on December 5 in all states except the Carolinas.

In June of that year Miss Stuckslager was going to New York for a few days, so she packed a medium-sized suitcase, put on a charcoal-gray suit with a white tucked blouse and a soft black suede hat, or beret, and arrived at the Cedar Rapids station about 10:00 P.M.

The Cedar Rapids Pullman car was waiting there on a siding, although it wouldn't be leaving until midnight, when it would be picked up by the Columbine, a Union Pacific train coming from Denver, but she was tired and wanted a good night's sleep, so she got aboard, the porter checked her ticket and took her to her berth, a lower somewhere in the middle of the car, away from the wheels.

Being a neat and orderly person, Eke hated having a lot of clothes lying around in the berth with her, so after she had undressed and was in a white silk nightie and a dark blue and white polka-dotted dressing gown (known as a Pullman robe in those times) she packed up all the clothes that she had taken off and put the whole suitcase under the berth, leaving out some matching polka-dotted Pullman slippers and her hairbrush and toothbrush. Then she trotted into the women's room at the end of the car, brushed her long thick dark hair and tied it back with a ribbon, brushed her teeth, and returned for the night.

She fell asleep in a few minutes, and the next thing she knew it was morning, and the porter was shaking the green curtain and saying, "Time to get up, miss, it's six-thirty and we're right on time. Arriving at seven." She thanked him through the curtains, and pushing them back, reached down for her suitcase. It was gone.

Evidently someone had come through the car during the night and had made off with it, for it was never found. Eke was aghast at what had happened, but with her customary forthrightness summoned the conductor and asked to have a wheelchair brought to her Pullman car and gave her name and the Blackstone Hotel, where she would go when they arrived in Chicago. She also gave him her New York hotel in case the suitcase turned up, as well as her Pullman space on the Twentieth Century Limited, where she would be that afternoon.

She stepped off the train with her toothbrush in her Pullman robe pocket, handbag clutched firmly in one hand and her hairbrush in the other, climbed into the wheelchair, and was pushed into the station, taken down in the elevator to the taxi stand, and off she went to the Blackstone Hotel. There she took a sitting room for the day, ordered a Chicago *Tribune* and breakfast, and promptly at nine o'clock telephoned Marshall Field and Company. She asked to speak to Mr. Stanley Field, who was one of the top executives at the time.

He was a nephew of the founder, Marshall Field, and the two of them had come to Chicago in 1902, from Wales. Stanley Field was about nineteen or twenty at the time, and learned the business from the ground up. He was not only intelligent and smart, but also most charming, and it was a privilege to have him for a friend.

He was also a friend of Eke's and so in no time at all she found herself telling him of her predicament, and how she was supposed to be taking the Century that afternoon, and was planning to be at a dinner and go to the new Ethel Barrymore play the next night in New York, and what could she do, and would he help her?

He said, "Never fear, I'll see to it that you'll be on that train in a gray suit and carrying a medium-sized suitcase and wearing shoes. Now hang up and be patient."

The next thing she knew a nice-sounding woman called her and asked her a lot of questions: what was her shoe size, glove size, and so on, what cosmetics and perfume did she prefer, what sort of lingerie did she wear, and even would she like a book to read on the train that night, and did she need any medicine, aspirin tablets, or castor oil or anything?

About twelve-thirty there was an important-sounding knock on the door, and when she opened it there stood three women and a bellboy, each carrying bundles and packages, the bellboy carrying the medium-sized suitcase as well.

The first one introduced herself as Miss Marr, the buyer of misses' dresses, and the second was Miss Mooney, a saleslady who had picked out everything but the dresses, and the third was a Miss Allison, who was a dressmaker and worked in the alterations department.

Miss Marr had brought her a choice of suits and dresses and she ended up with a handsome blue silk suit that she liked much better than the stolen one, and the theater dress was also a good choice, it was saffron yellow, her favorite color, and everything fitted with a few minor adjustments. She thanked them all, signed the charge slips, and ended up by taking the ladies to lunch in the Blackstone's grill.

She went to New York and back in her new clothes without incident, and before she left Chicago for home went to thank Mr. Field for his excellent handling of her disastrous problem.

He told her that she had given him an idea that he'd never thought of before until she telephoned him. There should exist, for people in predicaments like hers, something whereby they could order things by mail or telephone, rather than use up the time of three women armed with an assortment of things and leaving the store as well as carrying them to inconvenient places.

"Not as big as a Sears, Roebuck catalogue," she remembers him saying, "but some sort of an illustrated booklet that would describe each separate article, give the sizes available and the colors, as well as the price.

"If we'd had a booklet like this, we could have sent a Western Union messenger boy over to the Blackstone and then you could have telephoned us your order after you had decided what you wanted."

Eke remembered suggesting that it would be a good idea to include descriptions of sheets and towels too, saying that her mother often had to write to Marshall Field's for more linens.

Thus did the mail-order catalogue come into style, and Marshall Field's was one of the first to have a good Christmas catalogue from which one can order everything except perhaps a live reindeer.

Nowadays everyone puts out a Christmas catalogue. I even received one from the garage where we buy gasoline showing pictures of antifreeze cans and gift-wrapped tires, but back in 1933 there were only Sears, Montgomery Ward, and a few others who sent mail-order catalogues, and they were published for farmers and backwoods people, not city dwellers. Miles Kimball was also one of the very first to put out a catalogue for gift ordering, but his things were usually $2.98 in price or less, sort of in the stocking-present category.

Neiman Marcus wins the blue ribbon for the most elaborate and expensive catalogue items. Remember the life-sized stuffed bear to put under the tree for the little wife? It had a diamond necklace around its neck, diamond brooches in its ears, and cost $1,000,000. And remember the His and Hers airplanes?

What else has changed our way of shopping besides these handy catalogues? Credit cards, that's what.

In the thirties there were no credit cards that I can recall except Air Travel Cards. These were issued in the 1930s and required a deposit of $500, but I don't remember knowing anyone who used one. The American Express credit cards didn't make their appearance until 1956. What did we do without credit cards?

When we traveled, our hometown bank gave us a Letter of Credit addressed to "To Whom It May Concern" saying that we

were good for $2,000 or $5,000 or whatever the amount, and that
our bank would fully reimburse whoever would loan us part or
all of this amount. This was usually in case of an emergency, and
we traveled with cash in a money belt or locked up in something.
I remember going to Austria and Germany in 1922 when post-
war inflation had hit both countries. We had one large sturdy
suitcase filled with nothing but paper German marks and Austrian kronen. Ever see a big bundle of ten-thousand-mark notes?
Just barely enough to pay for a continental breakfast for six people. Ever see a *million*-kronen bill? In Austria that wouldn't have
bought a plate of Wiener schnitzel.

We had charge accounts. They took no time at all. If you
were a well-dressed normal-appearing adult, you could march
into any big store and say, "I'd like to open a charge account,"
and some handy floorwalker (that would be today's section
manager) would obligingly take your name and address and
bank, and presto, you had a charge account. A few days later
you would receive a thank-you note from the store, suggesting
that you drop in any old time, and that you'd always be welcome.

When the bill arrived, and *all bills* used to arrive on the first
day of the month, you were supposed to pay it before the tenth,
but a great many honest citizens paid their bills weeks later and
no store made a fuss unless it became habitual. In that case you
were known as a "slow pay" or even a "poor risk" and your
credit rating had a black mark on it instead of a gold star.

When Saks Fifth Avenue opened its first branch store on
Chicago's Michigan Boulevard in the early 1930s, I remember
going to it the first or second week. I think that some of us had
made a special all-day shopping trip from Cedar Rapids.

Anyway, it was a beautiful new store filled with gorgeous
things and I was so carried away by the clothes that I bought one
lovely thing after another: a greige duvetyn (similar to today's
ultra-suede) suit trimmed with glossy black broadtail fur, a
brocade evening wrap with a shawl collar of dark mink, a long
gold-and-white evening dress with a cerise velvet sash, a thin, all-
tucked black crepe afternoon dress with long sleeves and yoke,
both of light-blue tucked crepe. There were also hats and shoes

to match, and I distinctly remember uneasily wondering how I was *ever* going to pay the bill, and right after that I saw another lovely item, but the bill was going to be so large that one more thing wouldn't really matter.

I already had a charge account with the New York store, so I had no trouble walking out in the new greige suit (it fitted perfectly) with a new black broadtail turban on my head, feeling as stylish as Mrs. Vincent Astor or Millicent Rogers or Ina Claire (all on the Best-Dressed list of that year).

When the bill arrived on November 1, it was well over two thousand dollars and I had just a little over three hundred dollars in the bank. Bravely I took pen in hand and sent a check for three hundred dollars to the Head of the Department of Accounts of the Chicago Saks, and explained apologetically in a letter on my best stationery that this was all the money I had in the world until January 15, and that I was terribly sorry about it, but that it was really Saks Fifth Avenue's fault for having such good-looking things, and that I was the Toast of the Boulevards of Cedar Rapids, if that was any consolation.

Straightway a reply arrived from some nice Saks executive (on his best stationery too), and he said that he and all his confreres were perfectly delighted that I had liked their merchandise so much and not to worry one whit about the bothersome bill until January 15, that he understood perfectly and in fact wouldn't even send a bill until then, and to drop in again any time, and signed it "Cordially yours," etc.

Needless to say, I've always had a warm furry feeling for the Saks stores ever since. If one did this sort of reckless charging today, the store would probably send you to their psychiatrist or else a house of detention, and certainly add an armed bill collector.

One day years ago, Mother commissioned Aunt Harriet Douglas, who had been visiting us in Brucemore, to buy a long list of things for her at Marshall Field's in Chicago on her way home to New York. She marched into the store from the early-morning Chicago and Northwestern train and spent a busy morning filling the shopping list. At one point she found herself on the ground floor in the silver department, where Mother had asked her to get two round silver trays, the kind that little sandwiches or cookies are passed on.

Aunt Harriet chose a suitable pair and said that they were to be charged and sent to Mrs. George Bruce Douglas, Brucemore, Cedar Rapids, Iowa.

The clerk said to her as she filled out the sales slip, "And you are Mrs. Douglas?" Aunt Harriet said that she was, signed the slip, and headed for the glassware department.

Before she arrived she was stopped by a floorwalker.

"I beg your pardon, madam." He spoke nervously. He looked quickly over his shoulder to where a lady was standing. "It has been reported to me by your salesman in the silver department that you are not Mrs. Douglas. The lady standing behind us overheard you say that you are Mrs. George Douglas but she says that she knows Mrs. Douglas and that you are not her friend at all."

Aunt Harriet explained that she was a sister-in-law, and identified herself properly and to the man's satisfaction. Then she went over to the woman who had reported her.

"And you're a friend of Irene's," she said pleasantly, holding out her hand. "Who shall I tell her I met in Field's?"

"Someone who is too red in the face to give her name," she answered, and hurried away.

While we are on the subject of credit, it occurs to me that in Great Britain things were utterly different. Merchants there sent out bills annually, or sometimes semiannually. And a lot of Americans practiced this same way of paying. A friend of mine after she graduated from college worked for Georg Jensen, and when someone named W. R. Hearst wanted to charge some expensive silver candelabras, she looked up his credit rating in a charge-account book and found that he hadn't paid his bill for nearly ten months, so she told him that she didn't think Mr. Jensen would allow him to charge anything more until he cleaned up his overdue back bill.

Luckily she was young and pretty and Mr. Hearst was much amused, and someone intercepted.

The strangest experience that I ever had with a bill happened in New York City at the Ambassador Hotel back before World

War II. The Ambassador was a small elegant hotel on Park Avenue and Fifty-second Street with an enticing little bar all full of black lacquer furniture and banks of cool green ferns. There was soft piano music and a marble fountain, and I'd been invited to have cocktails there by an aunt of mine one summer afternoon.

I was living on Park Avenue and Fifty-eighth Street at the time, so I walked to the Ambassador, naturally, and never bothered to bring along a handbag, just wore some dark glasses and a pair of white gloves and carried a handkerchief. I found my aunt at a table for five, the other three girls with her were all first cousins of mine, one was her daughter and the other two were a daughter and a daughter-in-law of another aunt of mine, if you follow me.

I hadn't seen any of them for ages, I'd been living in Chicago and they were in Connecticut and Washington, so it was a jolly family reunion, and we all drank tom collinses and gin fizzes and got caught up on the family gossip. When it was time to leave a waiter appeared with the check and my aunt pointed to me and the next thing I knew, there it was staring at me from its plate, and me without a nickel.

Puzzled but undaunted, I asked the waiter for his pencil, turned the check over, and wrote on the back:

"Dear MGR—Am stuck with this check and need yr. help! Please open a chg. acc't for me at once. I live at 470 Pk Ave. and can chg at Plaza and Hamp. House. Pls. tip w'tr $3 & my thnx."

I signed my name and handed it to the man, pulled on my gloves, and stood up. Before I had reached the doorway the waiter was back, gave me a dazzling and knowing smile, and off I went.

The next morning in the mail was a letter welcoming me to the membership list of Ambassador Hotel charge-account holders from the manager, and his postscipt suggested that if I'd drop in penniless, any old time, but preferably alone, *he* would like to buy me a drink.

Another enormous change in the way we live has been caused by paper and plastics, the throwaway things that we are all so accustomed to these days. Imagine packing back in 1933: dresses wrinkled least when they were surrounded by tissue paper, especially where the folds were. Shoes went into felt or cloth shoe bags, each with a drawstring. Toilet articles went into an oilcloth case or box that sometimes fastened with snappers or buttons, and sometimes with a brand-new invention: the zipper. These zippers were unreliable then, and if in a hurry, always chose to get stuck. Engineers call this I.O.I.O., meaning the Innate Obstinacy of Inanimate Objects.

There were no plastic garment bags, no fold-over luggage, no handy hang-up anything. People motored with coats hanging on wire coat hangers, swinging in the back seat somewhere, and it looked terrible and sloppy.

The first plastic that I ever saw was cellophane, and it was wrapped around each *green*-and-red package of Lucky Strike cigarettes. It was a terrific novelty, and at first we used to save each wrapper, smooth them all out flat, and keep them until we had thirty or forty. Then they were folded, each one a certain way, so that it hitched onto the next one, and all together they made a beautiful iridescent hatband, or perhaps even a belt if one had a safety pin (Scotch-tape not as yet having been invented).

We *did* have a forerunner of plastic and that must have been invented at the beginning of the century: celluloid. It was used to make "dresser sets," which might consist of a hairbrush, a comb, a clothes brush, a buttonhook with a celluloid handle, a round box with a hole in the top in which to poke hair combings, and finally a lovely hand mirror, each piece with a hand-painted blue monogram. Celluloid was usually ivory colored and always opaque and shiny, and I believe that it was highly inflammable. I recall several gruesome tales of women having a water wave for their hair, and having it set with celluloid combs. Then, when they sat under a hot dryer, the combs exploded and they were more or less scalped.

Besides this early plastic, there were paper things, nothing like the paper dresses of today and the fancy paper plates and tablecloths and so on, but we did have paper napkins for picnics, and paper hats for birthdays and oiled-paper bright-colored umbrellas and parasols from Japan, and in the thirties disposable tissues bowed in, things like Kleenex and Kotex and Tampax, and finally throwaway diapers for babies.

Before their entries we used washable cheesecloth squares (hemmed by hand if we wanted to be really elegant) to remove cold cream or suntan oil, that sort of thing, and women (before Kotex, etc.) and babies used cotton *serviettes* (elegant term) for sanitary napkins, or diapers made of a pebbly porous material called bird's-eye.

These undisposable and necessary articles had to be washed of course after each use, and before the automatic washing machine they presented a dreadfully tedious task.

Nearly everything that we took for aches and pains in those days was completely different from now except a few things: we still take aspirin, and many of us gargle with good old Lavoris when we have sore throats, and milk of magnesia is still around.

However, nearly everything else was different, and much worse. Castor oil, for example, was perfectly frightening to take, especially for little children. It was not only a hideous shade of greenish brown, it also smelled horrible. Perhaps you have smelled it at the Indianapolis automobile racetrack, where it is used for cars because it is the best lubricant? It was also a powerful laxative, and to be given a tablespoon of castor oil was Operation Horror. Cascara was better, it was a pill; and Castoria was fair. Cod-liver oil was awful. It was taken as a tonic, a builder-upper, and it smelled quite naturally of fish. After a mouthful, the patient smelled of fish and everything he ate tasted of fish for the rest of the day. Scott's Emulsion was only slightly better.

If you had a cut finger it was painted with bright orange-red Mercurochrome, or a purple antiseptic called gentian violet, which turned the flesh a brilliant purple. If you had a stuffed-up nose the doctor sprayed your nasal passages with a ghastly brown liquid called Argyrol. Iodine also stained wounds and scratches brown, and so did tincture of benzine.

However, there was one very nice medicine and it was for women only, and in delicate wording the label on the bottle suggested that it be taken at "certain difficult times of the month." It suggested taking two tablespoonsfuls in a little water before meals, and to repeat if necessary. It was known far and wide, and was called Lydia E. Pinkham's Vegetable Compound.

I knew a nephew of Lydia E. and he was an undergraduate at

Princeton when I was in college. I went to several football games with him and he always brought a bottle of Aunt Lydia's famous medicine along. The first time that he brought this out of his pocket I almost expired with embarrassment, but to my surprise he told me that it was actually nothing more than an old-fashioned cocktail, made of pure Kentucky Bourbon whiskey with some herbs added, rather like Angostura bitters. On a brisk fall day in a cold stadium it made one feel all warm and furry inside, and I can see plainly how many housewives (many of them married to Methodist and Baptist ministers) wrote ecstatic letters of praise to Lydia. There was even a song about her. I can remember the chorus:

> Sing, oh sing to Lydia Pinkham
> And her love for the human race
> She invented the Vegetable Compound
> And the papers all published her Face. [Some face.]

The thing that we probably took the most of was bicarbonate of soda, just plain old baking soda. It was the normal thing to take for indigestion. They say that Calvin Coolidge (who believed implicitly in "home doctoring") took sodium bicarb for his chest pains and subsequently died of his heart attack.

In 1940 when I first went on the board of directors of a family wholesale drug company, the medicine that outsold everything else was aspirin. However, it was soon replaced by vitamins, which became the *rage*. These were replaced for a while (the company does business mostly in the state of Michigan) by a widely advertised tonic known as Hadacol. For several months the company shipped bottles of it by the gross to every drugstore in the state. It turned out to be rather like Lydia E. Pinkham's product: mostly alcohol but not nearly as tasty.

I almost forgot to tell what we took years ago for hangovers. Bromo Seltzer was popular, but lots of people also took drops of aromatic spirits of ammonia, stirred into a half glass of water or even into a little Coca-Cola. Other people swore by something called a "prairie oyster," which I think was a whole raw egg covered with Tabasco sauce. The most popular of all the hangover remedies, however, was undoubtedly the famous "hair of the dog."

There are so many more things that have changed the way of life, everything from panty hose, frozen foods, and radar ranges to macro-balloon energy sources, computers and heart transplants and lasers and cobalt rays, that if I went on further this chapter would get too long and dull, so I will only say that there are so many *conveniences* in today's world compared to 1933, and so much better and faster communications, and traveling, and built-in home entertainment (what could be better than turning on the television on a rainy night and being able to see the entire movie *Oklahoma!*).

10

Aviation

"ALL ABOARD!" shouted the conductor, after consulting his watch, which said precisely 6:05 P.M. Then he signaled to the engineer, the brakeman waved his red lantern, and the two swung aboard as the De Luxe Limited glided out of New York's Pennsylvania Station and headed west, stopping only to pick up passengers at North Philadelphia, Washington, D.C., and Baltimore, Maryland, before proceeding with no further stops (except for fuel) until morning.

And this is a chapter on *aviation?* Yes, it is, and the train was known as the Airway Limited, and I was one of the passengers on it, and the year is sometime in the early 1930s.

After we had left the station and zoomed into the tunnel under the Hudson River and were bowling along over the Jersey Flats, dinner was announced and we Air-Rail passengers went promptly into the diner, ate our dinners, and turned in for the night, for we were all to be called at 6 A.M. and were disembarking at a brand-new stop: Port Columbus, Ohio.

There were twelve of us in all, and after an early breakfast in the diner, we arrived at this no-longer-existent stop at 7:55. Here we and all of our luggage were taken to the Columbus airport (a few minutes away) in station wagons owned by Transcontinental Air Transportation, Inc., and there awaiting us was a large Ford Tri-Motor plane.

We were greeted by the captain and copilot and helped aboard up a little ladder by our steward, and were each assigned to a lightweight wicker chair fastened firmly to the floor, each one next to a large window. Our seat belts were fastened and we were all given sticks of chewing gum, and with much shouting and waving, the door was slammed, the propellers cranked up one by one, and off we lumbered with clouds of dust rising behind us, and the motors roaring and vibrating terrifically.

Each "Tin Goose," as the planes were called, held twelve passengers, and in an incredibly short time, four lengths of the plane, off the ground they went, climbing steeply. They took off at a speed of sixty miles an hour, and cruised noisily at about eighty-eight miles per hour, at an altitude of around seventeen hundred feet. They could fly this way for five hundred miles (about four hours' flying time) without refueling.

As a matter of fact, the past tense isn't correct: there are still twelve of these corrugated-aluminum crafts actively flying in the United States (example: Island Airways of Lake Erie), and no one knows how many are still flying in Mexico and South America.

I remember they were a bargain, too, their original cost being $55,000, another thing about the Tin Goose that was most appealing. It had, as all large planes did at this time, an Artificial Horizon. This one was made by the Sperry Corporation, and the rear horizon face (like a rearview mirror in an auto) was tinted a delicate sky blue and instead of a marker at the pivot point there was a dear little airplane.

It was probably the most reliable plane of them all until the DC-3 turned up ten years later. It had only one drawback besides its sounding like a boiler factory (it had cables banging outside on the fuselage as well as the three clanking engines) and that was that the pilot had to be lean and thin, otherwise he couldn't squeeze in behind the control wheel, especially if it was pulled back for a three-point landing.

Off we went at 8:15, and the steward served us hot coffee from a thermos bottle after we were airborne. We came down at Indianapolis, Indiana, for a few minutes and then on to St. Louis, Missouri, a little after noon. Lunch was put aboard there, and we all enjoyed sandwiches and pickles and more coffee from the thermos. Then on we flew to Kansas City, Missouri, and Wichita, Kansas, and at 6:24 P.M. reached an unnamed airport in Oklahoma where we were met by two Aero Cars (those would be station wagons), which took us to Harvey House in Waynoka, Oklahoma, where we dined.

This Harvey House was a part of the Waynoka station, as I recall, and from there it was just a short walk to the Pullman sleeping car waiting for us on the Atchison, Topeka and Santa Fe railroad tracks. I fell asleep (I was a dead bunny, I was) so fast that I don't know what through train picked us up, but I imagine it was the Chief, and the next morning we were again routed out and off the train in Clovis, New Mexico. We breakfasted in another Harvey House and Transcontinental Air Transportation, Inc., again got us to an airport, called Portair Landing Field.

The day was much the same as the day before. Off we went at 8:10 A.M., stopping at Albuquerque, New Mexico (wonderful mountains), and then Winslow, Arizona (those sandwiches again), then Kingman, Arizona, and finally, after a fast glimpse of the state of Nevada, the plane crossed the Mojave Desert and we finally landed at the Grand Central Air Terminal of Glendale, California, at 5:52 P.M. Pacific Time.

It took me a week to recover. Besides being quite deaf from the roar of the motors, and dizzy from the constant rolling and yawing, as well as a little queasy from the more gentle motion of the trains at night, I ended up just plain tired from all the hectic rushing from one moving object to another.

It saved thirty-six hours, and I was glad that I'd done it once, but *never again*. The next time I went to California I took one of the new diesel trains, the Union Pacific's City of Los Angeles, which saved almost as much time, and was an earthly Paradise with its white and red wines with dinner and its comfortable bed and smooth roadbed.

However, later on that summer found me taking flying lessons at a small airport north of Chicago called Palwaukee. I got talked into it by a group of enthusiastic friends: it was the latest thing to do, it was "the bee's knees," "the cat's pajamas," "the snake's hips," anybody who *was* somebody *flew*.

We assembled at Palwaukee Saturday afternoons and Sunday, wearing helmets and goggles and leather jackets and *pants*, and there were five men, five girls, ten of us, and the ringleader (who had already soloed) was the husband of my long-time friend Patty Chapman. Theron Chapman said that learning to fly taught you how a plane cannot *help* but fly, and one mile up gave you nine miles to glide down. If you had a good instructor, and did what he said, flying was as safe as sitting in the Old North Church.

Our teacher was one Dwight Morrow (no relation to the Honorable Dwight Morrow, who was Ambassador to Mexico and father of Anne Lindbergh), and also an excellent man. We learned the purpose of the ailerons, the rudder, the stick, and the elevator, and we knew about lift and drag, thrust and gravity.

My training plane was a Curtiss Robin and, as I remember it, had only three things on its instrument panel: an altimeter, the rpm gauge, and the oil-pressure gauge. There was also a compass but there was so much metal in the plane that it never worked accurately.

It was a biplane with practically vertical takeoff. As soon as it achieved a speed of sixty miles per hour, you pulled the stick back and up it went, into the air slow and steady, rather like the funicular that takes you up Mount Vesuvius.

I loved it. I loved my plane and flying and we all did. We flew with dual-control planes, the instructor Mr. Morrow or one of his men sitting behind us. First we learned to fly in a straight line, by following a highway or a railroad track. With a crosswind it was difficult in the beginning; we would drift away from the road, then overcompensate, causing a series of zigs and zags.

Then we practiced huge figure-eights up in the sky, as well as various turns. Every once in a while the instructor would turn off the engine and yell "Forced landing!" and we would quickly look over the ground below and pick out a proper spot (there were many golf courses handy) and glide down until the man started the motor going, and back up we would sweep.

After each lesson we would all gather at someone's house or apartment and talk about aviation. Nothing else seemed interesting, and the people who didn't fly were oddballs, and to be avoided whenever possible.

Before the end of the summer, actually it was at a point when my own logbook showed that I had nine and a half hours of flying time, all the lessons stopped, and we never flew our own planes again.

"Thee" Chapman, who, as I said, had much more flying time

than we beginners, had a most terrible experience. He was flying solo one Sunday afternoon, away from the rest of us, and in fact was exploring the shoreline of Lake Michigan along by Lake Bluff and Lake Forest and Highland Park. Suddenly a fog enveloped him, appearing from nowhere at all, and materializing so fast that in a few seconds he was bumping around blindly. When he adapted himself to what had happened he had no idea whether he was heading south or east or west. He flew high to get out of it but nothing happened, then tried as low as he dared, also with no luck.

After a few more struggles in the thick, billowing, impenetrable white mist, he gave up, pointed the plane toward what he hoped was the lake, and bailed out from an altitude of 7,500 feet, the highest that his Stinson would go.

Contrary to his fears, he parachuted safely down into a cornfield a few miles west of Fort Sheridan, but the plane, instead of zooming out over the lake, crashed into a woods up north, just over the Wisconsin border.

It was several hours before we found that he was safe and I remember so well how awful we all felt as we sat around the flying school's log room, or whatever it was. We knew that his plane had crashed and burned up but it was a long time before we learned that Thee was alive.

He had sprained his ankle when he landed, and had to hobble very slowly through various pastures and fields until he reached a farmhouse. It had no telephone but the farmer drove him to a nearby corner store, where he called his wife, Patty. She came and picked him up and took him at once to the Highland Park Hospital, and only then did he remember his flying pals, all smoking endless cigarettes and sipping Cokes furiously.

We heard the news with the greatest relief, all shook hands and departed. I resolved to skip flying then and there and I think the others did too.

By 1936 the memory of the noisy and fatiguing airplane and the dangers of being the pilot began to fade, and I changed my mind about flying. As more and more friends flew in commercial planes there began to be something very alluring (as well as practical) about walking onto a plane at 4 P.M. in New York and walking off in Chicago at 8:33 P.M. and being able to sleep in one's own bed, rather than having to undress and dress, and carry all those little toilet articles along; so June 1936 found me returning to Chicago by American Airlines in the very latest of planes, the DC-3. It left from Newark Airport and headed for Buffalo, every seat taken, and it seemed quiet as a Packard limousine compared to the wobbly Tin Goose and smoother too. It had a handsome stewardess in an equally handsome uniform who took good care of us, and we reached Buffalo safely at 6 P.M. after veering over Niagara Falls at 2,000 feet for a quick glimpse.

Almost all of the passengers got off, leaving two or three men sitting separately up in the front, and me alone back in the tail. We took off again, heading for Detroit, where, according to the timetable, we were due to arrive at 6:50 P.M. Off we flew, all was well, the seat-belt sign flashed off and I settled back, but it flashed on again, in a few minutes we ran into dark murky clouds and rain, the plane wallowing along like a seagoing tug. I tried to read and pay no attention but it seemed to get worse, and the clouds got darker, with lightning shooting around now and then. I looked at my watch: it said 6:30. Twenty minutes more, I told myself, and we'd be on the ground.

However, we flew on and on. I began to jitter as we lurched about, and just as I was going to ask the stewardess why we weren't making a descent, the pilot's buzzer sounded, the signal for her to come to the cockpit. (Remember, there were no speaker systems in those days, no pilots saying, "Folks, there's a little turbulence ahead, but we'll be out of it shortly," etc. etc.).

The stewardess went immediately forward, unlocked the door (customary in those days), and let herself in, carefully locking it behind her.

I was *frantic*. It was already 7 P.M., then it was 7:10 after an eternity, and finally it managed to say 7:15. Meanwhile the weather was no better, and furthermore, to my fevered imagination the engines sounded strained and belabored.

A horrible thought occurred to me: The two pilots and the stewardess had quietly bailed out, had landed safely somewhere in the Detroit area, and we were careening along somewhere north of the border, perhaps approaching wild Canadian timberland.

I was just on the verge of waking up the dozing passengers forward when the pilot's door opened and the stewardess appeared. I could have kissed her.

"What's happening?" I asked her as she came alongside. "Why aren't we in Detroit?"

She looked at her watch. "We're a few minutes late but we'll be in a little before seven o'clock."

Then I suddenly remembered about the change to Central Time, and the time for us was only 6:30, and just then the plane nosed forward slightly as we began the descent to Detroit.

We reached the Cicero airport in Chicago exactly at 8:33, and I tottered off vowing that rather than go through the past two hours again, I would travel hereafter by horse, or even perhaps by covered wagon.

What were airports like when commercial aviation was in its infancy? Most of them were perfectly terrible. Some were just a grass runway with a hangar and a wind sock, some had rickety wooden sheds filled with flies, furnished with a kitchen chair or two and a bench. The sheds gradually grew larger and became buildings. Some had lunch counters and waiting rooms that looked like station waiting rooms with a ticket-office–check-in counter.

Passengers walked (or ran when in a rainstorm) out to their plane and got into it by climbing up a small stepladder. To get inside they had to stoop over to get through the narrow side door, and still bending nearly double, pulled themselves along up the steep aisle, finally managing to crawl into their seats. The floor of the plane was level only when it was up in the air.

I remember running a distance of at least four blocks once at Chicago's brand-new airport, O'Hare, to catch a plane to Florida. It was ten below zero and a fierce icy wind was blowing. All of us raced across the flat frozen ground and I didn't warm up until we were just landing at Miami Airport. It was a shock to climb out into 80-degree weather, carrying a fur coat and again trudging for a long distance to the airport building, in the hot sun.

There were no wheelchairs or electric cars, but in most places passengers who couldn't walk to the plane were taken out to the plane by some airport official's automobile.

The strangest airport that I was ever in existed high up in the Rocky Mountains: Knight, Wyoming. It was an emergency landing field (the highest in the United States) and next to it was a little farmhouse. I was on my way to California when the oil gauge on the instrument board showed that the oil pressure was dangerously low, so down we came, in a very short descent, and landed on a bumpy gravelly airstrip, taxied up to the farmhouse, and out we got, twelve passengers, as I recall. The plane was a Lockheed Vega and I believe we were on United Airlines.

The mountain air was freezing cold, but we swarmed into the farmhouse, and while the pilots had a look at the engines, the farmer's wife made coffee and we sat stiffly about, crowding the parlor and kitchen, some of us making trips outside to a chilly little privy. Very quickly our pilots appeared and announced that the oil pressure was perfectly normal; it was the indicator on the instrument panel that wasn't working and the plane could take off at once. *However*, due to the altitude, the air wasn't dense enough to take off with a full load, so another plane would be needed to come from Denver and pick up half of the passengers.

We drew lots to see who got to wait for the rescue plane and who could depart at once. Luckily I picked a winning ticket and we were off. We felt sad for the ones left behind as we taxied off; the copilot told us that they were probably going to sleep all night on the parlor floor wrapped in blankets, as to get a plane there before morning would be impossible. Emergency fields no longer exist—we now refer to emergency landings as *unscheduled* landings.

What sort of people flew in those days? Most of them were *young* and *daring*, and in a hurry. Also nearly everyone stepped into the nearest bar and had a least one stiff drink before going to the plane. The teetotalers probably took some phenobarbital or took along smelling salts (tranquilizers being nonexistent), and those prone to airsickness brought with them Mothersill's seasick pills.

There was another category of people who flew back and forth across the United States in the early days: movie stars. In fact, they actually made flying stylish in the 1930s. "I just flew in from Hollywood, folks, and my plane was a little late," was a favorite opening remark of any radio star from Kate Smith to Fred Allen to Eddie Cantor to Maurice Chevalier.

My Uncle Charles Pynchon was flying to California on business once and found himself sitting next to an attractive and quiet young woman. She didn't speak to him and spent the whole time looking out of the window. When the plane started over the Rockies it got rough and she became distressingly airsick.

Uncle Charlie was as helpful as could be: he got her a damp towel after she was over the worst of it, made her drink a little ginger ale out of a paper cup, and so on. He was a big handsome man with a great deal of charm, and by the time the turbulence had vanished and the flying was smooth again, they were enjoying each other's company very much.

When he went to the rest room some male passenger grabbed him and said, "You *lucky* fellow!" and when Charlie looked puzzled the man said, "You're sitting next to Greta Garbo, for God's sake."

He returned to his seat and Miss Garbo said to him, "Oh, I can tell by the expression on your face that someone has told you who I am. I'm so disappointed, as I was having such a good time."

He assured her that it would make no difference, that he seldom went to the movies, and would never send her a fan letter or be a bother, and that he was a happily married man living in Winnetka, Illinois, with a son at Asheville and a daughter at Dobbs Ferry.

She then asked if she could drop him off anywhere when they got to the airport, or was there *anything* that she could do for him, as he had been so nice to her, and he thanked her and said that his brother and sister-in-law were meeting him.

"*However*," Uncle Charlie said, "they might be *most* impressed if you would let me sort of escort you off the plane—"

"I'll be delighted to," she said promptly. "Furthermore, I'll snuggle up." She turned to him and added, with a mischievous smile, "You know, I'm supposed to be pretty good at that."

Uncle Charlie reported that the Harold Pynchons were waiting for him when the plane landed in Los Angeles, and that when they saw him leaving the plane with Miss Garbo clinging to him they almost expired.

The next day there were pictures all over the country in the newspapers, with captions like "Who Is Garbo's Newest Flame?" and "Greta Garbo and Mystery Man."

There was also another type of international air travel existing then: the airship. These German-made lighter-than-air Zeppelins made all sorts of trips from World War I on, and finally, in the summer of 1936, the huge new dirigible *Hindenburg* was put into regular air service on May 11 between Luftschiff, Germany, and Lakehurst, New Jersey.

During the summer the *Hindenburg* made ten round trips, carrying fifty passengers on a nonstop sixty-to-seventy-hour flight at a cost of $400 one way, or $720 round trip.

I never traveled on it, but knew several people who made the trip. There were only two complaints that I recall: luggage was limited to forty pounds, and there was absolutely no smoking except in a smoking room, which passengers entered through locked double doors. Remember that inside the *Hindenburg*'s silver cigar-shaped framework there was over seven million cubic feet of inflammable hydrogen, all pumped into sixteen cells or balloonets, as they were called. The passengers were frisked for matches and cigarettes and lighters as they boarded, and these were kept for them in the smoking room.

The great airship rode smoothly and comfortably above the storms, cruising at eighty miles an hour, powered by four diesel engines, each housed in a separate gondola aft of the passenger quarters.

What was it like to take a trip in this new airship in the summer of 1936? You purchased your ticket and arrived at the Frankfurter Hof in Frankfurt, and there, after a few hearty *Heil Hitlers* (you were in Nazi Germany, don't forget), all passengers were lined up by the customs officials and every piece of luggage and every package and handbag was thoroughly searched, every inch.

The *Hindenburg* was *enormous*, five city blocks long, seventy-five feet high, all shining silver except for huge red, black, and white swastikas painted on both sides of its mammoth tail. A brass band played as you climbed up the long stair to B Deck, where the chief steward greeted you and sent you with one of the six stewards or the one stewardess to your little inside double cabin on A Deck, one short flight up. There were twenty-five of these cabins, each with a narrow lower and upper berth, much like a Pullman compartment, with a washbowl and clothes hangers and two small cupboards, the walls covered with gray linen.

You left your coat and parcels and hurried out to the Promenade Lounge, where you could look down at the ground through the wide sloping windows. The long stairway was drawn up and folded away in a long slot flush with the bottom of the hull. Instead of the familiar "All aboard," the order for departure was "Up ship," and the liftoff was so gentle that there was no sensation of rising except that the people waving goodbye below grew smaller and smaller.

At an altitude of five hundred feet the great airship sailed over the Rhine in the gathering twilight, speeding along guided by a long string of little flashes, one beacon after another blinking from each hill. Up ahead you could see a great mass of lights spreading everywhere. This is Cologne and you could hear horns tooting faintly below, and even a few dogs barking. Then on to Holland (France had threatened antiaircraft fire if the LZ-129, the *Hindenburg*'s military name, ever flew over French soil), then proceeding on to above the English Channel and then on to the North Atlantic.

After leaving the lights of Cologne behind, it was time for all passengers to cross the companionway to the dining room on the other side of A Deck. All the single passengers sat with the captain at a long narrow table. Couples sat at tables for two, and families at their own tables. A supper of cold meats and salads was served, with wines and fresh fruit and cheeses, and afterward you could descend to B Deck, if you liked, where besides the smoking room there was also a bar, which remained open for the entire trip.

You could sleep comfortably in your berth, with its smooth linen sheets and light soft blankets; your shoes were shined during the night if you left them outside your door. There were seven toilets among the twenty-five cabins plus one shower bath, and besides the big lounge with its beautiful wall map of the whole world and all its seas and lands, there was a small room for writing. One passenger sent two hundred postcards, it is reported. Postcards could be sent by pneumatic tube pressure direct to the airship's own post office. You could spend a busy day reading and chatting and watching the angry waves of the Atlantic far down below. There was also a tour of the ship after lunch, and after a visit to the Command Gondola you could walk the length of the ship inside the dirigible on the catwalk that led back to the engines and all the way to the steps leading up to the nose cone and the windows on each side of it.

Late in the afternoon of the second day the airship sailed over Newfoundland and the next morning after breakfast the *Hindenburg* was flying over Boston, Massachusetts. You could see the crowds of people below waving, ships in the harbor saluting, and the planes flying around you like busy little mosquitoes. Everyone on board had an early buffet lunch after flying over Providence. Then came New York City, and you could see traffic actually stopping as you sailed down over Fifth Avenue.

At the end of Fifth Avenue the dirigible turned west and flew down the Hudson River over the transatlantic ships at their piers, past Wall Street and the Battery, Staten Island, and finally on down to Lakehurst, New Jersey.

Landing lines were dropped to the waiting ground crew and the airship was winched down to an air dock resting on a railroad flatcar. The tail was also winched down to another flatcar on the track 803 feet back, and when the bow and stern were both anchored, the *Hindenburg* rolled smoothly into the great hangar and you could disembark down the stairway to be greeted by waiting friends and relations. If you were going on to Chicago or California, American Airlines had a DC-3 plane waiting to transport you.

Meanwhile the *Hindenburg's* crew was busy tidying up the cabins and putting fresh flowers in the dining room and lounge, for the airship was sailing for Luftschiff (Frankfurt) at midnight with fifty new passengers, some of them already beginning to arrive at the hangar.

That was airship travel in the summer of 1936. As you know, the picture changed in 1937 when the first flight in May ended with a disastrous fire just as the *Hindenburg* was coming down for its landing in Lakehurst.

At the present time it looks as if the lighter-than-air ship is about to return to popularity, and especially as a carrier of cargo. Economically, it is practical, and engineers envision a huge dirigible, made buoyant by non-inflammable helium, carrying tons of cargo and never landing but sending the cargo down to its purchaser by parachute, in rather the same way that the big oil carriers never enter a port, but dispense their oil to smaller tankers that come out to get it.

What got me back into another plane after that frightening trip to Chicago? My husband and I were on a Caribbean cruise and when we arrived in Havana there was an airmail special-delivery letter from New York saying that our little daughter was ill. We jumped ship, took a taxi to the Pan American Clipper Pier, and boarded a Sikorsky S-4 Flying Boat, or Clipper, as Pan Am called it, heading for Miami Airport. This flight, by the way, was Pan Am's first *international* service. The big Clipper ship was tied up to a high pier, we were helped onto the top of the fuselage and over to an open hatch by a naval-officer type (actually our steward), and we descended by a steep ladder into the cabin. There were about thirty of us, each assigned to a comfortable seat, and we could look out the portholes and see the harbor and even Morro Castle. The captain welcomed us, it was all very nautical and shipshape. When we were all inside the steward hauled the ladder up so that it was flush with the top of the cabin, the moorings were cast off, and we were towed out to open sea by a sturdy little white tug.

Off it went, as soon as our propellers started turning, and we were skimming along the water. It was a long time until we took to the air, but once up there it was smooth and quiet and steady. I felt reassured about flying and enjoyed the ninety-minute trip very much more than I had expected.

Since then I've flown in all sorts of planes but the most memorable of the post-World War II commercial aircraft were *The President* and *Il Presidente*. They were four-engine Boeing Strato-Cruisers, and flew between Europe and New York, and South America and New York, respectively. They carried seventy-two passengers.

Not only were they cabin-pressurized and air-conditioned, but they were double-decked; that is, there was a small spiral stairway leading from the main deck down to the lower-deck cocktail lounge, where thirteen people could enjoy drinks together, mixed by the purser. It was not unlike the present bar of the 747s, where passengers climb a spiral stairway to do the same thing, but on a grander scale.

There was another great feature about them that attracted universal interest: they had *berths*, and just as in the old Pullman car there were uppers and lowers. However, there was a difference in that the lowers were just the same daytime seats that tilted back and stretched out into what were called "sleeperettes." The uppers were, however, full-length berths and there was an extra charge for them. There was also a ladies' dressing room as well as one for the men.

The President, as I remember, left Orly, the main airport of Paris, late in the afternoon, and dinner with champagne (and orchids and perfume for the ladies) was served on board. Then the plane landed in Shannon, Ireland, and we all got off and drank crème de menthes or brandy and coffee while the plane was refueled and the berths were made up.

Then off we went again, everyone retiring behind the handsome blue curtains, and the three stewardesses offering us magazines and extra pillows and even a little ladder with one step so that short people could get into their uppers. (We taller folk could do it with a quick jump.)

In the morning we stopped for refueling and breakfast in Gander, Newfoundland, while the berths were made up and the uppers folded into the side walls.

Then on we went to New York, arriving at Idlewild (the old name for Kennedy Airport). GW met me after we had gone through customs, and amazed me by saying, "Let's grab a little breakfast before we leave, wouldn't you like to? I had to hurry over my coffee, so that I didn't really enjoy it." And here I'd had breakfast *hours* ago and I was looking forward to a daiquiri on the rocks, with a lamb chop and some creamed spinach after. And thus entered the beginning of the jet-lag era.

There are still people that I know who have never flown. If you have never been on a plane, what is the best procedure for your maiden voyage?

First of all, fly on a great big jet, preferably a nonstop flight. The smoothest flight is that of the 747, or the DC-10 usually, and the pleasantest time of day for flying is early morning. Get a good night's sleep the night before, bring along some Dramamine in case you might be the airsick type, and if you are fearfully nervous, take a Valium or similar tranquilizer on your way to the airport, and stay away from any alcoholic drinks.

When you make your flight reservation tell the airline that it will be your first flight. They in turn will inform your stewardesses, and one of them will be on hand when you board the plane. She will explain the procedures to you as you go along, such as "What's that funny noise below just as we left the ground?" The stewardess' answer: "That is the wheels being drawn up hydraulically into the plane underneath us."

The stewardess will probably also give you a pamphlet that tells all about plane travel, and how the wings cannot possibly fall off, and how the engines are all taken apart after every so many hours of flying, and how careful the pilots are because the last thing on *their* list is to crash or be hijacked, and so on.

Stewardesses (now referred to as flight attendants) are almost without exception wonderful and nice and hard-working, and they are all trained to open safety chutes in ten seconds or less. How long have they been around? There were a few in the thirties, but as general standard equipment they've been around only since the end of World War II. The first one was hired by Boeing Air Transport, what is now United Airlines, and she was a registered nurse named Ellen Church. She in turn found seven more nurses and trained them for their new jobs. There are now over 40,000 of these capable young women who can handle anything from standing all alone in a bikini bathing suit on a jumbo jet in a place known as "the Pit," to warming up over three hundred dinners in a radar oven (ten dinners at a time) and sending them up by dumbwaiter to the galley, where the other flight attendants distribute them about, to stopping a water fight among a group of mischievous kids, to putting out a fire started by a slightly squiffed lady passenger who used her green wool topcoat as an ashtray, to saying to a man passenger, "Sir, you are not allowed to kneel and pray in the aisle. Will you please go back to your seat and pray there."

There is quite a difference between traveling on the speedy nonstop jets of today and the first flight that I ever made.

It was made in 1925 when I was in college. A barnstorming plane owned by a former World War I pilot, who was a stunt pilot as well, by the name of Swanee Taylor, was taking passengers up for rides at some fairgrounds in Poughkeepsie at the price of three dollars apiece, so a classmate named Dotty George and I bicycled out to the place and went for our first ride.

It was a *circus*. It was an open biplane of some sort, and we could both just squeeze in beside Captain Taylor, who turned out to be delightfully amusing as well as an excellent pilot. He flew us over our campus, dipping low into our dormitory-ringed Quadrangle and swooping in and out of it from different angles. It was so much fun, this buzzing of our probable friends, that we took off our shoes and threw them merrily out as we flashed by, hoping that someone would recognize us.

Bicycling home in our stocking feet afterward was not as much fun, and Richard Keene (Keene Little Richard, we called him), Vassar's manager of the grounds, called Captain Taylor and threatened to file a complaint if he ever came anywhere near the college again. Meanwhile we invited him to dinner, and everyone in Strong Hall (our dormitory) laughed all evening at his flying stories and his imitations of British Tommies and German and French aviators.

And to end this chapter on flying here is one that Swanee Taylor would have liked.

It's about a student who had been taking flying lessons in a dual-control fore-and-aft plane for weeks and weeks with a patient instructor and who was scared to solo.

His teacher was fed up, and decided to force him to solo by going up with him as usual but when they were aloft he would take out his own flying stick (they could be unhooked in some easy way) and tap the pupil on the shoulder to catch his eye, then toss the stick away, fold his arms, and sit complacently back.

He told a friend of his about his little scheme and the pupil overheard or got wind of it in some way. They got in the plane at the next lesson, and when the man tapped him on the shoulder and threw the stick overboard, the pupil nodded and reached down and held up his flying stick and threw it over too.

The instructor, most fearfully horrified, bailed right out. The student, who had taken along an extra stick, brought the plane in for a perfect landing.

ও 11
Café Society

A SUNDAY NIGHT IN November 1940 found my husband and me dancing and drinking champagne at the Stork Club. Actually it was Monday morning, about one o'clock, and we had a ringside table on the dance floor, and were wearing dressy afternoon things because it was Sunday. I was wearing a two-piece dress from Hattie Carnegie which consisted of a black knife-pleated silk skirt, and the top was a very simple short-sleeved tunic of thin silver lamé, also with silver pleats around its lower edge. Instead of a hat, I wore a little black veil (the latest thing) that fitted over my hair, and was trimmed with a few little black velvet ribbon bows. GW was in a dark suit and white shirt, and wore a fresh white carnation in his buttonhole.

Did we look about the same as nowadays? Yes, as far as dress is concerned, but there was a difference: make-up and hair. The ladies of 1940 wore white make-up, and their lipstick was a much darker red. Highly lacquered fingernail polish matched the lipstick, fingernails were longer, and hair was always curly; permanents were a part of life unless one had naturally curly hair. If you had dark hair, it was worn down to the shoulders, parted in the middle or at one side, in order to look as much like the debutante Brenda Frazier as possible. She was the glamour girl of this time for the younger ones; the older women tried to look like the Duchess of Windsor, who was similar to Miss Frazier in her chic way. The men had very short hair, the crewcut was in great vogue, and all men except musicians and foreigners were clean-shaven.

Blondes had permanents too, and tried to look like Ginger Rogers or Greta Garbo or Tallulah Bankhead. Speaking of permanents, I, who luckily had natural curls, was getting a shampoo one day at Elizabeth Arden's and had an operator whom I didn't know.

"Whoever gave you your last permanent certainly did a very poor job," this woman remarked. When I told her that I'd never had one, ever, she said, "Oh, that explains it."

We had dined at Lüchow's (a splendid restaurant, and still going strong) and afterward had gone to a crazy, undescribable extravaganza called *Hellzapoppin*, which was playing nightly in the Broadway theater district. It was the second or third time that we had seen it, and after that we had arrived at the Stork Club, still laughing and wiping the tears from our eyes.

Why had we come at this late hour, with Monday morning just around the corner? Because it was Balloon Night. Over the dance floor and high up next to the ceiling was a great big string net, and nestling inside were fifty or sixty large colored balloons, each one containing a slip of paper. At exactly 2 A.M. the music would stop, all the ladies present would get out on the floor (some even kicked off their shoes) with their arms stretched upward, the drums would roll *fortissimo*, and slowly the net would open and the balloons would come floating down. We ladies could each grab as many as possible, *but* should the balloon break, the gift on the slip of paper was no good.

The trick was to have a table close to the balloons, and have your husband or escort sitting at it ready to receive the balloons passed to him. Having had some experience as a basketball jumping center, I could almost always capture a balloon or two. Then we sat exhausted and disheveled, with busted balloons lying all over the dance floor, until the captain came to our table, broke the trophies with a sharp pencil, and read off each prize. It was the most exciting moment.

"Aha, madame," he would exclaim. "You have won Luncheon for Four here at the Stork any weekday this coming week." A waiter accompanying him would hand you the invitation.

Or: "You have a bottle of Sortilège [a speciality of the club] coming to you." And the waiter would hand you the gift-wrapped bottle of this delicious French perfume.

And once in a big red balloon that I'd managed to snatch out of the air was: "Madame, you have won the first prize. Congratulations." I was led out to a vitrine in the foyer which contained five or six pieces of real jewelry and I chose a handsome and large gold-link bracelet.

While this was going on, the floor was cleared and the music was gaily playing. Lots of us would dance, others had chicken chow mein and a final drink. We used to get home disgracefully late, never before 3 A.M.

It was fearfully clever of Sherman Billingsley, the owner, for it was always jammed, while most nightclubs were deserted on Sunday night by 11 P.M.

Mr. Billingsley had some other smart tricks too. On each table was a small white card in a little stand stating that Table Hopping was Forbidden. Anyone who broke this rule was never allowed to enter the Stork again. There was a remarkably astute man by the name of Joe Lopez who stood in the foyer and knew who was welcome and who wasn't.

His boss was just as astute, and never forgot the people who were polite and well behaved. He had signals to the headwaiters. If he touched his left ear, possibly it meant: "Give those girls at table 22 each a gardenia corsage!" If he rubbed the side of his nose, it might be the signal to send a bottle of champagne to another table.

Debutantes were usually allowed to go to the Stork Club after somebody's big ball at the Ritz or wherever, mainly because their parents knew that they'd be looked after properly. I remember going there once after the coming out of a younger friend. There were three of us girls with five stags, and as I had known Mr. B. since the days when his nightclub was an excellent speakeasy, he thoughtfully sent over a bottle of champagne. One of the other two girls in our group, whose name was Mary Katherine, managed to get herself fearfully squiffed (plastered, we used to call it) in no time at all, and as she began turning pea green our captain and I took her to the ladies' retiring room (that's a new name for an extra-fancy rest room). He steered her firmly and inconspicuously into a little secret elevator, me following, and when we reached the second floor he put her into

the capable hands of a large experienced maid who told me to
return to my table and come back in an hour.

When I returned, Mary Katherine was lying on a chaise
longue sipping black coffee, and outside of looking pale, seemed
fine.

"She should go home right now," the maid said. "Mr. Billingsley has telephoned her apartment, and her mother is expecting
her, and Mr. Lopez will send her in the limousine." The maid
smiled knowingly and added, "This happens now and then." The
Stork Club certainly gave its clients T.L.C.

There were so many spots in 1940 and with so much variety
that it is hard to narrow the list down to a few favorites. Fifty-
second Street was almost solid night entertainment all the way
from Fifth Avenue to Eighth Avenue. I remember the Famous
Door and the place where Nat King Cole played the piano and
another where Maxine Sullivan sang. The names changed, and
the people moved from one place to another, but the variety
was unlimited. There were "racy" spots (the word "porno" was
unheard of), and there was every nationality: El Boracho, Ruby
Foo's, a Russian spot called the Yar, etc., and featuring everything from singing waiters to spots where bells rang when someone pulled the chain in *le petit endroit* (that's French for you-
know-where). There were also the huge ballrooms ranging from
the ten-cents-a-dance types to the elegant ones with the big-name
bands: Harry James, Tommy Dorsey, Glenn Miller, and dozens
more.

But these night spots were mostly for the out-of-towners.
Where did we go, we who lived here? Besides the beloved Stork
Club there was a more sophisticated counterpart, John Perona's
El Morocco, or its nickname, Elmo's. And there were the supper
clubs. A typical evening on the town might be dinner at "21,"
also known as "Jack and Charlie's." It is still at 21 West Fifty-
second Street, just as it was back in 1930, when it was a speakeasy
(the best) known as the Puncheon Club. The food and service
has always been triple A, and always will be, I hope. After dinner
we might taxi up to a nightclub at 480 Park Avenue known as
Larue's, where a small but excellent orchestra led by Eddie Davis

played gorgeous dance music, and the place was usually filled with stags and old friends. Then for a change we would move on to the Ruban Bleu, a supper club not too far away. Here there was no dancing, but background music by the Norman Paris trio, as I remember, piano music by Julius Monk, and every once in a while a song or a funny monologue or act. The entertainment was continuous, the air was blue with smoke, waiters squeezed through the little empty spaces all evening with their trays of drinks.

This was Café Society—staying up all night and restlessly moving from place to place? Dressing up in full evening regalia and sitting *à deux* at a specially reserved banquette here and a ringside table there, and ending up joining friends for supper at a table for eight somewhere else? Yes, generally speaking, that was what was called Café Society. Why did we do it? What was the big idea?

It resulted from a combination of circumstances, I think. We were the first generation to move from the big old stately mansions into smaller houses or apartments. When I was a little girl most of the children that I knew and played with in Chicago and New York, for example, lived in houses on the South Side in Chicago, or in New York on Riverside Drive or somewhere along Fifth Avenue. By the time I was graduating from Spence these families had nearly all moved to Park Avenue into apartments like the Avignon and Sherry's from East Forty-eighth Street up, and in Chicago they were switching to Lake Shore Drive and North State Street.

What was the reason for this change? Cost mostly, even for the rich. Lots of these town houses had stables attached to them and carriage houses, usually with quarters for the coachman and his family. With the advent of the automobile there was too much extra space. A stylish new compact apartment with lower maintenance and no taxes and the family limousine resting comfortably in the rented stall of the neighborhood garage, became the new life style.

With the exception of some enormously rich families, almost all of the apartment owners needed fewer servants. In most cases gone were the billiard rooms and the recreation rooms and play-rooms, to say nothing of guest rooms and sewing rooms and con-servatories. This in turn changed our generation's life style even more. If the parents were having a dinner party, for instance, the children presented a problem: Where did they eat? What could they do with them? As we grew older, very often we were taken out. We ate supper in the Mary Elizabeth Tearoom or the Woman's Exchange Restaurant, and our chaperone or our gov-erness took us to the movies afterward.

When we began having dates with boys it was perfectly natu-ral for us to *go* somewhere. We were all used to it. Conse-quently, those of us who could afford to ended up by dining out in good restaurants as often as possible, as well as staying out dancing and being entertained.

When I first moved to New York from the Middle West I was single and unattached and had decided to live in New York per-manently; it was more interesting (GW lived there!) than Chicago and I'd always loved it anyway, so I found an apartment at the Hampshire House, a brand-new hotel in those days, hand-somely decorated by Dorothy Draper, and moved in.

After I'd unpacked and settled in, hired a dog walker for Wil-bur, my blond cocker spaniel, and bought some bar equipment and flower vases and put cigarette boxes and silver-framed pho-tographs around, I went up to East Sixty-third Street to see my friend Newby Murray, who was laid up in bed, there being something wrong with his right leg.

After we had exchanged greetings and he'd told me of his health and how he'd he laid up for several months, he gave me some excellent advice, for which I've always been grateful.

"You don't know enough people in New York, men in partic-ular, to have a good time," he told me. "To go out every night of the week, or at least to be *asked*, requires knowing dozens of men, literally dozens."

I nodded. "You're right," I said, "but what good would it do me even if I did know dozens? Girls do not call up eligible bach-elors and say, 'I'm in town, honey, and how about taking me out tonight?' You and my cousins Johnny Hamilton and Rudy

Montgelas are the only men that I know well enough to call; anyone else I wouldn't dare."

In those days girls who telephoned men were considered fresh, pushy and gauche.

"You men are lucky," I added. "If you want to go out on the town, you reach for the telephone. We ladies get to sit and stare at it hoping that it will ring."

"When I am bored with all the girls I know and want to meet someone new and fascinating, do you know what I do?" he asked.

"I suppose you telephone a pal and ask him to get you a blind date," I suggested.

"Certainly not," he replied. "I do just what I expect you to do also. I go to a cocktail party. That is how I meet attractive new girls. That's why all the guys I know go and stand around at those things."

He looked at me very seriously. "Go to cocktail parties *at once*. Even if it's one given by your Great-uncle Moses or your old Latin teacher. You can never tell who will be there. Stand in the center of the room, don't hobnob with the other girls, stay by yourself, and look elegant and interesting. I always go up to a single girl who looks that way, and if it turns out that she actually *is* elegant and interesting, I ask her to have dinner with me."

I said that I'd give it a try and he added a further suggestion: "Wear something that attracts attention or can start a conversation."

"Something like Salvador Dali's pet ocelot?"

Newby shook his head. "Nothing dramatic. Something nice that could receive a compliment. Perhaps a sort of trademark that you'd be known by. There's a young married lady called Tokyo Payne who goes out a great deal dressed in oriental style. This is an extreme, but as she is short with dark hair, it is becoming, and she is always getting mentioned in Cholly Knickerbocker's column." He smiled and gave me a wink. "Just think! Being in the *American* in his column or mentioned by Walter Winchell or Mark Hellinger is what everyone in Café Society hopes for. It's the ultimate, better than being seen sitting at those front tables at the Colony while having lunch or dining at the Plaza's Terrace Room on the first terrace."

We both laughed, and I remember thinking how silly I thought "Café Society" sounded. My mother would have been amused and puzzled, for how could *society*, or rather people *in* society, attend functions in public places where everyone else could come too?

Yet they did exactly that, and some of these "beautiful people" acquired so much notoriety that their names became household words. Everyone knew Brenda Frazier and Shipwreck Kelly, and if they were seen dancing at the Monte Carlo, then the Monte Carlo became jammed. The same went for the Orson Munns, Jerome Zerbe, Mrs. Harrison Williams and Mrs. Julien Chaqueneau and I don't know *who all*. Some of these even employed press agents to see that they were constantly kept in the public eye.

Meanwhile, back to the lowlier members of this society, or perhaps the lowliest, how did the cocktail-party circuit that I embarked on work out? The answer is: *magnificently*. Mr. Murray's advice was superb, and it wasn't more than a few weeks before I was buying a larger engagement book, more white gloves, and more satin evening slippers.

I had been to perhaps four or five cocktail parties before I discovered one essential addition that contributed to the success of any female member of Café Society, something that Mr. Murray wouldn't have anticipated: I needed to arrive on the arm of an escort.

At the first cocktail party of all, I had gone with a married couple. I was dressed as elegantly as possible in a black Jane Derby trimmed all around the edges with a border of narrow black lace. My conversation starter was a so-called cabbage rose: real pink rose petals from three roses, and wired together in some way so that it looked like one big full-blown sweet-smelling rose, pinned to my shoulder. I had a jolly time, met some nice people, including a gent that I'd met a year before who asked me to dine with him. I said fine, but just then up came the couple, who insisted that they were expecting me to dine with them and it all became very awkward. "We asked you first!" "Oh, but really—" Etc.

What we did I've forgotten, but I resolved to go to the next one by myself. This was worse. It was a small affair and when it grew late I had a terrible time, with nearly everyone there offering to take me home or suggesting that we all go somewhere together.

After trying again, this time sneaking in late and trying to leave unnoticed in a large group, the hostess stopped me and told me that I couldn't leave. Would I please stay and have a bite to eat and make a fourth at bridge? At another similar affair almost the same kind of thing happened. People feel sorry for the single girl, and the nicer people are, the more awkward the departures become. Never again would I come alone was my next resolution.

Two days later I had an inspiration: Ted Peckham, the founder of the first New York escort service. After explaining my troubles to him on the telephone he agreed to supply me with an assortment of male escorts for any and all functions as needed. He even opened a charge account for me so that no embarrassing money would cross any palms.

"What if my escort gets drunk, Mr. Peckham?"

"Never fear. My boys are only allowed to drink one weak highball at a cocktail party, and one highball an hour if it is an evening affair. Remember, they are at work and will lose their jobs if they don't obey orders."

It turned out that three young men took turns being the escort, and they were all polite and nice-mannered with dark suits and short crew-cut hair. They cost $7.50 per cocktail party, a flat fee whether they stayed and took me home or not. They were $10.00 in a dinner coat and $15.00 in a white tie with an extra charge per hour after 11 P.M.

After we became friends the things that I learned about the escort business still continued to fascinate me. Movie stars, for instance, had big and steady accounts, usually arranged for by the star's agent. When Sonja Henie, the blond ice skater who turned into a movie star, appeared in public she dressed exactly as the beautiful blond snow-and-ice queen should look, always in white sparkling dresses, trimmed with ermine and usually crowned with a diamond tiara. She was always the only girl accompanied by five or six gallant and handsome men, all in full dress. Mr. Peckham's boys loved her and the glass of champagne each hour.

Other movie queens came from Hollywood and did the same thing, hired several of them, but none of them were as friendly and nice as Sonja or as lavish with the champagne or danced as well. Furthermore, she liked to go to the Hotel Commodore and dance to Benny Goodman's music besides being seen at the Empire Room and the Persian Room and the other proper places.

Mr. Peckham's boys had one job that they all loathed: the lonesome older "grass widow" as divorceés were often called. These women were perfectly awful, especially if they were loners. Mr. Peckham tried to be very careful not to do business with many of this type who had established a bad reputation. Some had already become drunk in nightclubs, and the maîtres d'hôtel tipped off Mr. Peckham. With many, however, the escorts learned by experience and Mr. Peckham listed them "X" and soon had a well-filled little black book. Two or three lonesome well-to-do middle-aged widows signing up for two or three escorts was different. They usually went to a merry but corny place like Bill's Gay Nineties or the Hawaiian Room in the Lexington Hotel and spent a happy nostalgic evening enjoying the singing waiters or the hula maidens as they sipped a glass of ginger ale or Aloha Punch.

For the rest of the year I used the escort boys, at first two or three times a week, then less and less as I began to know more people. However, for a long time afterward I used to see them with other clients and we would wave and shout merrily the way old friends do. Later on, when spring arrived, I was invited to Long Island for the weekend and who did I run into at some cocktail party in Westhampton but Mr. Burns and Mr. Gregg, both from Peckham's. This time it turned out they were not escorting a soul, they were honored guests. It seems that they were both struggling young lawyers in the same firm, and to make extra money worked as escorts several evenings a week.

Back to Café Society again, is there any advice that I can give besides recommending the escort service for the single maiden of today? Of course there is, first of all what to do in a nightclub when in a dilemma. What, for example, if you are tired and want to go home and everyone else at your table is bright and tiddly and full of pep? The quick way is to get up from the table, saying that you are off to the ladies' room. Leave the place at once, telling the maître d' that you went home, should anyone ask.

What if you are out with a man who gets taken unexpectedly drunk, passes out cold even? The answer is the same: tell the maître d' and go home. I've had this same thing happen just recently. A friend of mine from the Middle West was in New York about six months ago and asked me and GW to dine with him. GW was away, so I met Jim alone at a restaurant that he suggested.

He was sitting at the bar when I arrived, greeted me enthusiastically, and announced that he was celebrating the fact that only two hours ago he had sold his company to one of the large tobacco companies, and that he was not only rich but also free and retired. He was also drunk, and before he'd even had a bit of his crab-meat cocktail he slid off the banquette and was out cold on the floor.

Off I went to the maître d', who said that Monsieur was an old client of theirs and that he knew his credit-card numbers and not to worry. He also asked if Monsieur was not stopping as usual at the Waldorf, which I knew to be true, whereupon he bade me adieu and said to leave everything to him, that even now Monsieur was almost on his way to the Waldorf.

What if you have a late date with a dream man? How can you get rid of the early date gracefully? You can pretend to be coming down with the flu and send him off feeling sorry and sympathetic, but the chances are excellent that no matter where you and the dream man go, the early date will be sitting at the next table. There is nothing you can do except tell it to him like it was, as pleasantly as possible.

Once I had a cocktail date with a British man named Reginald Brackenbury. I was to meet him at the Plaza in the main lobby at

7 P.M. At 8:30 I had a date with GW, who at this point was rapidly on his way to becoming Numero Uno in my books. I sat waiting in the lobby of the Plaza until almost 8 P.M., but Mr. Brackenbury never appeared, so rather crossly I wandered over to Chez Nino's, where I was to meet GW, and sat listening to Rudy Timfeld play the piano until GW appeared.

"How was your cocktail date?" was the first thing that he asked me after we'd exchanged greetings.

It would have been nice to have given a dazzling smile and the word "great," but instead I said, "I was stood up." Thank heavens I did, for two hours later the man came up to me in the Club Eighteen and said, "My dear, where *were* you? I waited and waited at the Plaza, and you never came." It turned out that he had seen a large "P" on the canopy of the Hotel Pierre and thought it was the Plaza.

Several years before this, and this will be the last advice for the last dilemma, sister Barbara and I and three friends of ours (Princeton, 1929) from Washington, D.C., were invited to dine and go dancing with a very correct New York girl named Jane Van Cortlandt. We had dinner at her apartment, as I remember, and afterward she announced that she was taking us to a most exclusive club located on the top of the Hotel Pierre. It would be filled with the top social elite of New York and, of course, she realized that we wouldn't know anyone there, we being from Iowa and other places. We were not to worry, however, she would see that we were properly introduced, so that hopefully a few stags would cut in on Barbara and me, and our boys could also circulate.

We all squeezed into her smart little dark-blue limousine, driven by her very own chauffeur, and timidly arrived at the club's large ballroom. Before we even reached our table we were greeted by joyful shouts from people at tables along the way. Between the five of us we must have known half the crowd there. Friends from Lake Forest were at one table, a whole bunch from Washington at another, Vassar and Farmington and Princeton were represented everywhere. We all had the pleasantest evening possible except poor Miss Jane, who knew nobody but us, her hick guests from the sticks.

I hope that she learned something from her evening with us. At any rate, we said goodbye to her at the Pierre and off we went to a supper club, where we stayed for hours drinking champagne and talking.

Why they were called supper clubs we'll never know. I never saw anyone even eat a cracker in one, ever. However, I remember sitting in the Ruban Bleu in June 1940, just after Paris fell to the Nazis, and heard Jerome Kern's song "The Last Time I Saw Paris" for the first time, sung by a most elegant blond soprano (I forget her name), and how we were all stunned by it. We were with our French cousin, a refugee from St.-Rémy-les-Chevreuses (near Versailles). The Germans had occupied her villa there in May, she had fled to Marseilles, and had just arrived in New York. I think that she went to the Ruban Bleu every night for weeks after that just to hear the song.

There were always so many good entertainers there: I can particularly recall Casper Reardon, who plazed jazz on the harp, things like "Ain't Misbehavin'" and "I Can't Get Started with You." Then there was Bruz Fletcher, a crazy little man who sang "Just Bring Me a Lei from Hawaii" (I've wanted a lei for so long) and other spicy ballads. Greta Keller sang her lovely Austrian songs there, and Paula Lawrence her mad, mad songs, and Los Indos, four Incas in magnificent war paint, sang and played their strange instruments, and many others, thanks to Mr. Monk and his excellent taste.

War clouds were everywhere, in the Near East, Norway, and in early 1941 the terrible bombing of Coventry. I remember about this time GW saying to me that we were going to be in the war too, it was just a matter of time, and that he was going to Washington and volunteer for a job in the U. S. Navy, preferably in the Bureau of Naval Personnel. This he did, before the end of the year, but nothing about it changed our life, at least for a while. He wore no uniform, and worked in an office just across Park Avenue from the former office of his advertising company, and I remember that we celebrated the change by going to see

Ethel Merman in *Panama Hattie,* and then to the Persian Room, and on to a nightclub called Café Society after.

If I could go back to that dazzling year for just one day, where would I go and what would I see? First of all, I would get up and put on my best black Jane Derby dress, add a string of pearls, some white gloves, and don my new jacket: a hip-length affair made of platina fox, a gray mutation fox that was not only the latest thing but also warm and furry. Then I would lunch at Chambord's, a French restaurant with delicious food, over on Third Avenue under the old elevated tracks.

Then I would go to see Greta Garbo in her new movie *Ninotchka;* or perhaps if it was Wednesday, a matinee day, I'd go to see Grace George in *Kind Lady* (arrr-what a play that was). Then I'd hurry home, catch the latest war news on the radio while dressing for dinner. It would be a white-tie full-dress affair, and GW would have thoughtfully sent a small corsage of the latest thing: a spray of little green orchids, which I would pin on the right shoulder of my long white silk Fortuny dress. With this dress, I would wear my new glass slippers. They weren't glass, really, just clear plastic and probably the same thing that is now used to hitch together six beer cans, but in 1940 shoes made of this were "the cat's meow," and in the Lucite heels of each, a little artificial forget-me-not was imbedded.

We would dine in the Irridium Room (now the King Cole Bar) at the St. Regis while watching a small ice show or a dance team known as the Del Marcos, perhaps with three or four other couples, and then on to a small dance to which we'd all been invited at the Crystal Room in the Hotel Ritz (it used to be at Madison Avenue and Forty-sixth Street). The orchestra would be Meyer Davis' or maybe Eddie Duchin's or Emil Coleman's and it was the most beautiful room in which to dance or just *be.* Its chandeliers and fluted gold columns and marble walls gave all of us an air of great elegance too.

After that we might have gone up to the Cotton Club in Harlem, or down to the Hotel Bervoort in the Greenwich Village area. Thinking about how late it would have been makes me feel worn out, but before I would have folded up I still wouldn't have minded a final nightcap at our favorite spot, the Stork Club.

Our friend Finis Farr had, years before, written an article for *The Saturday Evening Post* saying very nice things indeed about Sherman Billingsley and his Stork Club, and why it was so successful. I remember that among the reasons he gave was that each table at which customers were sitting must always look as if they had just sat down: clean ashtrays, spotless linen, no empty glasses waiting to be taken away, fresh flowers, and also spotless waiters. The article also mentioned that the rooms were redecorated every few months. The dance room would be blue for spring, while the Cub Room would be all in gold, and upstairs the Blessed Event Room (that was for private parties) would be in green and white stripes. By summer it would be all different. Mr. Farr's sketch had made him and all of his friends very welcome at the club ever since.

The Stork Club has, of course, long been closed now and Mr. Billingsley has died. A place like the Stork Club probably couldn't exist today, but a very nice thing has come about on the spot where it used to be. William S. Paley bought the property, the building was torn down, and Mr. Paley, in memory of his father, turned it into a little park. Should you walk along Fifty-third Street between Fifth and Madison avenues, you will see people sitting at the tables there, enjoying green shrubs and trees, the pretty waterfall and the pleasant atmosphere.

✑ 12

City Hall

WORLD WAR II CAME to the United States with the bombing of Pearl Harbor on December 7, 1941. It was like any other winter Sunday, as GW and I lunched at the Harvard Club with my godmother Aunt Bessie Campbell and her son Douglas Campbell. After lunch GW said for me to go along home; he thought he'd stop at the office for a moment to see if all was well. That was the last time that he had time to speak to me for almost a week. When he reached the office no one was there, but all the telephones were ringing and red lights were flashing on the Washington Hot Line. Japan had attacked us.

Our life changed with a bang. Having a husband who arose at dawn's early light and sometimes didn't come home at all was mighty different, and I, along with most of the other ladies of New York who had the leisure time, dropped all social activities and went to work for the AWVS: The American Women's Voluntary Services.

A week and a day after Pearl Harbor found me working as one of Mayor La Guardia's receptionists down in New York's City Hall. When I went to the AWVS office to volunteer my services, the lady who interviewed me turned out to be a friend of a friend, and she sent me down to City Hall in a station wagon with five or six other volunteers, telling me that the Office of Civilian Defense had telephoned a few minutes before and asked for some AWVS women to work in City Hall.

I hadn't seen City Hall since boarding-school days, and hardly knew where it was located, but I did remember that Mayor La Guardia was known as "the Little Flower," that he was supposed to be an excellent mayor and was about to serve his third term, and that he was very short, was crazy about music, and liked to go to fires. But whatever did he want us girls for and how could we help at a place like City Hall? It all seemed silly to me.

A half hour later I changed my mind. When we arrived at City Hall a uniformed woman police officer met us in the rotunda and conducted all of us (some coming from Brooklyn, Queens, and other areas, forty in all) upstairs to a room that is used by the City Council. There we were all given Civilian Defense uniforms of gray-blue covert cloth, with caps to match, and when dressed in them were marched down and into the Mayor's big high-ceilinged office, and were arranged in a big wide circle curving around his desk. As we stood there feeling self-conscious in the strange new uniforms, he appeared from out of nowhere, and made the best little speech I've ever heard.

"Those of you who came to have a look at New York's Mayor may now leave," he said, standing short and dark and businesslike, yet good-naturedly, in front of his desk, and turning from left to right for all of us to see him, "as well as those of you who are planning to go down to Florida later on this winter, and you ladies with small children that require daily care won't fit in here.

"We're at war, as you all know. City Hall has always been run by members of the police force, but now there is danger in the city and the police are needed elsewhere. Our tunnels and bridges must be guarded, there are possibilities of air raids, sabotage, even attacks from submarines and unmanned missiles.

"You women are desperately needed to run City Hall at once." He paused and looked us over carefully. "How many of you have a college degree?" he asked. There were seven of us who raised our hands. "I will take these ladies for my own office," he said. "The rest of you will be divided among the other offices in the building, Mr. Stone, my executive secretary, the City Planning Commission, the City Council offices, and Captain Harten of the police head office."

Then he said in Italian, "How many of you speak Italian?" I raised my hand excitedly. Then he asked the same thing in Yiddish and got a hand from a Mrs. Felder. "I will take these two ladies for my appointments, getting each person in and out of my office according to schedule." He turned to us. "Lieutenant

Stoffers, my aide, will help you, also Miss Schwartz here, who with Captain Harten is responsible for my appointments."

I've forgotten what else he said now, but we all became his fans. Then he shook hands all around, thanked us for coming, and disappeared as quickly as he'd come.

I went back uptown later with Betty Felder, who lived in an apartment near ours, and we decided to team up and help each other learn the names and faces of the people who would be seeing His Honor. At this time, GW had a Chrysler limousine driven by an affable chauffeur named Tony, and Betty and I drove down to Lower Manhattan every morning, side by side in the back seat. Our conversation probably went something like this:

"Betty, who is the Fire Commisioner?"

"He is Patrick J. Walsh," she answered, and then she said to me, "What does he look like?"

"He's large, has a red face, quite bald, and speaks with an Irish brogue," I replied, and added, "Who is Stanley M. Isaacs?"

"He's a Borough President," she said. "Queens?"

"No, I think he's Manhattan." Then we'd look in the Little Green Book to make sure.

"Manhattan," Betty said. "Describe him."

"He's dark, with a mustache, and gray hair at his temples. He wears a tweed overcoat. Now you tell me the Police Commissioner."

"That is Lewis Valentine," Betty answered. "Who is Commissioner Wilson?"

"He is the Commerce Commissioner or is it Taxes? He's good-looking too. Who is the Treasurer?"

And we would both answer together, "Amerindo Portfolio!"

He was our favorite, both because of his name and because of his courtly manners. I used to see him frequently, dining in the Oak Room bar at the Plaza. He was charming.

By the end of two weeks we were doing a good job, and knew the regular appointees like Comptroller McGoldrick and Billy Rose (chairman of I-Am-an-American Day) and Mr. Arthur Wallender, who was going to be a special Commissioner of Defense. We also knew the five Borough Presidents and greeted them politely with "Good morning, Mr. President," as well as the other VIPs: Commissioner Feeley (Markets), Dr. Gonzalez (the Coroner), and Judge Lefkowitz.

We also had to know where to send people who wanted a copy of a birth certificate (126 Worth Street) and where to get a marriage license or even where to get married. That was easy, for Mayor (that's what we all called him, just Mayor) married anyone free of charge himself in his big beautiful room right there in City Hall every Saturday at high noon. There were many couples who took advantage of this, and he performed a very dignified and touching ceremony each time. He ended with a word of advice about it taking two to argue, and that mates should *respect* each other always. Then he gave them his blessing, and added that his marriages had a reputation of lasting forever, and for them never to let him down.

About this time food rationing began to be talked about. I've forgotten when it went into effect, but it was considered *dastardly* to hoard.

At the entrance to Mayor's quarters was a gate that opened electronically (by us Civilian Defense ladies) and every day there always appeared a few crackpots who insisted on seeing His Honor, for some very important reason. Whoever was on gate duty would explain that Mayor La Guardia saw people by appointment only, and to please write a letter, stating the reason for the interview, etc., etc. This usually worked well, but there was one case of a woman from Brooklyn who came every day, and begged us to let her in for just a moment to see the Little Flower, that she couldn't confide in anyone else, and she was in great trouble in her home over in Brooklyn.

Finally we got nice understanding Lieutenant Charlie Stoffers (our boss, really) to talk to her, and he in time persuaded her to tell him her problem, swearing that he would act as a go-between.

Imagine what it turned out to be: Mrs. Pezzogrosso, for that was her name, had been doing a large amount of hoarding; in fact, her basement was stacked with canned foods of all kinds. Knowing that the Little Flower would be sympathetic because they were both Italian, she had come to tell him that her cellar had been flooded by a broken water pipe and now the labels had all washed off the cans, and she couldn't tell what was in any of them. Charlie got rid of her by telling her that Mayor was born in Arizona and brought up in New York and his mother was Jewish and that the only way to find out what was in the cans would be to consult the American Can Company or the Continental Can Company, suggesting that they might have a secret marking on them telling what was inside.

The variety of the people who came to City Hall was amazing. I remember one day when Virgil Thomson, the composer, came and sat in a corner of Mayor's office all one day. He was composing a tone poem about him, and needed to feel the City Hall atmosphere. Madame Chiang Kai-shek was there, cardinals and admirals and boys' choirs, and graduating nurses from Bellevue Hospital, and even four jeeps loaded with soldiers who drove up the steps of City Hall (simultaneously) to bring greetings to Mayor from the commandant at Fort Dix. (They ruined the steps, too.)

The most popular visitor who ever came to City Hall was former Mayor Jimmy Walker. The word would get around that he was coming, and everyone who worked there flocked around to listen to him. He had charm, all right, and was funny too.

Monday, February 9, 1942, was terribly cold, about ten above, and it was a busy morning at City Hall with appointments coming and going. Each one lasted for fifteen minutes, unless otherwise noted, and if someone overstayed, Mayor got up and walked out himself (through his private door).

He also had a trick which hurried the appointments. He turned up the thermostat and the room became broiling hot. Then he took off his coat, put his glasses on the top of his head, and nodded for one of us to bring the victim or victims in. Besides this, the chairs that his guests sat in all tilted forward a little (the front legs have been sawed off an inch or two) and this made sitting somewhat of a strain.

On this cold afternoon, Mayor's office was 85 or 90 degrees and he was meeting with some judges. Suddenly, the ticker-tape machine started ticking. It was the Fire Department's, and as the tape rolled out I picked it up and read: "2:30 P.M. S.S. *Lafayette* on fire Pier 90." Our mayor liked to be notified at once of all important fires, but the *Lafayette?* I'd never heard of it. Then *crash*, it dawned on me the *Lafayette* was the *Normandie*, the biggest ocean liner (83,423 tons) afloat. When France fell, the United States had taken it over and it was being made into a troop ship.

I tore the tape off, pasted the message onto a white card, then walked quickly to the coat room, got my coat and hung it over the railing by the electronic gate, and signaled to Tony, who was waiting in the rotunda with several other chauffeurs, that I would be leaving in a few minutes. Then I alerted friend Betty, who ran for her coat, while I tiptoed into the side entrance of Mayor's office, approached his desk, and put down the little card. He pulled his glasses down and read the message, stood up at once, and marched out, saying over his shoulder that he'd be right back. I stood aside while he strode out, picking up his large black ten-gallon hat on the way, slamming it on his head (he never wore a top coat), and jumped into his little blue two-seater squad car, with his chauffeur John Peluso at the wheel.

However, it wouldn't start. Meanwhile Betty and two gentlemen from the press (there was a newsroom just to the right of the main door in the rotunda) and I had piled into the Chrysler and were pulling away when Mayor hailed us. He jumped into the front seat, turned to me, and said, "What is your driver's name?" "Tony," I replied, and he said, "Thank you, if you don't mind I'll tell him how to get there."

All the way up the West Side Highway at seventy miles an hour (or better) we careened, with headlights blazing, and horn blowing, and Mayor yelling, "Faster, Tony, dammit. Faster, Tony, dammit. Faster," into Tony's right ear.

We arrived before the Fire Department, before anyone else, and sure enough there was the great ship with flames flickering inside, we could see an orange glow from the whole long line of portholes. Mayor marched up the gangplank and went right on board. Betty and I followed, but never got there, as Fire Commissioner Walsh arrived just then and dashed past us, almost knocking us flat.

After that, fire boats, fire engines, and police cars thundered up from every direction, and cars containing Admiral Adolphus A. Andrews, Commander of our Third Naval District, and the Port Authority Commissioner. The four men (almost like the Charge of the Light Brigade) stood on the burning deck arguing furiously.

Admiral Andrews announced that he was in charge, as the ship belonged to the Navy; Commissioner Walsh said that it was his responsibility, seeing that it was on fire; Port Authority Commissioner McCloskey said that he was in charge because the ship was in his port; and Mayor said he was in charge.

It was so cold that Betty and I went back and sat in the car, watching workmen climbing down a rope ladder to Twelfth Avenue from the bow of the ship. By 4 P.M. everyone seemed to be off the ship, and it was obviously beginning to list to port. The fire boats got the fire under control at 6:30 P.M., but there was so much water inside that it finally tipped over at 3 A.M., February 10, and lay there depressingly black and quiet, its three huge smokestacks just touching the water. It lay there for weeks.

What happened to this 83,423-ton ship that was supposed to be able to transport 15,000 troops to the battlefront? Salvage work began in the spring, but it was not until October 1943 that she was righted and towed to the Brooklyn Navy Yard. There was talk of rebuilding the *Normandie*, but due to the lack of manpower and materials, the 60-million-dollar ship was finally sold for scrap in 1946 for the sum of $160,000.

City Hall was back to normal the next day, and so busy that Mayor had no time to eat his lunch. Usually one of us Civilian Defense girls would rush in with his chicken, lettuce, and tomato sandwich on a hamburger bun, and hot coffee (sent over from Schrafft's), and he would eat it in between appointments.

On this afternoon, among other visitors, Mary Pillsbury Lord arrived (the flour of Minnesota, as we used to call her when she came a-visiting in Cedar Rapids) in Mayor's office. She was the president of New York's Junior League at the time and I've forgotten the purpose of the call, but when she saw me (I came in just as she was leaving) she grabbed me in surprise.

"You!" she gasped. "What in God's name are you doing here?" Her voice carried clearly across the room.

"Quiet," I murmured. "I'm a Civilian Defense volunteer, that's all."

"We have much to catch up on," she said as I helped her into her coat. "How about lunching tomorrow?" I shook my head. "Then what about a drink with us Sunday afternoon?" We were outside by now, and arranged something. When I returned to the office, Mayor looked up and said, "I see that you know Mrs. Lord." I explained that we were old friends from the Middle West.

During the next hour some Washington officials had an appointment with Mayor, and among them was Mr. Ralph Bard from Chicago, who was then Assistant Secretary of the Navy.

As I was helping them out of their coats at the entrance, Mr. Bard said, "Hello, Mrs. Williamson, I was hoping I'd get to see you here. Your cousin Jim Douglas said you were working here, and sends his greetings, and love. Grace too."

After they had left, Mayor peered at me over the tops of his glasses.

"I see that you are a friend of our Assistant Naval Secretary. And I suppose you know the Undersecretary and Secretary Knox as well?" I remember turning the color of a ripe red tomato.

"It's a t-t-terrible coincidence, but yes I do," I stammered. "My husband works for Mr. Forrestal in Washington, and Frank Knox is from Grand Rapids, where my mother came from."

He nodded and pushed the button for Betty Cohen, his personal secretary. When she came in he said, "Betty, Mrs. Williamson will no longer bring me my lunch, tell one of the chauffeurs to do it instead."

"Gosh, Mayor," I said. "I don't mind the lunch a bit, it's a pleasure, and having the men do it will slow up the war effort, won't it?"

He didn't answer, but merely said, "So your husband is in Washington?" I replied that he came up Saturday night and went back Sunday evening, usually.

"You must find it lonesome during the week."

"Yes, but I'm so busy and I like my job so much that I manage." I smiled.

"You really like the job?" he asked anxiously.

I thought for a moment and then said, "When I wake up in the morning I say to myself, 'Thank God it's morning so I can get up and go down to City Hall.'"

He beamed with delight. Then he said, "Perhaps sometimes during the week if you're not too tired, would you go to an evening benefit with me, as my Civilian Defense Aide?"

"I'd be honored," I said.

April 10 was my first evening as Mayor's aide. Dressed in my freshly pressed best uniform, I met him at the Waldorf-Astoria, where the Norden Company of New York City received the coveted Navy "E" award ("E" standing for excellence) for their outstanding work in manufacturing the Norden bombsight, a top-secret device for dropping bombs with uncanny accuracy used by all the Allied bombers. As I recall, the various parts that made up the bombsight were all manufactured in small factories and machine shops in Manhattan, mainly in the garment district, and for a long time many of the employees had no idea what they were helping to make.

Now the bombsight had been made public, and here were all the employees sitting in the Waldorf ballroom, and on the flag-draped platform, with several admirals, the officers of the Norden Company, including Mr. Norden himself, several senators and commissioners, sat Mayor La Guardia, with me standing behind him as tall and military-looking as possible.

The whole evening was broadcast (live, of course, in that time) on station WNYC, and Mayor made an excellent speech, describing the big navy-blue flag with its white anchor and huge white "E" that would fly triumphantly over the Norden Company until the end of the war, given to the company by the grateful Navy, and saying that all New York was proud.

When the ceremonies were over Senator Alben W. Barkley of Kentucky came over to greet Mayor, and after shaking hands Mayor said, "Alben, I want to present you to my aide Mrs. Williamson."

Senator Barkley said politely, "How do you do, Mrs. Williamson. It is nice to meet you, and what a very handsome uniform you are wearing."

"It's the New York Civilian Defense uniform, and the Mayor chose them himself," I told him.

"I hope you will take good care of him," he said pleasantly as he took his departure. "You know, he's the best mayor New York has ever had."

Mayor winked at me and said, "He says that to all mayors."

There were all kinds of evening outings after that; I remember Mayor conducting the joint Fire and Sanitation bands at the old Metropolitan Opera House one evening, the bands in the orchestra pit, and Mayor waving his arms wildly while standing on the podium. And where was I? In the prompter's box, the little low place front stage center, watching a large group of GIs on stage singing "This Is The Army, Mr. Jones" (no private rooms or telephones). This was a Red Cross benefit, and the sort of thing that took place in Queens and Brooklyn and Staten Island, too.

As the war wore on, and increased in intensity, Mayor decided that he wanted to be a general in the Army, that he knew Italy well and could help immeasurably when and if the Allies invaded Italy. As a young man he had worked in the American consulates in Trieste and Fiume, and later had commanded troops in World War I on the Italian-Austrian frontier.

One day he had an appointment in Washington, and went down to see the Secretary of War with high hopes. He left by plane from brand-new La Guardia Field early in the morning, going straight to the airport from his own quarters. He telephoned from Washington later and said that he had been turned down flat and would somebody please meet his plane, and gave the arrival time.

"You will meet him!" Charlie Stoffers pointed his finger at me. "Any of the rest of us he would swear at, vent his spleen, throw things. He'll be awful mad, but you will keep him on better behavior."

"Gee, I feel sorry for you, Mrs. Williamson," said John Peluso as we drove away from City Hall in the squad car. And behind us were various staff members waving goodbye sadly.

I met the plane, nervous as a girl, and Mayor waved his hand when he neared the gate. Instead of being angry he was pathetic, and I felt like crying over his terrific disappointment.

"Well, I guess the only uniform I'll be wearing for the duration will be one from the New York Department of Sanitation," he said sadly. Then he stopped and turned to me.

"Henry Stimson gave me the greatest raking over the coals that I've ever had." His voice shook with emotion. "He told me to go along home and to forget that being-a-general business. Said my job was here, and not to bother him again."

"Mayor, I know just how disappointed you feel. What you need most of all right now is to have a drink with a friend. Will you have one with me?"

He nodded dumbly. We squeezed into the front seat of the squad car and went to the Hampshire House (where I was living) and sat in the little bar in a quiet corner while he tossed off two double scotches. "I don't like the taste much, but I certainly enjoy the effect," I remember him saying. We talked about music and how much we liked it, and then Commissioner Robert Moses (his closest friend) arrived and the two of them went off together, Mayor looking far less woebegone.

I was very fond of him in every way, and everyone who knew him felt the same way. However, after working in City Hall for over a year and a half, I began to realize that he was ill. I think he was in pain much of the time. And after the war, in 1945, all the Civilian Defense people who had worked for Mayor during the war gave a great big reunion party in a private room at the Waldorf, but alas for all of us, he never showed up. He had, it was revealed later, cancer of the pancreas, and he died in 1947.

ᥱ᥍ 13
War, Work, and Play

EARLY SEPTEMBER 1943 found me in Washington staying at the Carlton Hotel. I was house hunting, and was actually waiting in the lobby for a real-estate friend to come and pick me up.

Dressed in a red-and-white summer dress, I was standing at the reception desk leaving a message or something when I heard a voice say, "My goodness, it's Mrs. Williamson and what are you doing in Washington, and whatever have you done with Mayor La Guardia?" Standing in front of me was Senator Barkley.

I was speechless. I finally managed to gasp, "*How?* How do you *do* it? I-I-I'm not even in my uniform."

"My dear," he said, "it's my business." We shook hands, and I explained that I had left City Hall but would return should my husband go overseas.

He said, "Welcome to Washington," and off he went. (The next time I saw him he was President Truman's Vice-President and I've forgotten where it was, but he still remembered me and my name. He was fantastic.)

GW and I rented a little furnished house on Leroy Place and settled ourselves in Washington on a kind of month-to-month basis. The schools were crowded but Holton-Arms, a nearby private school, accepted our nine-year-old daughter.

It was heaven all being under one roof after nine months of constant commuting. Friends were turning up in Washington from all sorts of places, others were leaving. If you moved every time your husband was transferred it was known as camp following, and there was a lot of that going on. Washington was so crowded that strangers shared double beds in hotels, and friends who came to Washington cadged sofas in living rooms when they couldn't get into a hotel.

Actually, New York was almost as bad. At the Hampshire House, where I'd been living all spring, every apartment was taken, and some had even been converted into separate rooms. The manager, Vincent J. Coyle, an old friend of ours, complained bitterly one day about an eccentric old lady who had a large apartment up on Fifth Avenue somewhere in the Eighties or Nineties, and who also rented (by the year) an apartment with living room, dressing room, bedroom, and bath in the Hampshire House just in case she happened to get tired after shopping in the Fifties and wanted to stop in and rest and have a cup of tea: sort of an emergency stopping place, complete with a kitchenette too. I was horrified at such extravagance, and said so.

"We've written asking her to relinquish it, saying we'll even substitute a little studio apartment, but she doesn't answer," he complained. "She's only used the place twice this year so far. Oh yes, I forgot to say that she has *two* apartments in the Fifth Avenue building. One is for her, the other is really just a warehouse where she keeps her collection of oriental rugs."

The last had a familiar ring. GW and I turned to each other and said simultaneously, "Lillian Timken!"

"That's right," said Mr. Coyle. "Don't tell me you know her?"

"Indeed we do," my husband replied. "She is my aunt's best friend. We'll tell her to give it up at once."

"You're right about Mrs. Timken being eccentric," I said, "but she is also very kind and nice."

"Tell her how many young couples need a room for just a night or two: soldiers who are going overseas and may never get back, and young navy officers who are here for a short leave. She'd be God's gift to the Armed Forces as well as our room clerks."

Mrs. Timken gave the apartment up the next day, Mr. Coyle sent her some flowers, and we went back to Washington feeling like Boy Scouts who have done exceptionally good deeds.

At the end of 1942, the war became more dreadful and serious for us Williamsons. GW left for London early in January. It was a matter of the greatest secrecy and we left Washington ostensi-

bly going to New York for a business conference at the Third
Naval District. When we arrived we stayed at the Gotham
Hotel, and I went out at once with his best blue navy lieutenant's
uniform and overcoat, took it to his tailor and had the two gold
lieutenant's stripes and all the gold buttons taken off, and plain
black ones substituted, and bought a red and navy-blue foulard
necktie.

Then I shopped for flints (scarce in Britain), and extra batteries, and padlocks, and vitamin pills, while GW bought long lightweight woolen underwear at Abercrombie & Fitch, soap, woolly
socks, and a supply of ball-point pens.

To get all this into one footlocker took a lot of huffing
and puffing, but we managed, and I saw him bravely off at 8:45
A.M. on January 12, went back up the hotel steps after his taxi
disappeared and to the now lonely room, and tried to eat some
breakfast, but instead had a good cry. Just then the telephone
rang, and there was GW telling me that due to Atlantic weather
conditions (he was flying, and on a commercial airline) he'd had
a twenty-four-hour-reprieve and would be back from La Guardia
in a few minutes.

I powdered my nose happily, descended to the lobby, and he
was back at 9:30. We lunched in a dark corner of the Baroque
restaurant, and afterward he bought me a huge pale amethyst
ring in a pawnshop on Sixth Avenue as a present, and also as a
weapon. If any wolf got fresh, he said, it would be as useful as a
brass knuckle. Then we sneaked into the St. Regis for cocktails
and to a Broadway play called *The Doughgirls* (the first time I
ever saw Arlene Francis) and retired after a late visit to the Plaza
Oak Room bar.

The next day exactly the same thing happened: another
reprieve, due to the weather. It was wonderful, but agonizing,
and we spent another day ducking in and out of dark little bars
and restaurants, GW still in the sober dark civilian outfit that
make him look like someone's British valet on his day off.

The following day the black moment arrived, and he left as
usual at 8:45, but did not return. I went back to Washington on
the 4 P.M. train, feeling shattered and blue, and stayed that way
while I packed everything up and moved out of the nice little

house. It was very confusing, as the new tenants (also a navy couple) moved in at the same time I moved out. They had been evicted from their hotel, due to GW's delayed departure, and were most annoyed by me and my luggage right in Their Way, and in Their House.

Meanwhile my husband, I learned later, arrived safely in Bermuda, had a swim and spent the night there, and flew nonstop the next day to Portugal (a neutral country). When they neared the Portuguese coast their plane was surrounded by three Messerschmitts which flew as close to their plane as possible, with German soldiers inside glaring at them through their binoculars. Luckily our Bermuda passengers looked extremely neutral, and as their plane began the descent to the Lisbon airport, the Messerschmitts flew away. The next day he was in London, after an uneventful flight.

Back to the Hampshire House I went, driving the car myself because it was an efficient little Chrysler sedan (known as CarLar), the big limousine having been traded in and Tony having gone to work in the New London shipyard. I was arrested for speeding on the way. The speed limit all over the United States was thirty-five miles an hour (to save precious gas, which was now rationed), and I was clocked at thirty-eight miles an hour on an almost empty road in New Jersey. One result of gas rationing was that we all learned how to siphon gasoline from one gas tank to another. After accomplishing this mouth-to-rubber-tube starter-offer it was well to refrain from smoking for half an hour, and the gasoline taste was best combated by a swallow of dark rum.

It was less lonesome to be back in New York, and I returned to City Hall and worked there nearly every day. Everything in the way of food was getting scarce, and red stamps and blue stamps were being issued for rationing. Blue stamps limited the amount of canned goods that each individual could buy; red stamps limited meat and butter and fats. Coffee also became rationed, as well as sugar. Cigarettes were getting harder and harder to find. Finally shoes were rationed, and this was a real problem with a daughter who was ten years old and growing like a whole garden of weeds.

One of the hardest things for us civilians was *travel.* Trains were jammed with troops and so were planes. There was a priority system that worked from top VIP on down. If you were a five-star general, for instance, you carried a priority of A-1, which meant that you could "bump off" anyone from any plane or train except another five-star general.

The War Production Board assigned priorities, and many important businessmen had very high ones too. I imagine that Mr. Benjamin Fairless, who was president of Bethlehem Steel Corporation, carried an A-1 or A-2, and I know that Donald Douglas of Douglas Aircraft rated high.

Those of us housewives who worked at part-time volunteer jobs rated *zero,* and we rode on slow trains that stopped every few miles, and some of the cars actually were so old that they had gas lights and even wood-burning stoves. Most of us brought food along because the diners were so crowded; consequently, there were mice in the berths at night, which was worse than a Peeping Tom. I remember posters everywhere urging us to stay home and let a tired soldier on leave have your berth instead.

A friend of mine, Dougie Browning, who lived in Washington in the middle of the war, received a telegram from the boarding school in Texas where her son was, saying that he'd been seriously injured in some kind of a chemical explosion, and for her to come at once.

She dashed out to the airport as fast as she could, found that there wasn't a chance of her getting anywhere *near* Texas, in fact, she couldn't even get a space on a plane to Newark or Philadelphia.

Some marines overheard her and felt sorry for the plight that she was in. It seems that about thirty of them were leaving in a few minutes for Galveston, Texas (her son was nearby in Houston), and they decided to smuggle her on board with them. Luckily she is tiny and slim, and they marched onto the plane, two-abreast, with Dougie in between four marines, who were holding her firmly by her elbows in some way so that her feet weren't touching the ground. Aboard the plane she sat on the floor, with a marine jacket covering her when anyone passed by. She said they treated her wonderfully well, and after they hustled her off at some marine air base they found a station wagon that was going to Houston and she got a free ride in it all the way to the school.

Another thing that was hard to find in those strenuous days was liquor. All invitations to cocktail parties were BYOL (bring your own liquor) and it was quite fun swapping around. Once after returning to Cedar Rapids I remember going to something festive with a bottle of brandy. It was the only thing I had and I never drink it, but some people were so pleased to see brandy that I traded one shot of it for as many as two or three shots of Bourbon.

Iowa had (and still has) state-controlled liquor stores, and there were three or four of these in Cedar Rapids. One was on the wrong side of the tracks; that is, across the Cedar River in a poor part of town. To our joy we discovered that this delightful store had cases of Johnnie Walker Black Label for sale. It was incredible, as the store near Brucemore had nothing to offer for a while except sacramental wine, Dubonnet Blonde, and some gallons of California sherry.

The war news was depressing in most of 1943, and it looked as if it would be such a long, long war. I managed through the winter and the spring and the summer, spending most of the summer in Chicago, or rather in the guest house of my James Douglas cousins in Lake Forest, and all of a sudden one day late in August came a telegram from GW saying:

DARLING I AM LOOKING FORWARD TO A VERY HAPPY WEEKEND

That was all. Apparently it had said much more but it had been highly censored. Mail was so unreliable that I didn't think he knew where we were, but after reading the exciting ten words over twenty more times I decided that he couldn't possibly have a very exciting weekend except with Who Else But Me, and that we'd better get to New York at once, the day being Wednesday. By calling the Quaker Oats Company and talking to their man who arranges for company officials' transportation (I pulled wires, I did), we left in style on the Century that afternoon, and were installed in the Hampshire House Thursday, and sure enough he arrived Friday morning, and the weekend was a *rip-snorter*.

I remember we went to *Oklahoma!* and dined on steak at "21," where GW was greeted as "Commander," much to his delight, and went to a nightclub called the Monte Carlo, where he was addressed as "Admiral."

Then he went to Washington, and I commuted back and forth for two weeks, and then he was gone (complete with Christmas presents, including a red felt stocking to hang by a chimney with care).

The less said the better about the rest of 1943, and most of 1944. I was more lonesome than before, and moved to Cedar Rapids, teaming up with sister Barbara (whose husband was in Guadalcanal), and cousin Eleanor, who shared her house with us. Altogether there were twelve of us, including five children, three nurses, and a cook named Grace.

It was so *different* from Washington and New York. The war was as remote as the Wars of the Roses, there was meat, there was bacon, there was black-market gasoline around (no need to go to the War Ration Board to get gas for a long trip the way I'd had to in order to get to Iowa in Car-Lar).

Also, it was nice being among old friends again and we all managed to get along, and when spring came sister Barbara and I, and the children, moved to Pasadena, as her husband Gail, had returned from the South Pacific.

There I found myself a most interesting volunteer job with the Red Cross. It involved going to see the nearest of kin of all men from the Los Angeles area who were in prison camps in Germany. Each POW was allowed to receive one food package a month from the nearest of kin, but it had to conform to strict rules, otherwise it would be confiscated right in front of the poor prisoner. (The Red Cross learned this from a prisoner who had in some way escaped from Stalag 2.)

It was my job to call on each of these people (mostly mothers) and beg them to send ONLY what was allowed. It required great tact and friendly persuasion.

"My Johnny could never *stand* chewing tobacco, let alone cigarettes, how ridiculous can you get?"

"Mrs. Jones," I would answer politely, "even though he doesn't smoke himself, the prison guards do, and the cigarettes are very useful as a *bribe*." Then I added, "The chewing tobacco comes in a little sack and is prized for that."

Or this kind of thing:

"I don't understand why I can't send my son a big can of sardines, they are his favorite food. Also what's wrong with sending salt and pepper?"

"Surely you don't want him to have to stand and watch the package that you sent him with his favorite food be swept into the wastebasket right before his eyes?"

A shake of the head.

"Pepper is forbidden, as it is regarded as a weapon. Shaken into the eyes of a guard, it can blind him. This seems to have happened with great success at some point. Large tin cans can also be made into weapons. You can send a *little* can. They are allowed, and the boys have even cut them up to make Christmas-tree ornaments."

"Ball-point pens are forbidden. Instead, why don't you put in some pencils, of different colors?"

"Wrap the bottle of cough medicine in Kleenex and then add a roll of absorbent cotton around it. If the cough medicine is really straight Bourbon whiskey add a little artificial red or green coloring to make it look authentic, and get a real druggist's label for the bottle."

"Stick whole peanuts, in the shell, in all the nooks and crannies of the shoe box [that was the proper size allowed]."

It was fascinating. I've forgotten the ingredients now, but by sending some spools of thread, some paper clips, small tubes of a certain kind cardboard, and so on, a real live radio could be constructed by a prisoner, one that would pick up the Armed Forces Radio Network, and the POWs of Oflag prison 3, for example, could hear such cheering things as that Foggia had fallen to the Allied forces in Italy, and that the Russians had reached Kiev on the Dneiper.

The job was rewarding all right, and I felt that I was helping in my small way, but it was a ten-hour-a-day job. There was literally no gasoline available in Los Angeles area, so I went all over the map by bus. The time that I spent at bus stops waiting to get from Glendale to Burbank and from there to Torrance and then on to Redondo Beach and finally back to Pasadena was interminable, but I knitted things and read every scrap of newspaper that I could lay my hands on. The Normandy invasion had started on June 6, and that is about the only thing that I thought about when I was by myself.

There was one other thing that I knew about during the spring and summer of 1944 that is fascinating, to say the least. A Pasadena friend of mine had a husband who was also an officer in the Navy and also stationed in Britain, and he knew an officer in the Air Force who had the job of flying some very important general back to Washington, then was flying to the Los Angeles area to pick up a new part for the submarine *Blackfish*'s conning tower, which had been damaged in some way. There was room for Stan to go along, rather like a stowaway, only he actually had the nod from his commanding officer. This secret leave happened now and then and was known as "basket leave," the secret papers being in the bottom of the letter basket on the stowaway's desk, in case something went wrong and he never got back. When he returned, he threw the papers away, and no one was the wiser.

Stan telephoned his wife from Washington and told her that he would be in California on February 4, that it was *top secret* and if she told a soul he would be court-martialed, but that there was a motel between Glendale and Pasadena called the Mountain View, and for her to get a room there under the name of Mr. and Mrs. London, and wait for him there.

She promised to say nothing to anyone, of course, and went off at the appointed time saying that a girl friend was down from San Francisco and that she was off to Beverly Hills for dinner and the night.

She switched to a rented car after she left, and with dark glasses on and a scarf hiding her hair, she registered in at the Mountain View, almost expiring with excitement. Stan arrived, they spent a happy night together, and she arrived home the next day in time for lunch.

There was only one thing that made it complicated: she became pregnant. At first she hadn't worried about it, feeling that it was borrowing trouble and that the war news was getting better, and that Stan would perhaps be transferred to some post where she could join him and then pretend that the baby had arrived early.

When I turned up in California, she hadn't told anyone, or even seen her doctor. I mentioned something about GW almost getting a "basket leave" at one point, but then it had turned into a courier mission instead, and she broke down and told me her problem. Here she was, nearly five months along, what should she *do?* What *could* she do?

Stan and GW were both at sea, presumably off the coast of Normandy somewhere, neither of us had heard a word, no V-mails, no letters or cables, nor had anyone else. I remember that we had dinner together at Don the Beachcomber and talked about her problem until nearly midnight.

There was one thing that made it all right, we decided. She and Stan had done nothing wrong; therefore, she at least should pay a visit to her obstetrician at once. Ethically, doctors cannot talk and her secret would be safe with him, and Stan would approve of this too, and maybe the doctor would have a suggestion, such as hiding her away in a little infirmary in the foothills somewhere near, perhaps pretending that she had a mild case of—of—well, leprosy was the only thing that we could think of.

Her figure was still good enough to remain unnoticeable, but it wasn't going to last much longer. "Maybe you should start wearing painter's smocks tomorrow, and just keep a-wearing them," I suggested.

"I could say that I have some sort of a rash, poison oak maybe?" she said. Then she laughed. "My mother and sister Jane and everyone else in the family would become suspicious at once, and none of them can keep their mouths shut. It will get all over southern California in six hours flat."

"You could go to Cedar Rapids and spend the remaining four months with my cousin Eleanor. She would love the intrigue and would keep quiet, and probably even has a bassinet and a few baby carriages in the attic. That family never throws anything away," I said. "You know, it's not such a bad idea, that. Eleanor is also a very experienced nurse's aide. Do you know anyone in Cedar Rapids?"

"No," she replied, and we talked on and on. We finally decided that she should think about it for a few days, and that we would dine again the following Sunday night.

That was Wednesday June 21, and the very next day the strangest thing happened which indirectly affected Stan and Florence, and their weighty problem (no pun intended, I apologize).

I came home from Red Cross work about five o'clock, took a bath, and started getting dressed, for sister Barbara and her husband and I were going to a dinner party at seven.

Barbara and I were both in the dressing room discussing what to wear or something as mundane, when I suddenly had a great desire to play the radio. I can't explain it, but it was so strong that I hunted around the bedroom until I found a little portable one. To plug it in necessitated moving a big heavy chest of drawers, which I did, then I got down on all fours and plugged it in.

"What on earth are you doing?" Barbara asked.

"I don't know," I said truthfully. "Just thought I'd like to hear the radio." I felt sheepish as I turned on the switch, especially when all I got was a voice saying, "Ho-ho-ho, I'm Singin' Sam, the Barbasol Man," or some such inane thing. However, I left it on, and returned to get dressed.

Then Gail came into the dressing room in his handsome lieutenant commander's uniform, and as Barbara and I put on last touches of powder and lipstick, and were chatting away, we all three distinctly heard the words "Gregory Williamson" on the radio. We dashed out of the dressing room and stood huddled around the little radio. My first thought was that GW had been killed in the invasion and that they were announcing a memorial service for him. But the next voice we heard was another commercial, something about "Lucky Strike Green has gone to war . . ."

We were *wild*. I should add here that Gail and GW roomed together at Leland Stanford, and that I had met GW when he was best man in their wedding.

Finally a voice interrupted whatever was going on next, and said, "Ladies and gentlemen, we are waiting for a broadcast from London, an interview with Lieutenant Commander Gregory Williamson of the United States Navy, who has been on 'The Lucky T' [the cruiser *Tuscaloosa*] during the Normandy invasion. Please stand by until we can get a clear signal."

We were late for the dinner party but everyone cheered when we arrived. I was walking eight feet off the ground myself, and couldn't remember any of the broadcast or anything that he said, but he was safely back. And that also meant that Stan must be safely back too.

Florence, who was also at the dinner party, and I had a little chat in a corner after everything had calmed down, and she said she had decided then and there to write him, now that he was on dry land, and dump the whole matter in his lap.

She got a letter off the next day through a friend of ours, Commander John Hayward, and the letter was delivered to Stan in London the following day, and Stan went to his commanding officer and told him the whole story and guess what.

The nice commanding officer procured for Stan a "compassionate leave," which the Navy grants in an emergency, such as a death in the family or a tragedy of some sort or when somebody is in a jam like Stan and Florence. Stan arrived on Sunday and they politely asked me to dinner, as planned, and I refused, saying that I was starting to pack in case I would soon be returning to Washington.

As it was, GW didn't get back until late August. After a thirty-day leave, blissfully spent in Sea Island, Georgia, I found myself happily house hunting in jam-packed, overcrowded, war-rationed Washington.

With good luck it wasn't too long before we discovered a dear little brick house smack next door to the empty Japanese Embassy—just the place to walk our dog—and in no time at all the movers were carting all our scratched-and-marred worldly goods (fresh from two years in storage) into the house, and Bessie, our new all-time favorite cook, was unpacking pots and pans while taking little sips of tea laced with rum (sometimes in Bessie's case it was rum laced with tea).

"Madam"—Bessie was the formal type—"best if you'd find us a grocery store in the neighborhood, for soon I'll be wanting to telephone an order." I told her that I'd go over to Magruder's and establish credit, open a charge account at once.

"Madam." Bessie looked at me scornfully. "Better if you'd get us a smaller store. That Magruder sends all the best things to them embassies. We'd be lucky to get cat food from them."

"We'll be lucky to get any meat at all," I said, "we have so few red stamps. However, you're right. In a smaller store we'll be treated as more important customers. I will buzz over to Georgetown and find us something."

Bessie held up a hand in protest. "No, madam. Georgetown is also too fashionable. Go over to Columbus Avenue, find a privately owned grocery store where them big tall apartment buildings are."

She was right. I found a place there called Shapiro's Market and introduced myself to Mr. Shapiro himself, a dark harassed-looking little man in his thirties. "Sorry, we can't take any more charge accounts," he said promptly. "The bookkeeper will leave."

"Oh, come on." I gave him what I hoped was a dazzling smile. "Just one more account won't hurt her; besides, we'll be very good customers. My husband is just back from two years in Great Britain, where he ate nothing but brussels sprouts. He is hungry as a wolf. Also we know lots of people here and expect to have a lot of dinner parties."

A crafty look crossed Mr. Shapiro's face. "How much does your grocery bill usually run?" I had no more idea what any family grocery bill would run to than a horse. After three years of camp following and living in hotels and motels and visiting and moving I didn't dare even to guess.

Again I tried the dazzling smile, and then had a dazzling idea. "Our bill should be about the same as the Turkish Embassy's." I spoke casually. A flash of a gold tooth and the account was opened.

I explained that we would not be able to buy any rationed meat; the few red ration points that we had would have to be used for butter (our daughter had gone off to boarding school with extra red points from us at the request of the school). "But we don't care," I finished heartily. "We'll subsist on fish and oxtails and anything that you can supply." At his suggestion I left our pathetic little booklets of red stamps with the bookkeeper (Mrs. Shapiro), to be doled out when we needed butter, and returned to the new house to unpack barrels and hang pictures and read *Cluny Brown* by Margery Sharp in the coffee breaks.

A few weeks later, all settled in and acting like a native again, I was lunching at the Statler with a cousin from Akron who was in Washington on business. He worked for the Quaker Oats Company, at that time in the container division, and was all excited about a new package. "The Robert Gair Company," he volunteered, "has an experimental machine that can make a transparent rigid plastic box so cheaply that we are thinking of packaging puffed wheat and puffed rice and even rolled oats in them. The customer can see for himself what the cereal looks like—also can see the premium teacup or plate in the Mother's Oats package. What do you think of the idea?"

"The customer can also see a dead mouse or a boll weevil should there be one inside," I suggested. "I think it's a fine idea. Would it sell more oats?"

"We'd market-test it first and see," he said. "The Robert Gair people are of course wildly enthusiastic. If we decide to do it, they'd make a fortune."

I said I'd never heard of them. "It's an old company. They've made boxes and such for years and years. Their common stock sells on the Big Board—around five dollars a share or less."

"Let me know what happens," I said, and he said he would.

Later that afternoon found me in Shapiro's Market staring fixedly at a shelf towering with packages of Quaker Oats' Puffed Rice, trying to visualize them in the see-through box, and who should find me there but Mr. Shapiro.

"What can I do for you today—a little cereal perhaps?" he inquired.

I explained why I was staring, told him about the plastic box, and even mentioned the low-priced Robert Gair stock. He seemed interested and said he'd heard of the stock but never knew what it made. "Well, if the Quaker Oats Company does decide to use this transparent packaging, and if my investment man approves, I'm maybe going to buy some Robert Gair stock and make enough money to rent the Japanese Embassy," I told him.

"Let me know if you do," he said, and I saw the gold tooth gleam as he turned away.

The next time that I was in New York I asked Stu our investment counselor about the stock. "Listen," he said, "that's a terrible company. No matter what kind of an order they'd get or what kind of a package they'd turn out, they wouldn't make any money—they've been trying for years and years and nothing happens—leave them alone."

I promptly forgot about Robert Gair for several weeks until I noticed that the stock was going up. It crept quietly from 4½ to 5 one week, then maddeningly rose to 5½ the following week and 6 the next. I was so irritated by it that I resolved not to look at any stock beginning with "R" for the rest of the year. However, I couldn't help peeking now and then, and sure enough—there was old Robert Gair common selling at 7¼, and just before Christmas it went to 8.

Meanwhile, although I never did hear how many dinner parties the Turkish Embassy was giving, we were entertaining busily and I would guess that we were giving them stiff competition. With Bessie dreaming up tasty dishes in the kitchen, and an easygoing red-haired waitress named Lillian (oh, those broken dishes) in the dining room, and a cleaning man known as "Smelly James," who came the following morning, we had six or eight for dinner once or twice a week all that winter.

And all the time that the Allied forces under General Patton were marching nearer and nearer the Rhine, and General MacArthur's men were getting closer and closer to Manila, and our Russian allies were approaching Berlin mile by mile from the east, we in war-rationed Washington were eating better and better—we, in this case, meaning us and our guests—thanks to Shapiro's Market.

When Bessie ordered for a Saturday-night dinner party, she always telephoned on Friday. Mr. Shapiro himself took the order.

"We have a very nice five-rib roast of beef today," he would volunteer. "How would you like to have me send it over?"

"But our red points—can we afford it?" Bessie would ask.

"Now you just let me worry about that," Mr. Shapiro would answer unctuously. "And how are you fixed for butter? I'd better send you an extra pound."

At first Bessie and I worried ourselves sick—we were sure that we couldn't afford such extravagances—the Ration Board would be knocking on our door any day and we'd be hauled off to jail. But nothing of the sort happened, and Mr. Shapiro continued to offer us delicious goody after delicious goody—bacon, soap flakes (very rare in those days), filets mignons, potato chips (I hadn't seen any of these for years), and cartons of real cigarettes—Luckies and Chesterfields instead of those Coffeetones and Hushpuppies—or whatever they were called that most people were trying to get along with (they tasted as if someone else had smoked them first), if they were lucky enough to find a cigar store that had some for sale.

It was not only fun for us but also a lot of fun for our guests—it was a joy to watch the incredulous expression on the faces of newly returned navy and army officers, especially those who'd been stationed in London, when they saw one of Bessie's succulent-looking sirloin steaks, sizzling in butter and surrounded by delicately browned mushrooms and shoestring potatoes.

We continued to eat in this Lucullan manner through the winter and into the spring. By V-E Day, when no FBI men had appeared to question us and no word had come from the War Ration Board denouncing us as scofflaws or black-market users or whatever we were, we breathed more easily, and by V-J Day we were actually believing that in some mysterious way either our red points secretly multiplied when lying quietly in their books the way rock crystals do under the right circumstances, or our blue points (there were more of them for each person than red, and I think they were for canned peaches and things like that) had turned red.

It turned out to be nothing like that. A month or so after the war was over GW was out of the Navy, we had sold the cute little brick house, and were off to New York. I dropped in to pay the final grocery bill and bid Mr. Shapiro a fond farewell.

"Meat will still be rationed for a few more months," he told me, "so here is the name and address of a grocery firm in New York which is run by a friend of mine. I've made arrangements for him to look after you." I thanked him enthusiastically, told him he was a real pal and that I'd never forget him, and timidly asked for the ration books. As he handed them over he remarked casually, "By the way, did you realize that you owe me twelve hundred red points?"

My heart sank. Of course I knew it—I'd been kidding myself for months—only what could I do? Furthermore, it was all Mr. Shapiro's fault for egging me on. I had a fast vision of myself being escorted into the paddy wagon with people throwing tomatoes and rocks at me while flashbulbs popped.

Mr. Shapiro's gold tooth showed itself briefly in a quick smile. "However," he said, "I've decided to cancel the whole thing, and you don't owe me anything. You see, after you gave me the tip on Robert Gair I bought two thousand shares—also bought five hundred for the missus, paid a little over four dollars a share for them. I figured here was a tip right from the horse's mouth for Gair." He laughed merrily at this show of wit and I noticed now that he had three gold teeth, not just one.

"I sold a thousand shares at eight and a half," he continued. "Last week I sold the other thousand at thirteen and also the five hundred of the missus. It sure was the best tip I got and the missus thanks you too. Best tip I ever got."

A Sobering Thought for Today: If Robert Gair had gone down to 2½, for example, instead of up to 13, would Mr. Shapiro have given us and our guests ptomaine poisoning?

14
Tea in Tigertown

WITH THE WAR OVER, GW decided not to go back into advertising, and after considerable looking around during the winter of 1945 finally went into the electronics business in (of all places, I said) Philadelphia. We knew no one in the City of Brotherly Love, and its Main Line seemed far away from the towers of Manhattan and our friends there, so we did what a lot of other people did, and are still doing; we picked out a spot halfway between: Princeton, in Mercer County, in the state of New Jersey. In 1947 there was excellent train service to both New York and Philadelphia, each being less than fifty miles from Princeton. The Pennsylvania Railroad had trains stopping at Princeton Junction every half hour, and one could also go to New York on the Reading Railroad, especially if you wanted to end up in the Wall Street area. I remember the four o'clock from New York (to Philadelphia). After lunch in New York and shopping, one could take it and get to Princeton at 4:50 P.M. It had a bar car too.

Besides the people like us who moved to Princeton because it was halfway between Philadelphia and New York, there was the author John O'Hara, who said that he'd moved to Princeton because it was halfway between New Brunswick and Trenton. At any rate, the population when we moved there was probably about six thousand people in the summer, and about ten to twelve thousand in the winter, when the university students returned from summer vacations.

In the Princeton University Library, in the Rare Books Room, there is a most delightful letter from Thomas Jefferson, a reply to a lady whom he knew, who had written to ask him what he thought of the College of New Jersey (as it was called then) and should she sent her two sons there? He replied:

You ask me what I think about sending your sons to the College of New Jersey in Princeton, and I say very definitely no. The climate is perfectly terrible, they will get swamp fever and the ague.

YOURS TRULY T.J.

President Jefferson was right. The humidity is still atrocious at times but air conditioning has of course made living there in the summer possible. We bought a large white Georgian house on the highest spot in Princeton, the old water tower had been just across the street, and water towers were always built on the highest place, if you remember your physics. So we stayed fairly cool being on a hilltop close by the Princeton Graduate School, where one could go on Wednesday evenings in the summertime, and participate in square dancing on the green.

I was simply wild about the new house, and couldn't believe our good fortune: it was exactly the same house as a big white house on S Street in Washington that I had tried to buy back in 1944, but too late, someone beat me to it. I soon discovered why.

The Princeton house was built by Colonel George B. McClellan, an ex-mayor of New York City (his father was one of Abraham Lincoln's generals), who from 1911 to 1930 was a member of the university faculty. President Woodrow Wilson appointed him senator from New Jersey when a senator died, and his wife was so loath to leave her beloved house in Princeton that he duplicated the house for her in Washington.

We moved happily in, painted the shutters black and the house itself a nice clean white (instead of a dirty and yellowish white), painted the front door a mellow cranberry red (that is for good luck), shined up the brass door knocker, and put pots of round boxwood bushes on each side of the door.

Much to our surprise, shortly thereafter we began to have callers. Ladies came in twos, or singly, and they stayed and chatted for a few minutes, and departed after leaving calling cards. (I had to get out a silver card tray, actually, a silver butter plate.) Most of the callers were neighbors, and one of the first was a Mrs. McClure, a most charming lady, from across the street, whose husband had gone to the North Pole as a young man with Admiral Robert Edwin Peary and was presently a professor emeritus of anthropology at the university. Shortly after she had come and gone, another nice neighbor arrived with some yellow flowers, and a calling card saying that she was a Mrs. Harrison. The next caller made things puzzling, as her card said that she was a Mrs. Harrison McClure Thomas. It turned out that it was pure coincidence, but for a while I was all shook up.

There were church calls, and Vassar alumnae calls, and one from the wife of our new friendly family banker. These had to be returned within ten days, according to Emily Post, so all dressed up in our best white gloves and armed with some freshly engraved cards from Cartier, daughter Margot and I set out to return the calls. We got as far as a Mrs. Foster's house down the street. It had rained hard the night before. I slipped in her muddy gravel driveway and sat down with a thud, ruining the cards and the gloves, besides spraining an ankle.

I limped home and gave up. Instead of returning the calls I invited everybody for afternoon tea. In those days having three or four friends in for tea was a normal thing. Now it's so rare that it's a Lost Meal, and why is this? We had servants, that's the answer. The downstairs maid always got to shine up the silver tea set, slice the lemon, fill up the cream pitcher, put the kettle on, whip up some dainty little cucumber sandwiches, get out the best teacups and some little lace-trimmed napkins, put everything on a large tray and get it all into the living room, and then later on, get it all back into the kitchen again.

Back to the Princeton callers: I remember one call far worse than my falling down at Mrs. Foster's. When Dr. and Mrs. Einstein first came to Princeton in 1933 and moved into a house in the same neighborhood (he was invited to be the director of the Institute for Advanced Study), everyone welcomed them in the same pleasant way.

The owner of the largest house in our area was Mrs. Allan Marquand, who lived in a beautiful estate called Guernsey Hall, and had been away when the Einsteins arrived in Princeton. When someone mentioned having called on them, Mrs. Marquand said that she was planning to call on them the next day. Knowing that she was a diabetic and on a very strict regime, her friends told her to be sure not to call too near mealtime, that they were very hospitable and served all kinds of dangerously rich food.

Mrs. Marquand thanked them, and decided that 2:30 P.M. was a safe time to call. Her chauffeur drove her to the unpretentious yellow house at 112 Mercer Street, where the Einsteins greeted her cordially.

"Sit right down here, Mrs. Marquand, and talk to the good Doctor," said Mrs. Einstein after they reached the living room, "and I will go and make us a little collation!"

"Oh, please don't, Mrs. Einstein," Mrs. Marquand said quickly, and explained why. Mrs. Einstein paid no attention.

"No one leaves this house, Mrs. Marquand, without a little something to enjoy together. I will be just a moment."

Mrs. Einstein marched into the kitchen, and Mrs. Marquand said that she could hear the fridge door opening and slamming shut, then egg beaters whirring, and then drawers opening and closing, cupboards too, then more egg beaters. Finally Mrs. Einstein appeared with a tray, beaming and smiling, and set it down proudly. On it were three plates, each one containing a magnificent snow castle of a dessert. Angel food cake with ice cream and frosting swirled about each, and on the top ramparts sat rows of little candies of various colors.

Mrs. Marquand took her plate and politely ate a spoonful, then started to put it down, murmuring, "That was perfectly delicious."

"No, no, no!" Mrs. Einstein exclaimed excitely. "Here in this house we only allow empty plates, Mrs. Marquand. Remember, there are little children starving in Germany." Dr. Einstein nodded in agreement.

Rather than hurt their feelings the poor lady ate the whole concoction, arose and said her goodbyes as quickly as possible, hurried into the car, and said to the chauffeur, "The Princeton Hospital, the emergency entrance."

She went home after having had her stomach pumped, and I imagine remained pretty much shook up for several days, but fortunately her health remained good.

We had other kinds of callers too. The worst kind, in a way, was during the football season. Every Saturday afternoon after a big home game, people who had driven to Princeton to see Dartmouth or Yale or Colgate or Penn try to beat Princeton, or maybe had come to see their Alma Mater beat Harvard said to each other, "Whom do we know in Princeton where we can go and have a drink while waiting for the traffic jam to calm down?"

"Aha, I know!" someone exclaims. "The Williamsons!" And someone else is saying, "Aha, I know! The Delongs!" or "The Starkeys!" or "The Rulon-Millers!"

And sure enough, a half hour after the end of the game would find nearly every house near the stadium filled with a noisy happy mob of people, lapping up the scotch and the Bourbon, jamming all the available bathrooms, and some of them staying on and on until it became dinnertime.

Some of them we were overjoyed to see, some had already been invited and had accepted, but there were some who brought along four or five strangers and hadn't come to see us at all.

After one Yale-Princeton game (our second or third) I remember that we had eighty-nine for a buffet supper, to which we had invited and expected only twenty. And when I went upstairs to my own little pink-and-silver dressing room there was a perfectly strange older woman in a black satin dress being sick to her stomach in my washbasin. (I don't care for this sort of thing at all.)

GW and I decided that we'd had it for a while, so the following year we bought two big wooden sawhorses to block the entrance and exit of the driveway, hung a red lantern on each and pulled the shades down in the house, and turned off the porch light. We did this every Saturday afternoon when there was a game. It worked magnificently. And what if we *invited* someone to come for a drink, what about them? We had, in our cyclone fence, a gate (usually locked) that the gardener and his crew used. It led to a small turnaround with room for three or four cars on the garden side of the house. The invited people came in that way and walked up the terrace steps and scratched on the french windows. Once, when this secret gate was open after a game, and we were merrily dining with some Washington visitors, a great big deer wandered in and made himself comfortable trampling around and eating up a great many rhododendron leaves. We had a perfectly awful time getting him out: the Fire Department finally lassoed him in some way.

In a way, the nicest guests of all were the undergraduates who came to see us. They came strictly by invitation, and most often because friends of ours would write us. The typical letter went something like this:

"Johnny will be a freshman at Princeton this fall. Will you two keep an eye on him for us? Don't go to any trouble *at all*, but sometime maybe he could bicycle over and meet you, just so you can see what a handsome young man he is getting to be, and also we'd feel more comfortable about his knowing you, in case something awful happened in this crackpot world that we live in," etc. etc.

We dutifully met these children every time we received this kind of letter, and at first we did everything wrong. It took about three years before we became experts.

The proper way to entertain these eighteen-year-old freshmen is to invite them for dinner on *Sunday* night only, for that is the night that they don't have much to do, the weekend is over, the girls have gone, there's a let-down feeling. They might even feel a little homesick.

Next we always invited Johnny or Harold or Billy to bring along his roommate or best friend. We usually invited three pairs at a time, and had them come at six-thirty. For cocktails we served each boy a weak scotch and plain water, no other choice except a soft drink if they preferred it. The drinks came in all made, and we found that no one got tipsy on these. The trouble we had previously had now and then with cocktails, and mixed drinks, I cannot *describe*.

At seven-fifteen dinner was announced and into the dining room we went. We served two courses only, and it was always the same thing: roast beef first, with Yorkshire pudding, browned potatoes and gravy, plus a green vegetable. The last was more for us, as the boys seldom took more than a small polite spoonful. Then the second course was vanilla ice cream and a thick chocolate mint sauce (made by melting up chocolate peppermints in a double boiler and adding extra chocolate sauce).

With this we served a sponge or angel food cake, and both courses were passed twice.

Then we adjourned to the library for coffee, and GW always had a large collection of liqueurs, which he offered in very small glasses, telling a little about these after-dinner drinks from all over the world, what they are made from and where they are made; such as Cointreau, which is made from a secret French formula, the basic substance being distilled oranges, and is manufactured six miles away in Pennington, New Jersey.

Then promptly at ten we would both stand up, just like President and Mrs. Coolidge, and one of us would say, "Good gracious, here it is ten o'clock and we are keeping you from doing all sorts of things. How inconsiderate of us."

Then we would both keep moving out toward the hall, help them into their coats, shake hands, and open the door wide and literally *steer them out firmly.*

One evening, I think it was the first time that we had freshmen to dinner, they stayed until after one in the morning. No one wanted to be the one to say, "Well, fellows, it's getting pretty late, and tomorrow's Monday and maybe we should be going—" We finally had to do it ourselves.

One last thing that I remember about those well-meaning and delightful but unpracticed boys: It was wise to put away delicate *objets d'art*, especially the ones sitting on end tables. Eighteen-year-old boys are clumsy as can be. Their big feet and big hands have not been that way very long, and they don't manage them well, especially when there are six or eight of them, and in a strange house.

The nicest thing of all about Princeton is the people, and it has always been that way, I understand. It is a perfect combination of interesting citizens, almost all of whom do something that makes them worth knowing.

Looking in my engagement calendar at random, I find a dinner party that took place two years ago that illustrates what I mean. Present were a former member of the Atomic Energy Commission and his wife, a former governor of New Jersey and his wife, an architect and his wife (who writes novels), the headmaster of a nearby boys' school, a lady pollster, and the retired librarian of Princeton's Firestone Library and his wife.

Another dinner, at the Nassau Club in Princeton last year, included a former Ambassador to Canada, an ex-Princeton football coach, two men who write market letters for two different brokerage houses, and the ex-head of one of the largest insurance companies, all with their wives.

There is one anecdote regarding a distinguished Princeton scientist that I'd like to tell about, and then I'm through with this semi-name-dropping, or whatever you call it.

One afternoon back in 1950, GW and I were invited to have a cocktail with neighbors of ours, Henry and Elizabeth Chauncy. He was at the time the head of the Educational Testing Service, which makes up exams for colleges and schools, all sorts of things like that, and they were nice neighbors in every way. They had invited one other couple, also neighbors, whom we had never met before and who also turned out to be delightful: the distinguished scientist J. Robert Oppenheimer and his wife, Kitty, who was eminent in her own field of botany.

We settled down with our drinks and I remember that we were talking about some current book, and someone said that it was the kind that was dull enough to put down anytime, but nonetheless worth reading.

"Bedside reading," I suggested.

J. Robert nodded. "Yes, I know just what you mean."

"What do *you* read for bedside reading?" I asked him with great curiosity.

"I read dictionaries," he said promptly.

"What sort of dictionaries? What one are you reading now, for example?"

"Well, all last week I read the Turkish-English, English-Turkish dictionary, and enjoyed it very much." Then he smiled and added, "It was a pleasant coincidence because a Turkish science professor turned up here just as I'd finished it, and we were able to understand each other pretty well."

I was almost speechless, but managed to gasp out the words: "How did you know how to pronounce the words, and do the grammar?"

"That's easy," he replied. "In every dictionary there is a pronunciation guide as well as a list of the letters of the alphabet, and how to form plurals, and diminutives and augmentatives, all that sort of thing."

"What are you reading this week?" I inquired in a quavering voice.

"The Hawaiian," he said, "and believe me, it's a terrible language."

I went home feeling mentally retarded, and still feel that way, especially as I pick up my nice book about Eskimos or the history of the Colosseum before turning out my bedside lamp.

The first time that I ever came to Princeton was in 1926, and it was to the university's spring house parties. In reality it was the spring prom, and *the* nicest weekend of all. The pink magnolias were out, it was May 1, and the grass was green. All of us girls were dressed in our best outfits as we first sat beside the tennis courts and watched the finals, and later went off to the polo field, to sit on the grass or in someone's car to watch the final polo match.

I remember that my best watching or spectator outfit was my Mrs. Franklin suit. This was the Pucci or Leonard costume of its time. Mrs. Franklin's things were hand-knit, and were usually two-piece affairs with skirt and top. My best one was a pale yellow, and the top had some knitted-in (or intarsia) black-and-white birds flying along over the right shoulder. With it I wore a yellow straw hat trimmed with some yellow daisies with black centers. There were two other girls in our group from the Quadrangle Club wearing Franklin things almost identical to mine; it was sort of a spring uniform.

Later we dressed up for the dinner dance in the club, most of us wearing long dresses of pastel colors, and each girl wearing a corsage that was sent by the man who had invited her to the house parties. In those days corsages were mostly roses or gardenias (orchids were for movie stars, then), or possibly freesias, and once in a while a pale-pink camellia. When my sister Margaret went to proms most of the girls wore violets: they were the *rage.* How come they are never worn any more? Because of a play called *The Captive.* Helen Mencken starred in it on Broadway, and it was very daring indeed. She was a lesbian, and her girl friend always sent her violets. The result: nobody would be seen dead wearing violets. Why don't girls wear corsages any more? One reason is the materials that our clothes are made of; they are thinner, there isn't enough to pin on three white gardenias. You need a black velvet dress with shoulder pads to carry around a load like that.

After the dinner dance at the club with its large and pleasant stag line we went to the Dillon Gymnasium, which was all trimmed with cherry blossoms and forsythia, and dancing there was everyone in the university as far as the eye could see.

We didn't get back to the club until five in the morning. My feet were tired from dancing so much, but I don't think I ever had a better time. It seemed as if I'd danced with almost everyone that I ever knew. As we said in those days, I had a "lamby" time.

Now let us turn the clock ahead to 1953 and there in Princeton at the same spot, the Dillon Gymnasium (destroyed by fire in 1944 but completely rebuilt), our daughter attended a prom with a beau named Ralph Condit. She came down from Bronxville, where she was a junior at Sarah Lawrence, and the weekend was the first one in May.

However, the girls were far less dressed up than we had been. Bermuda shorts and huaraches, with a Brooks sweater, or a plain tailored shirt, were the uniform of the day. In the evening, for the big dance, she and all the others dressed informally, the girls in short dresses with short sleeves, for the most part. Margot wore a pale-blue dress with a matching jacket and short white gloves, looking pretty as a picture and neat as a pin.

She too arrived home around five in the morning, and around noon, when she got up, I asked her what kind of a time she had.

"It was divine." She rolled her eyes. "I don't think I ever had a better time. Ralph really grabs me."

"Who all did you dance with?" I asked.

"Just Ralph" was the answer.

"Good heavens!" I exclaimed. "Nobody else? Didn't you get bored?"

"Of course not," she replied. "Ralph is a neat dancer, really *neat*. Oh, we did get asked to double-cut once or twice for a few minutes, but it was just to be polite."

Times change, for sure, and they go right on changing. Ten years ago they abandoned all proms at Princeton, and half of the clubs no longer exist. If there was any dancing in the hippie days it was done barefoot and in the traditional blue jeans. I understand, however, that there are some very nice-looking girls and boys on the campus these days. Perhaps the lace parasol and the dress with the ruffled train are on the way back.

$\mathscr{e}\!\!\mathscr{r}\!\!\mathscr{o}$ 15
Still Traveling

INSTEAD OF ENDING the book with a wedding and everyone throwing Puffed Rice (that's a tradition of long standing in our family) at some happy bride, I will end this reminiscence with one more anecdote about the toilet.

Mademoiselle Suzanne Bonnecaze, whom I have known off and on for some time, has for many years been a governess for small children; she spends many months in New York and Long Island and New Canaan, and the two of us often have tea together at the Hotel Plaza's Palm Court on her day off.

Mam'zelle B. is as conservative a spinster as I have ever known, and is rather frightening in appearance: tall and thin, with white skin, piercing black eyes, and an aquiline nose. I've never seen her except in a gray *tailleur* with low-heeled black pumps, a black toque, black veil, and black umbrella.

Just after the war, Mam'zelle B. finally heard from her sister who had been living in Tirana, the capital of Albania, and learned the sister's Albanian husband had died, that the sister was poor and very sad, and not very well, so she decided to pay her a visit. It took a great deal of time and red tape to get permission to go behind the Iron Curtain, but at long last she was free to go, and left from the Gare de Lyon in Paris, on the famous Orient Express, one fine evening at 7:28.

She went at once to the *wagon restaurant* for dinner, after leaving her luggage in her *wagon-lit appartement*, and when she returned after a delicious dinner, her berth was all made up for the night. Mam'zelle B. before getting undressed went to the W.C. at the end of her car, for French *wagon-lits* have only washbowls in their compartments. She always was, and still is (I imagine), scared of germs, especially on strange toilet seats which are used by unknown women and, what is worse, men, so she had taken the precaution of cutting out a lot of paper toilet-seat covers for train travel, and had used back copies of the Paris newspaper *Figaro* to make them. Hence when she trotted down to the *cabinet* she carried one with her.

The next day passed uneventfully, and she read and enjoyed the trip across northern Italy, got off at Milan for a little promenade in the station, and enjoyed the Italian food from the *vagone ristorante*.

At Trieste all the windows were blacked out as they crossed the border into Yugoslavia, and the whole train remained lighted only by electric light until they reached Tirana.

Meanwhile Mam'zelle B. had kept herself busy reading and sleeping and making her little *sorties* to the white-room-with-the-tiles, each time with a fresh newspaper cover for the toilet seat.

At last she arrived in Tirana, and was taken with the other passengers to the police to be searched for contraband material. The women (there were six others who had disembarked at Tirana) were all taken into a dressing room where to Mam'zelle's horror they were all ordered to disrobe completely. There was nothing that she could do about it, and the stern police matron threatened to yank off her clothes fast, so quickly and purple with embarrassment she found herself stark naked, hat with veil still on her head and handbag in one hand.

When they all were in line they were ordered "Forward, march" through the dressing room's farther door, to be inspected by the chief inspector, a man in uniform sitting at a desk, flanked by four policemen.

Every woman passed the inspection except poor Mademoiselle Bonnecaze. While the others were all back dressing, she had been detained as a probable spy. Why was this? On her derrière there seemed to be some secret messages. More police inspectors were summoned and poor Mam'zelle found her rear end being examined very carefully with a magnifying glass. She was almost fainting away when suddenly they all began to laugh. One inspector (who could read French) discovered that he was reading the want ads of last week's *Figaro*.

Before ending this add-a-bit-here and add-a-bit-there book

(little girls in my day were often given an add-a-pearl necklace by an aunt or a grandmother, and on birthdays or for Christmas, relatives or friends would add-another-pearl, which is the disjointed way this book materialized), I would like to report that I am still traveling most happily, and would like to end with a few words of advice for those just beginning their travels.

First of all, a word about clothes and packing. I always decide on a basic color for shoes, handbag, and traveling costume, let's take navy blue. Then into a brightly colored medium-sized rectangular suitcase I toss in as many as eighteen or twenty short, silk-knit or silk-type-knit dresses, some with long sleeves, some with short, and a few with matching jackets. I add a couple of bright prints with navy backgrounds, and a few with white backgrounds, plus one plain all-navy dress, the kind that Italian ladies wear with the string of pearls and white gloves. I try to keep the prints of the dresses all in the same tones, blues and greens and mauves, for example.

Then into an equally brightly colored and therefore easily identifiable duffel bag I put a pair of navy-blue pumps and a pair of white ones, each with Velcro patches on the toes. Then I add a plastic bag full of various buckles and ornaments, all with Velcro backing and all in colors to match the dresses. Next I include two or three evening bags, plain slim clutch bags, one covered all over in tiny blue and green sequins, one of satin, and one covered with cultured pearls.

I put in a sweater or two and a reversible navy-blue and white silk waterproofed coat, a little pillow in its own traveling case, some stylish semiprecious jewelry such as a necklace of pearls, lapis lazuli, and jade (but no gold or diamonds that would catch the eye of the brigand).

After adding my toilet articles I am ready to go, with my wrinkle-proof wardrobe that matches up easily and needs almost no care. And the last item of all would be the bag I carry. It is of navy-blue leather, a product of Roberta di Camerino, a Venetian designer who knows the exact size that a handbag should be. The bag has four different sets of handles. I would attach a pair that are striped rose and blue and pack the green and turquoise set, the purple and lavender, and the navy and white.

Next, instead of traveling all over the place (if-this-is-Wednesday-it-must-be-Belgium style) I would choose a place somewhere that is historically or topographically interesting, or both, with a variety of things to do, and then go there and stay put. Furthermore, the town should be small or medium-sized. Let's say that you live in Florida and have a month's vacation in August. I'd suggest going to Lucerne in Switzerland, for instance. You'd have a complete change; lofty snow-capped mountains, different weather with fog and cool mountain air, freshwater lakes, and walking around up and down hills.

What if you live in the Middle West and don't see many broad expanses of water? Then I'd go to the Greek island of Rhodes, or maybe an island in Hawaii. Perhaps you're from Boston and want a different place for a winter sojourn? Try spending a fortnight in Luxor, Egypt. You're fond of golf? Go to Gleneagles in Scotland. Sailing? Copenhagen. Gambling? Swaziland.

Why do I suggest going to a small or medium-sized place instead of a large one? In general, it is easier to make friends and get along in the smaller towns. But what if you find yourself in Milan, Italy, all alone, knowing nobody? Go walking, sticking prudently to the big wide boulevards and two-way streets. What if you can't walk or don't like to? Get the hotel doorman to find you a limousine and go driving. GW and I walked over Beirut once several years ago, and I've never forgotten what a beautiful city it *was*. Last spring I did the same thing in Port Said, where one can buy Mother's Day cards with Arabic greetings on them, something a little different.

Once years ago Dr. John Marquis and a close friend of his, Dr. Burkhalter, arrived in Rome for the first time, something that they had been looking forward to greatly. They were both Presbyterian ministers from Cedar Rapids and Dr. Marquis was also the president of Coe College. They checked into their hotel, a small one in the general neighborhood of the Vatican, and after hanging up their overcoats they rushed out to see the glories of the Eternal City. After a trip through St. Peter's and a visit to the Sistine Chapel and few other historic spots they became tired and hungry enough to want to return to the hotel. Their hotel? Dr. Marquis looked blank. What was its name?

"Never fear," Dr. Burkhalter said, "I wrote it down." He fished a paper out of his pocket. "Here it is: Albergo."

"And I know the word for where in Italian." Dr. Marquis chuckled. "It is *dove*." He went up to a passerby and said politely, "*Doe-vay* Hotel Albergo, please?"

He was greeted with a stare, then a laugh and a fast departure. Dr. Marquis tried again and almost the same thing happened. A crowd began to collect, and finally the police, who explained that *albergo* is the Italian word for hotel.

The two men ended up at police headquarters with an officer telephoning to each hotel on a long list of numbers. He finally located the right one shortly before midnight.

What memorable places and incidents would I like to see again or repeat if I could? The list would be so long that you would be reading on past midnight, so I'll only mention a few. First I'd like to be once again in a sailboat race up in northern Michigan on a summer afternoon with the whole fleet of six-meter yachts that we used to race, about fifteen sloops in all. The breeze would be fresh, the blue waters would be sparkling, and I would either be at the helm or maybe handling the Swedish jib. As we went over the finish line ahead of all the other boats the little brass cannon on the judges' boat would sound off and everyone would shout congratulations and our hands would be trembling with excitement. We would have won the race for the coveted Conover Cup, the most important race of the summer.

Next I'd find myself in Guatemala listening to a twelve- or fourteen-man marimba band, all of them playing away on one great long marimba, dressed in bright colors and playing their favorite song. Marimba music is "super-duper."

One of the things that I'd like to do over again if I could, as it was such fun, happened back in 1964. I had written a book and it had just come out in the bookstores, only I had been up in Michigan and hadn't seen a single copy anywhere. I arrived in New York and after getting settled found myself on a Madison Avenue bus going uptown on an errand. To my joy and delight there was a lady, and a *very* nice-looking one at that, sitting just opposite me reading my book. Furthermore, she was laughing. It was truly one of life's greatest moments.

Years ago another happy time occurred that I would love to repeat if I could. I was back in Cedar Rapids visiting for a few days and went in to the Merchants National Bank to cash a check. Mother's cousin Mr. James Hamilton was president of the bank at the time and he waved a greeting when he saw me come in.

"Hello, cousin Jimmy," I said politely as I approached his large impressive desk, located in the center of the bank, where he was reading the Chicago *Journal of Commerce*, and I imagine radiating confidence among the depositors.

We exchanged greetings and then he said, "I want you to meet my new vice-president. I consider him a very able young man who will someday take my place." He took me over to a small room opening off the main floor and introduced me to a tall very large man, saying, "Coke, another member of the family. Ellen, this is Mr. St. Elmo Coquillette." Then he walked off to his desk. Coke turned out to be perfectly charming, great fun, even, compared to stern cousin Jimmy, and I sat down for a minute and asked him how he liked Cedar Rapids. I ended up by staying all afternoon.

His desk, besides the usual papers, had on top of it a box of crayons and some bottles of colored ink and even a paintbrush or two. When I asked if he were an artist, perhaps a Sunday painter, he told me about Mr. Egbert P. McMuffin, the president of the bank in What Cheer, Iowa, a small town near Cedar Rapids.

It seems that Mr. McMuffin's bank had an account with the Merchants, and in those days it was customary for outlying banks such as his to send all their customers' checks to the Merchants every day for clearance. Everything was perfectly fine about Mr. McMuffin's customers but not the checks themselves.

Mr. Coquillette, or Coke, as I soon found myself calling him, showed me a pile of What Cheer checks. On each check was a large portrait of old bald-headed Mr. McMuffin, smiling away at us with a toothsome smile, his black eyes snapping with an overeager look. His face covered most of each check.

In the 1930s a check with anything printed on it other than a conventional frame around the edge was unheard of; this was the height of bad taste.

"I have to get him to change the checks at once," Coke said with a chuckle, "but I can't mention it or tell him not to. He might resent it, and then we'd lose the account." He paused and added, "It's a good account."

"What on earth will you do?" I couldn't imagine being in a worse dilemma.

When Coke told me his plan I was lost in admiration, and spent the whole afternoon in the bank, as I said, following his scheme to thwart Mr. Egbert P. McMuffin.

In a small borrowed office, with all the crayons and pencils sitting in front of me along with piles of the checks from What Cheer, I added fierce mustaches, fancy bow ties, long eyelashes, and so on to each of Mr. McMuffin's etched portraits.

Some were really gorgeous. I remember sparkling earrings and black Clara Bow curls on one, a red rose in the blacked-out teeth of another, dunce caps and sunbonnets here and there. Coke had all the good ideas, and I never had a better afternoon, and needless to say Mr. McMuffin's checks changed back to the ordinary kind the following week.

After that I'd be transported to the island of Cyprus and it would be in early March, when the yellow mimosa is in bloom and all the little yellow daisies are carpeting the fields, and in Famagusta I would order a picnic lunch of cheese and bread and olives and wine, and take it to the ruins of Salamis, which is where the great naval battle was fought between the Persians and the Athenians. There I would stay all afternoon sitting in the sunshine and looking out to sea.

Then I would be in Venice, sitting in a small outdoor café in the Piazza of St. Mark. It is full moonlight and the sky is dark velvety blue, there are little lights in all the windows of the Doges' palaces, and in the square is the huge Citizens of Venice Symphony Orchestra. A tenor is introduced, the conductor picks up his baton, and accompanied by this 186-piece orchestra, the singer renders the aria "Nessun' Dorma" from Puccini's opera *Turandot*. He sings beautifully, and when he finishes there is thunderous applause, so much so that happily he sings the whole thing over again.

I don't know whether I'd be in Interlaken in Switzerland watching the Jungfrau turning pink in the sunset, or riding horseback on the beach in Santa Barbara at low tide, or fishing for tarpon in Boca Grande on a spring evening, but I know that I would end up dining with GW, just the two of us, in some quiet elegant little restaurant, perhaps at George's in Rome with Michele pouring the wine for us, or the Laurent in New York with Jerry looking out for us, or even the Grey Gables in Charlevoix with Leona bringing a carafe of the local Cask wine (product of Paw Paw, Michigan) to our table.

Two last bits of advice and I'm through with this long ramble through the twentieth century: Get busy cultivating younger friends early. Make lots of them, keep in touch with them. Remember that friendship is like a little flower and needs sunshine and water and pleasant words.

And one other thing—if you can't afford to go first class, travel with children: nice, well-behaved ones who will get ice cream given to them and rides on the funicular, also maybe *you too*.

Dear Reader: I have enjoyed writing this book and hope to see you someday somewhere, perhaps sipping champagne before takeoff in a waiting Concorde. Wherever it is I will be wearing a Ken Scott silk-knit short dress with a black background and printed all over with large bright rose-red carnations.